Praise for *Raising the Curtain*

T0355457

"I'm excited about this book—I don't think there's anything like it out there. I Google things, but would have loved to have a book like this so many times."

—**Dane Toney, project and media specialist at Attack Theatre**

"This book is a needed offering in the world. It's so important and it really will help."

—**Stephanie Martinez, artistic director at PARA-MER Dance Theatre**

"As we know, nearly every aspect of modern life intersects with technology—and the performing arts are no exception. Brett Ashley Crawford and Paul Hansen, in their excellent new book, *Raising the Curtain*, remind us that this can be a good thing! Each thoughtful and thorough chapter artfully demystifies the ever-changing landscape of our digital world—and provides clear examples of how to best deploy software and other applications in a way that makes work easier and more efficient for artists and arts administrators. Dr. Crawford and Mr. Hansen have cut through the noise and demonstrated a true philosophy around technology in our field, while also showcasing real, actionable tactics that can be implemented into your practice right away."

—**James McNeel, managing director, City Theatre Company**

"I think this book is great—something really special here."

—**Juan José Escalante, executive director at Miami City Ballet**

"This book offers a framework and guide for people in [performing arts] institutions for ways how technology can aid their organizations."
—Scott Penner, freelance set and costume designer

Raising the Curtain

Technology Success Stories from
Performing Arts Leaders and Artists

Brett Ashley Crawford, PhD
Paul Hansen

WILEY

Copyright © 2024 by John Wiley & Sons, Inc. All rights reserved.

Published by John Wiley & Sons, Inc., Hoboken, New Jersey.
Published simultaneously in Canada and the United Kingdom.

ISBNs: 9781394203536 (paperback), 9781394203567 (ePDF), 9781394203550 (ePub)

No part of this publication may be reproduced, stored in a retrieval system, or transmitted in any form or by any means, electronic, mechanical, photocopying, recording, scanning, or otherwise, except as permitted under Section 107 or 108 of the 1976 United States Copyright Act, without either the prior written permission of the Publisher, or authorization through payment of the appropriate per-copy fee to the Copyright Clearance Center, Inc., 222 Rosewood Drive, Danvers, MA 01923, (978) 750-8400, fax (978) 750-4470, or on the web at www.copyright.com. Requests to the Publisher for permission should be addressed to the Permissions Department, John Wiley & Sons, Inc., 111 River Street, Hoboken, NJ 07030, (201) 748-6011, fax (201) 748-6008, or online at www.wiley.com/go/permission.

Trademarks: WILEY and the Wiley logo are trademarks or registered trademarks of John Wiley & Sons, Inc. and/or its affiliates, in the United States and other countries, and may not be used without written permission. All other trademarks are the property of their respective owners. John Wiley & Sons, Inc. is not associated with any product or vendor mentioned in this book.

Limit of Liability/Disclaimer of Warranty: While the publisher and authors have used their best efforts in preparing this book, they make no representations or warranties with respect to the accuracy or completeness of the contents of this book and specifically disclaim any implied warranties of merchantability or fitness for a particular purpose. No warranty may be created or extended by sales representatives or written sales materials. The advice and strategies contained herein may not be suitable for your situation. You should consult with a professional where appropriate. Further, readers should be aware that websites listed in this work may have changed or disappeared between when this work was written and when it is read. Neither the publisher nor authors shall be liable for any loss of profit or any other commercial damages, including but not limited to special, incidental, consequential, or other damages.

For general information on our other products and services or for technical support, please contact our Customer Care Department within the United States at (800) 762-2974, outside the United States at (317) 572-3993 or fax (317) 572-4002.

If you believe you've found a mistake in this book, please bring it to our attention by emailing our Reader Support team at wileysupport@wiley.com with the subject line "Possible Book Errata Submission."

Wiley also publishes its books in a variety of electronic formats. Some content that appears in print may not be available in electronic formats. For more information about Wiley products, visit our web site at www.wiley.com.

Library of Congress Control Number: 2024930675

Cover images: Curtain: © LEEDDONG/Getty Images
             Pattern: © piranka/Getty Images
Cover design: Wiley

Printed and bound by CPI Group (UK) Ltd, Croydon, CR0 4YY

C9781394203536_260124

Contents at a Glance

Introduction   xiii

Chapter 1   Getting on the Same Page: Efficient
             Internal Communication + Project Management   1

Chapter 2   Keeping Track of Everyone   27

Chapter 3   Growing Audiences + Donors: Tools + Tactics   59

Chapter 4   Making Magic: Enhancing Artistic Productions   93

Chapter 5   Defining Who You Are: Branding,
             Rebranding, + Residencies   125

Chapter 6   Extending the Stage: Digital Content,
             Education, + Touring   147

Chapter 7   The Arts Are for Everyone: Diversity + Accessibility   179

Appendix   Interviewees   203

Acknowledgments   231

About the Authors   233

Index   235

Contents

Introduction   xiii

Chapter 1   **Getting on the Same Page: Efficient**
                Internal Communication + Project Management   1
                Times Change, but How Do We?   2
                How Knowledge Systems Create Success   4
                Internal Communications: From Memos to
                  Email and Slack   8
                Managing the Workflow: Project Management Software   13
                    Asana   15
                    Airtable   15
                    ArtsVision   17
                Training   20
                The Selection Process   21
                Summary   22
                Takeaways   23
                Technology Solutions   23
                        Knowledge Management   23
                        Internal Communications   24
                        Project Management   24
                Notes   24

Chapter 2   **Keeping Track of Everyone**   27
                Structuring the System   30
                    Gathering + Cleaning   33
                Using Data Analytics for Strategy + Planning   36
                Data-Forward Company Culture   40
                    User Training + Onboarding   40

Privacy, Security + Legal Compliance   43
Artificial Intelligence: Automation, Machine
  Learning, + Chatbots   46
Selecting + Designing a CRM with a Robust CDP   48
Takeaways   49
Technology Solutions   56
  Structuring the System   56
  Gathering + Cleaning   57
  User Training + Onboarding   57
  Privacy, Security, + Legal Compliance   58
Notes   58

Chapter 3   **Growing Audiences + Donors: Tools + Tactics**   **59**
Marketing + Communications   60
The Customer Journey + User Experience Design   62
  People's Light   65
  Data and Automation   67
    TheatreSquared   67
Team, Tools, + Tactics   68
  Website   69
    People's Light   69
  Video   70
    Black Ensemble Theater   71
  Social Media   71
    Emmet Cohen   72
    People's Light   72
    PARA.MAR Dance   74
  Email   74
    Black Ensemble Theater   74
    People's Light   74
    Emmet Cohen   75
Subscriptions Are Not Dead   75
  Savannah Philharmonic   76
    Artists   81
    Artificial Intelligence—Now + the Future   81
Donations Adapt: Apps, Taps, Codes, + NFTs   83
    DipJar   84
    QR Codes   86
    NFTs   87
Takeaways   88
Technology Solutions   89
  Video   89
  Project Management   89
  Special Events   90

Artificial Intelligence   90
Email   90
Data Analysis for Marketing   90
Subscription   91
Customer Management Systems   91
  Project Management + Surveys   91

Chapter 4   Making Magic: Enhancing Artistic Productions   93
Set Design   94
  Czerton Lim, Freelance Set Designer for *Clue* at Indiana
    Repertory Theatre (IRT) and Syracuse Stage   94
  Scott Penner, Freelance Set Designer for *The Merry
    Wives of Windsor* at American Players Theatre (APT)   97
Costume Design   99
  Eric Winterling, Costume Creator   99
  Scott Penner, Freelance Costume Designer   101
Lighting Design   102
  Brandon Stirling Baker, Lighting Director for
    Boston Ballet and Freelance Lighting Designer   102
  Indiana Repertory Theatre (IRT) in Indianapolis   104
Video Design   105
  Benjamin Pearcy, Chief Technology Officer and Project
    Director at 59 Productions   106
  Jason H. Thompson and Kaitlyn Pietras, PXT Studio   108
  Lawrence Shea, Media Architect   112
Sound Design + Music Composition   114
  Indiana Repertory Theatre (IRT), Indianapolis   114
  Sartje Pickett, Freelance Composer + Sound Designer   115
  The Benedum Center for the Performing Arts   116
Playwriting, Directing, + Casting   118
  James Still, Playwright and Director   118
Takeaways   119
Technology Solutions   120
  Set Design   120
  Lighting Design   120
  Video Design   121
  Sound Design + Music Composition   122
  Playwriting, Directing, + Casting   123

**Chapter 5   Defining Who You Are: Branding,
                Rebranding, + Residencies   125**
Brand Style Guide   127
Branding Through Social Media   128
  Jane Monheit, Jazz Singer   128
  Chun Wai Chan, Ballet Dancer   131

Nina Yoshida Nelsen, Opera Singer   132
Stephanie Martinez, Choreographer + Artistic Director   133
Rebranding   134
Ballet RI   135
Detroit Opera   138
Residencies   140
Takeaways   142
Technology Solutions   144
Introduction   144
Social Media   144
Rebranding   145

Chapter 6   **Extending the Stage: Digital Content,
Education, + Touring**   **147**
Streaming + Simulcasts   147
Tradition of Capturing Dance at Jacob's
Pillow + Hybrid Festival   148
New York Philharmonic Media Wall +Digital Archives   150
Second Stage's Journey with Simulcasts   153
Digital Business Model at Boston Baroque   154
Digital Transformation at SFJAZZ   156
Expanding Content Use at Dallas Symphony Orchestra   160
Education, Mentorship, + New Work Development   162
Converting a Space into a Filming Studio   162
PNB Dance Film Festival   164
The Reiser Atlanta Artists Lab   168
Touring   171
Alvin Ailey American Dance Theater   171
Takeaways   174
Technology Solutions   175
Streaming + Simulcasts   175
Education, Mentorship, + New Work Development   176
Touring   176

Chapter 7   **The Arts Are for Everyone: Diversity + Accessibility**   **179**
Hearing + Vision-Impaired Audiences   181
Meeting the Needs of Artists with Disabilities   186
Podcasts + Live Streaming   188
The Score   188
Live from Emmet's Place   190
Green Room Meditations   192
Human Resources + Marketing   193
Bias in Written Materials   193
Color Blindness   194
Diversity of People in Images   194

Training   194
   Systemic Racism   196
   Additional Resources   198
Summary   200
Takeaways   200
Technology Solutions   200
   Meeting the Needs of Artists with Disabilities 201
   Podcasts + Live Streaming   201
   Bias in Written Materials   202
   Color Blindness   202

Appendix **Interviewees**   **203**

Acknowledgments   **231**

About the Authors   **233**

Index   **235**

Introduction

In the performing arts, our goal is to create great art and programs that connect with audiences and communities. Getting to opening night requires managing people, money, and materials. In other words, great art requires a great business model that includes the smart use of technology, from artistic creation to administration to community connection to reaching donors.

Digital transformation is continually changing how we make art, run businesses, and even live our lives. In this book, you'll find stories about nonprofit organizations, artists, and the technology they use to achieve success.

The performing arts are struggling to emerge from the COVID-19 pandemic in the United States and other countries around the globe. Audiences have yet to return to pre-pandemic numbers, subscriptions are faltering, and donors are receding. Bluntly, if you look at the numbers over time, the performing arts have been losing audiences and relying on long-term, big-money donors for more than a decade. Recent headlines in the media too frequently highlight organizations canceling shows, shrinking seasons, or ceasing operations altogether, striking fear in the hearts of many. There is a path forward. Lessons can be learned from the many organizations running efficient and effective operations—they pay their bills, run full seasons, and operate robust enterprises. These are the stories you will read in this book.

In our post-pandemic, AI-infused world, arts success stories are fueled by using technology and data in new ways to grow their business operations and innovate productions. Colleen Dilenschneider, a cultural leadership consultant who maintained an ongoing data analysis of audiences and marketing throughout the pandemic, found that organizations that invested in their infrastructure and continued engaging with their communities are finding audiences and donors return and even grow.

Harnessing technology to fuel success is the point of our book. We are both lifelong performing arts professionals working in production, management, and education. Our heart is in the work and the transformative power of the arts—we know that the performing arts can change lives. One of the keys to success, in our experience, is empowering people to use the tools available to them.

We're both "accidental techies" in our careers in the arts, filled with passion and curiosity. We discovered the efficiencies and impact that can be gained by using technology. We were simultaneously dismayed when we realized how many of our friends and colleagues were missing opportunities due to legacy (old) systems, missing integrations across departments, siloed systems, or the right tech in the wrong hands.

We have taken our combined 50 years of experience and added to it. Instead of offering two perspectives, this book brings together the innovative work of organizations and artists across multiple disciplines (jazz, symphony orchestras, choruses, contemporary dance, ballet, theater, opera, and more). Our interviews are with people working in jobs from marketing and fundraising to diversity, equity, accessibility, inclusion (DEAI), production, and information technology. The power of harnessing data and tech for transformational outcomes is revealed through their stories. Throughout the book, their words bring their work to life:

"The arts, by nature, are always evolving. You might take a piece of music that was written 400 years ago, and a new choreographer will take that music and create something that has never been seen before. We have to embrace technology in order to keep up with the evolution of the art form itself."

—Juan José Escalante, executive director, Miami City Ballet

"How you innovate is you solve the problems as they come."

—Denise McGovern, vice president of communications + media, Dallas Symphony Orchestra

---

"I use data to make strategic decisions as a leader in the organization. We serve our customers in the way that they have come to expect of the world. We exist in the same world as Amazon and Target and the rest of them. So, our interactions need to be the same."

—Larae J. Ferry, director of marketing, Alvin Ailey American Dance Theater

---

Raising the Curtain can't tell the story of every artist and performing arts leader finding success using technology. We have attempted, however, to provide examples of many different tactics, strategies, and tools. There are more examples of success across the performing arts than could ever be included in one book.

By providing a breadth of voices and experiences, *Raising the Curtain* serves arts administrators, board members, designers, and artists. We hope you'll find inspiration and solutions for your problem areas. This book can be read cover-to-cover or by diving into a chapter that covers a specific area you're working on.

New technologies enter the market daily. This book could never hope to be exhaustive in every solution, nor do we only highlight the most "cutting-edge" tech. We all know that whatever is cutting-edge today is soon considered the norm or, even worse, so trendy it quickly becomes obsolete. We also share how some of the simplest technologies are often the best for the job.

Finally, we know that stories of great success didn't just happen. Incorporating technology into a personal workflow or an organization is difficult. Change management is a considerable part of the process. Hence, many interviewees provide examples of successfully incorporating a particular process or technology. Training and skill development are essential, as is socialization across the organization in small steps.

Maintaining a digital ecosystem is increasingly the foundation of effective and efficient business practice. We wrote *Raising the Curtain* in an effort to demystify technology and support performing arts organizations and artists in their quest to find efficient and effective solutions to the problems they face. Although any technology described in this book may have a new version or be out-of-date by the time you read this book, we hope you'll use these stories for inspiration in the *way* it is being incorporated and as a starting point to find the right tech solutions for your needs.

Getting on the Same Page: Efficient Internal Communication + Project Management

Technology is a tool, a collaborator, that supports business operations in a significant but subtle way. While it would be wonderful to simply add on a technology to the workplace and have it magically solve our problems, that is rarely the case. Yet, when intentionally selected and implemented, technologies in the workplace have proven time and again that they can save time and headaches, therefore increasing the impact of our work.

In our experience as artists, freelancers, and arts administrators, the technology we use has often saved the day, but to be honest, it has also sometimes created massive headaches. This chapter will share our experiences as well as those of several theater, dance, and music companies. These success stories of creating and using institutional systems will reveal how they decrease "one more dead-end email chain" and increase clarity of purpose, priorities, and workflows.

The chapter begins with the frameworks of how our work systems and environments have changed over the years before we dive into knowledge management and how to increase institutional memory, efficiency, and job satisfaction day to day. The arts are a people business, so we'll also discuss how we can create better models for communication. The technology solutions that we'll investigate are software-as-a-service

(SaaS) models for workflow management. None of this works independently or is adopted without intention and training. The chapter wraps up with how to best train and maintain these systems in a world that is ever-changing.

Times Change, but How Do We?

Running arts organizations or pursuing artistic careers is far more complicated than most people think. Brett often equates it to running a start-up with a constantly changing product. But technology can help with the overall management of your creative enterprise. An early technology adopter, Brett began creating systems for documents and contracts in her first job in a three-person off-Broadway theater in the year 1992. This was the age of 3.5" computer discs that you inserted into a computer because the memory inside the computer was tiny and mostly used for processing. Of the three employees, only two were comfortable with computers. The artistic director was not, but he supported the time it took to implement the tiny system and liked that things could get done efficiently.

In a three-person organization, space was limited: a theater and a small office. While there were production meetings, staff "meetings" were more often conversations around morning coffee. The ease of communication was simple and production focused. Three brains, lots of three-ring notebooks, file cabinets, and one computer with 3.5" discs served as the knowledge system. It was fun but highly inefficient, with a lot of running up and down the stairs to the theater.

By 2006, Brett was the managing director for Imagination Stage, and the world had changed with respect to the technology available. But the systems that existed were happenstance. A system of shared knowledge of what goes where, how to communicate clearly, and how to prioritize still had to be created, communicated, and used. The company was also much bigger, with 52 full-time and 275 part-time artists, teaching artists, and over hire. Email predominated communication, and shared file folders on a server were common.

But problems existed. Younger staff had no sense of what the priorities were, especially which email needed the first response. Seniority, not mission or impact, often determined who had access for space. Eventually, a new software tool for space management provided a decision tree and transparency—40,000 square feet, seven classrooms, two theaters, and various other public spaces require coordination for facility management and maintenance. Additionally, the staff created a company-wide agreement for communication protocols (email priority systems, calendar appointments instead of email chains for meetings, etc.).

When Paul was the marketing director for a midsized dance company, communication about projects, workflow, and related responsibilities was not consistent. Even with an administrative staff of four, there was no system in place for sharing of internal information, which often led to duplicated work and missed opportunities. And often the first email in a chain was responded to instead of someone reading the entire chain on a given topic, wasting more precious time. Each staff member was great at what they did in their respective areas, but the lack of an organized system created more work and harmed efficiencies.

It is hopefully becoming clear that creating ecosystems of technology can make work easier but that doing so requires more than a standard, top-down approach. Senior and junior employees need buy-in and training. Any adopted technology solution will have to adapt over time. Hence, you will find ample explanations of not only useful tech solutions, but also conversations around how the employees are trained, how systems are created, and how the habits of work are changed, also known as *change management*.

It cannot go without saying that the global pandemic and lockdown had an immense impact on the way we all work. However, the need for clear and efficient internal operations existed prior to the pandemic. The only critical change noted over and over again in interviews was the need to rely on cloud-based solutions.[i] The organizations and individuals succeeded before, during, and after the pandemic because of clear and clean systems that could expand and contract as workflows changed.

Moving out of lockdown into the current day, hybrid and remote work continues to be a recognized and often successful solution for many organizations. But even if your organization has returned to 100 percent in-office, creating internal systems of knowledge sharing, communication, and workflow will undoubtedly contribute to greater success. The overarching system or technology framework has to facilitate person-to-person and team-to-team processes. And, most importantly, it must support the mission or purpose of the work overall.

---

[i] In this circumstance, interviewees were addressing external server–hosted content. Cloud computing can also be on-premises private servers. Hybrid infrastructures use both; internal servers are used for applications that have issues that must be addressed, and latency, governance, or security issues are better suited for on-premises operations. Video content for use in a production environment would meet that need.

How Knowledge Systems Create Success

Systems allow for work to proceed with ease. If an employee knows where to find a file, how to get the answer they need, or what the top priorities of their day are, work flows efficiently and effectively. The problem is that most organizations and individual businesses create "accidental" systems. These systems are created to serve the person who created them, with little thought to how they connect to the rest of the operations of the organization or fellow employees. We all know when something takes longer than it should, but it is rare that time is spent trying to fix the cause ("No one codified where to put the files in the drive"); rather, we often fix the system ("I'll put my work where I need it over here").

This is not a technology-based problem. When we had a world of documents, file folders, memos, and sticky notes, *how* the filing system was created was usually driven by one person in the organization. People who needed a file repeatedly would keep it (or a copy of it) on their desk. These breaks in the paper system would leave people looking for files, or lead to confusing the version history of a document ("How do you have the newest document—the file folder says the last one was edited on X date?").

It is also important to note that knowledge management has been a part of business structure for centuries, most often managed and transferred through a process of coworking and training. Small business owners would pass their knowledge on to the next generation through lived experience. Those working in trades would pass their knowledge through apprenticeship.

It wasn't until the 1990s that CEOs started talking about *knowledge management*—perhaps because the media and the web encouraged a new language for discussing the work of a new knowledge economy. According to *Harvard Business Review,* there are two approaches to knowledge management. When knowledge is managed in computer systems, it is a "codified" strategy. The second leans on the person-to-person transfer of knowledge, which if intentionally done is a "personalization" strategy. Choosing between the two is a choice and a strategy for a business. If a business wants to grow, codification is the right choice:

The codification strategy opens up the possibility of achieving scale in knowledge reuse and thus of growing the business.[1]

So what does it mean to *codify* your knowledge? In simple terms, it is a way of breaking down information (often stored in files or folders) into a transparent system that all the appropriate users can access to do their work and achieve their goals. For performing artists and organizations, often our collective shared knowledge exists in "siloes" tied to performances or shows. The following is a way of thinking about materials:

- Materials that will be reused by many people, teams, or departments.
  - Materials should be centrally located for all access (e.g., an employee handbook) or by department (e.g., a marketing style guide or logos).
  - Consider whether the materials will need to be updated and, if so, when.
    - If often, consider a wiki or internal-facing web page instead of a fixed PDF or other document.
- Materials that will be used once or within a time frame.
  - Materials should be located within a system of folders and names that align with the uses (e.g., 22-23 Production Name or 22-23 Season Marketing).
- People to documents: Create a flowchart of who uses or needs access to what materials and establish a permission tree that matches these needs.
  - Barbara needs to view document X. Donald needs to edit document X. Both have access to the document, but they have different permissions. Permission trees are important and need to be transparent (tell employees: you are being given *edit* access to Y drive and *view* access to Z). Permissions prevent accidental removal/deletion, but more important, they create a cleaner, expanded view and path for each employee. Employees see only what they need to do their work.

- Training employees is part of the strategy. Never assume anyone knows how to use your technology. They may be masters of the system at their previous position, but every software and codification is different. This is true regardless of age. No one is born knowing business technology, although we can all manage our personal devices. Employees still need a tutorial explaining how your company manages logins and how to navigate the system you or your organization have created.

- Buy-in/change management is necessary for effective implementation. Everyone has to use the system or it simply won't work. Creating rewards or positive public praise for people who use the system and add their materials appropriately is key.

The Producing Artistic Director and IT Director/Company Dancer at Attack Theatre were interviewed to gain a better sense of how knowledge management systems can work for a midsized contemporary dance company. Attack Theatre was founded in 1994 as a collaboration between two dancers, Michele de la Reza and Peter Kope. Its mission is to explore artistic expression in its commitment to remain curious in its investigation of new ideas; to artistically collaborate through deliberate, interdisciplinary partnerships; and to connect with local and global communities to provide accessible creative learning opportunities. To accomplish its mission, the company offers a performance season that includes original work choreographed by the company and collaborative work with other institutions, adult education courses, public school partnerships, and community education programs. The company also tours its work across the United States and beyond. As a midsized contemporary dance company with an operating budget of $1.2 million annually, it pays a staff and a company of dancers, with additional part-time staff totaling 13 and an additional 65-plus artists and teachers throughout the year. The company opened its first permanent home in Lawrenceville, a neighborhood in Pittsburgh, in 2021. A succinct description would be a company that is small with outsized impact and operations.

To achieve more than a typical company of their size might, Attack Theatre began investing in technology systems several years ago. The goal was to increase work efficiency. In 2019, they invested in Egnyte, a knowledge management system. Egnyte is a secure hosted file management platform. It includes layers of security, privacy, and compliance beyond a typical sharing/collaboration system with permission controls. The change to Egnyte saved time prior to the pandemic and was critical to operations afterward. As Dane Toney, a company dancer at Attack Theatre and its IT manager, explains:

> **Egnyte is pretty much our sole server. It houses everything—I mean everything. It was set up right before the lockdown. Before that all our servers were based on hard drives in the office. You could access them remotely, but it was very difficult and very, very slow.**

Speed is particularly important when working with larger files typical to a dance company like Attack Theatre. Content spans all documents, all music, video, photos, and archival materials.

When asked how moving to Egnyte revolutionized their work, both Toney and de la Reza note a multitude of impacts. For example, "We don't have 14 versions of the same document when editing grants" because of Egnyte's reliable version history system. Furthermore, it increases security and customization of users, which they find particularly helpful with an increased reliance on freelance workers. For example, Attack Theatre is currently working with an external public relations firm and graphic designer. They now share specific Egnyte folders with a specific permission level and an expiration date. This approach saves time and future headaches since there is no need to remember to go back and reverse permissions. Similarly, dancers have increased engagement in the system and access to files. De la Reza notes that "This changes communication flow and increased efficiency." Both Toney and de la Reza acknowledge that although Egnyte is powerful, it can take an additional level of training to understand a different logic and architecture. Admittedly, it is also more expensive than some of the integrated workspace solutions available to nonprofits. Toney notes that "Egnyte is expensive and powerful." They plan to continue to grow into using advanced tools of the system.

One of the oft-mentioned benefits of creating a system of organized and accessible materials is that employees can work independently. Providing the ability for staff to complete a project from beginning to end without waiting for someone to give them something, thus slowing down their process, increases worker satisfaction because they can self-actualize. Data from the "great resignation" of 2021 clearly demonstrated that people left jobs due to a lack of work satisfaction. Increasing a sense of satisfaction with one's work should, therefore, support internal commitment to a company. Creating a technology infrastructure that increases a sense of job ownership supports employee persistence. And it deepens institutional memory through actual documentation and human connectivity. De la Reza explains how this works at Attack Theatre:

> **Instead of calling someone and saying "Where can I find X?," they run a query in Egnyte. Institutional memory becomes more transparent. . . . [By] committing to these different technologies and the use of them . . . we're hopefully also preparing ourselves for a changing workforce. . . . Institutional memory is something that is so valuable.**

There are many other options beyond Egnyte. Big tech supports nonprofits through discounted pricing, from Amazon Web Services (AWS) to Microsoft Teams to Google Drive, among others. Regardless of where an organization stores its materials, the key to success is taking the time to codify the system and to train and reward individuals. This approach allows for high employee satisfaction, higher team morale, and a greater efficiency of work.

Whatever the system chosen, how we communicate across our organizations and how we communicate between our teams should integrate. This integrated system amplifies the efficiency and transparency available to any organization.

Internal Communications: From Memos to Email and Slack

As noted earlier, the performing arts is a people business—people working with people to make art for people. Effective and efficient communication is critical. When looking back on the heyday of the corporation, immortalized by television shows like *Mad Men*, we see that communication often consisted of watercooler conversations and memos from the boss. One offered informal and quick sharing of ideas or thoughts while the other served as a more formal notification, perhaps created in triplicate and saved for future reference. Business-to-business (B2B) communication occurred via telephone, meetings, or letters.

Business was disrupted in the 1970s and 1980s with the advent of the facsimile (fax) machine, which, over a phone line, could send a reproduction of a letter. It was so much faster than mailing letters. It also facilitated easy contracting and work across distances. It was so useful that it was still being used in the early 2000s by many, well after the advent of email, because it met the legal requirements of paper (Brett was faxing Actors Equity Association reports in the mid-2000s, and it was not uncommon to have to fax something for an international exchange as late as the 2010s!).

Email disrupted communications even more than the fax machine. Email was going to be the savior of all interpersonal communication. And it was—until it wasn't. In 20 short years, it became one of the biggest work inefficiencies used daily in the workplace. "Death by Email" was a common headline and generated the pursuit of the coveted "Inbox Zero." But email is only a tool and cannot take all the blame. It can be structured and used effectively, applying inbox rules, priorities, and other guidelines. Email's strength is its use as asynchronous communication. The problem is, we often use it as a synchronous communication path with an expected response. All of us, at one time or another, have expected someone to reply instantly or been expected to reply. You have likely had someone knock on your door with "I sent you an email 30 minutes ago, but I haven't heard back."

In people-driven, collaborative work that happens on a deadline, email falls short. It's linear and slow. While you can organize an email thread by a conversation, maintaining the integrity of a document passed through an email chain can easily become fraught with issues. Finding the information in an email that answered a question a few days and dozens of emails ago is often difficult. The list of potential woes felt by employees due to email is long. And, if the heart of our work is collaboration, then finding and using alternatives is increasingly common.

One way to solve the problem is using a solution for internal communications that moves immediate, bite-sized pieces of information to a more responsive platform. There are many options, from Slack to Teams to Yammer or HipChat or Mattermost. The increasing set of options reveals that these solutions work. These platforms also organize themselves into channels, allowing for self-sorted and easily searched information.

Email is not dead and remains necessary in the workplace. For communicating outside the organization, email is still critical. And email can still play a defined role in the internal operations of an organization, particularly for materials that don't require a quick turnaround, thereby leaning into email's strength. The key is creating standards and expectations of what goes where and sharing them with all users.

Using Slack or any of its work messaging siblings is easy. It is, essentially, threaded or "channeled" instant messaging akin to texting. It is not uncommon for small companies of two or three people to function using just texts. However, even small companies benefit from dedicated communication channels like Slack, as demonstrated in upcoming examples from Attack Theatre and Quantum Theatre. In fact, Brett started using Slack with a three-person enterprise in a university and was surprised at the immediate impact. It was particularly useful because of its natural content sorting and dedicated communication space outside of email.

Perhaps most importantly, unlike texting, work messaging systems are easily organized and searched. The ability to search is one of the reasons that Toney from Attack Theatre finds Slack to be a critical time-saving tool:

> With the amount we were texting each other and the amount we were emailing, things could easily be lost. And within text there's no search function, or at least I don't have a search function. So it's the amount of times I had to scroll through old text streams to find something in answer to "Hey, I sent a text. I don't remember what that number was but it was in a text message somewhere." It's like scrolling and scrolling and scrolling and scrolling to figure it out. So that has been the biggest benefit of just kind of keeping everything in its project and easily being able to search exactly what you need. For me, it was the biggest time-saver.

Attack Theatre adopted Slack only a couple of years ago. As de la Reza, one of the company founders, found, it took the usual transition for those used to an email-based culture:

> In the beginning, I was like, "Oh, another thing to check." And now I get annoyed that people send me emails; I'm like, Why are you emailing me? There's a Slack channel for this project, please put it in the Slack channel.

Once a company introduces a non-email internal communication tool like Slack, quite simply it completely changes their relationship to email.

Additionally, using a tool like Slack is good for project management and the primary reason many companies turn to it. However, it quickly changes the workplace culture and community. At Attack Theatre (and many others), there is a channel for company pets that actually gets the most activity (see Figure 1.1). All work and no play makes Slack a dull tool.

Attack Theatre's success as a dance company is similar to others. We interviewed Stewart Urist, former executive director of Quantum Theatre, because of the organization's very different work challenges and the solutions Slack afforded it. Urist implemented Slack when he joined the company. The organization's mission statement reads, "Quantum Theatre is a company of progressive, professional artists dedicated to producing intimate and sophisticated theatrical experiences in uncommon

settings, exploring universal themes of truth, beauty, and human relationships in unexpected ways." The organization has a physical office
but its work is site-specific. It has seven full-time staff; production staff
and artists are hired for shows. Urist notes that one of the biggest gains
from incorporating Slack is sorting and transparency: "The initial draw
was definitely addressing the clutter of an inbox intermixing very simple
emails or operational internal conversations from longer-term external
work. If it's all in your inbox, you have to have a system to organize that.
With Slack, those smaller conversations could be broken into separate
threads. It made it easy to be responsive to someone's simple one-sentence
question. . . . If it came in Slack, I knew it was one of my team members
who needed me right away."

Figure 1.1: An example of a Slack channel setup
Photo courtesy of Slack

At Quantum Theatre, the company used Slack as a front-of-house,
back-of-house communication tool. As a site-specific operation, traditional
headsets for communication are usually unavailable or nonfunctional
due to the limitations of the spaces. An example is the Carrie Furnace,
an historic steel blast furnace in Rankin, Pennsylvania, that has metallic
interference. Other historic spaces or schools have thick concrete walls
that inhibit signals for works that quite literally move you from room to
room. In those circumstances, Slack is used to run the cues for the shows.
According to Urist, "Most places we worked had Wi-Fi or a hotspot we
set up or with individual cell providers that had a signal. Slack was a
good way to communicate between front and back of house, and even
run the show" (see Figure 1.2 and Figure 1.3).

Figure 1.2: *King Lear actors outside the steel blast furnace*, directed by Karla Boos, at Carrie Furnace, Pittsburgh

Courtesy of Quantum Theatre

Although messaging tools like Slack seem intuitive, they still require intentional design, with a standard for channel naming and assigning someone to be in charge of starting/archiving channels. One common practice seems to be aligning channels to productions, as well as having a separate channel for administrative concerns. And, like any knowledge management system, establishing permission levels for each channel will help keep the mental load lighter. As de la Reza notes, "Archiving productions or projects once they are complete is essential to keeping a busy company's channels clean."

Training new employees on tools like Slack cannot be skipped, but it is not difficult. As de la Reza points out, "I think the training also relies on shared understanding of what channels are for and how to use it. I mean, it's not always what the technology can do, it's how we have a common understanding." At Attack Theatre, staff meetings include discussions about clarifications and improvements. For example, at one meeting someone mentioned there is a status button in Slack that would help people know if they should expect a response. Everyone agreed that would be useful. Additionally, due to the plethora of projects and programs, they created a naming protocol. All channels with education programs have "ed" at the beginning and all productions have "show," for example, #edduquesnepublicschool.

Figure 1.3: *King Lear standing inside the steel blast furnace*, directed by Karla Boos, at Carrie Furnace, Pittsburgh

Courtesy of Quantum Theatre

Managing the Workflow: Project Management Software

The three W's are critical pieces of workflow and collaboration: *who*'s doing *what when*. Project management software is a useful tool that provides clarity on the three W's for each employee and offers an organizationwide view for administrators. Furthermore, having a system that clarifies how an individual's work affects the larger project or organization results in increased worker satisfaction.

There are many benefits to creating a work management system. Perhaps first and foremost, it keeps work and goals all in one place. According to the Asana Anatomy of Work Global Index 2023 (download full report `https://asana.com/resources/anatomy-of-work`)[2], we spend 60 percent of our time every day *trying* to work—doing tasks like searching for documents, chasing approvals, and attending meetings—instead of performing skilled or strategic work. Teams lack alignment because tasks, files, and commutation are disjointed and spread across multiple logins and locations. Eliminating confusion increases team efficiency and effectiveness. Finally, when you provide greater clarity for the work, communication between team members and supervisors becomes focused and aligned to goals and tasks.

In the performing arts, it often feels as though everyone should know what to do—a rehearsal for an orchestra performance is similar in many respects. Many feel it should be a "rinse and repeat" mindset for a team. However, there are always exceptions to every "repeat." A workflow template could be used, but there will always be something unusual and different about a specific piece of music, a performance, a play, or a dance. That is why we make the art and why the audience comes back to see it. There is always something new to discover. The arts, especially the nonprofit arts, can benefit from a transparent workflow system.

The Anatomy of Work study determined that nonprofit organizations are typically highly collaborative workplaces but struggle to adapt to new business challenges. The nonprofit performing arts organizations are no different. From production to administration, teams of people collaborate. What is often lacking is a system for clear planning and management of individual projects.

Cloud-based software solutions offer a path for transparency and a shared understanding of goals, objectives, and tasks. But there is no silver bullet. The companies and individuals we interviewed for this book all have different preferences and solutions. Quantum Theatre utilizes Asana, Attack Theatre uses Airtable, and Aspen Music Festival uses ArtsVision, software that was designed to support the performing arts industry. Notable in all interviews, the key to success for a company is creating a culture around the technology. Any well-designed tool can be made to work, but it only works if everyone uses it and agrees to the terms. And the software must easily work within the systems created for storage and communication. De la Reza noted that at Attack Theatre:

Airtable's effectiveness is so much greater because Egnyte and Airtable interact and links in Slack. We have a system where we say you know if you're in Slack and you'll say, you know, "Carrie, could you please look at the budget for the draft budget for NEA," in all caps, and you put a hyperlink to where it is. If we had to attach things and upload things all the time, it would have just been an entirely different ballgame.

Asana

Asana is a cloud-based software that Brett has used since 2014 for the Arts Management and Technology Lab team at Carnegie Mellon University. The team meets weekly but otherwise operates remotely, connecting via Asana and Slack for all other communication. If a task requires a specific file, the file location is included in the task description as a hyperlink. What makes Asana work so well is the option for individualized views. Asana projects are essentially smart sheets that can be viewed in the way each user works best: list format, Kanban boards, or calendar format. It also allows users to see all their tasks in one place, called My Tasks, and to include personal tasks that are not part of a project, like a reminder to make an appointment for the eye doctor.

Urist at Quantum Theatre also utilized Asana for both administration and production. It was particularly useful for time-based work, from marketing and development to general event timelines and punchlists. For both large and smaller projects, there were tasks and milestones to mark key drop dates. Urist also used Asana for one-on-one and team meetings for collaborative agendas. Similar to the communication and knowledge tools we've mentioned, the Asana workspace can be managed by the organization's administrators who need to see everything, while specific projects can limit members and give permission to either view only or to edit. The view-only option is particularly useful for collaborators who need to know information but don't need to be able to work in the project. At Quantum Theatre they could manage projects that were production-focused (archiving when complete) as well as manage season or annual projects like an annual campaign or capital campaign.

Financially, Asana is well suited for smaller organizations because it is free, with a team size limit. It provides web access and mobile access for hybrid or site-specific work.

Airtable

As mentioned earlier, Attack Theatre accomplishes a lot for an organization of its size, primarily because of how Airtable makes its workflow so efficient. Attack Theatre uses Airtable for everything: auditions, education programs, human resources and contracts, productions, marketing, and fundraising. De La Reza feels one major success has been with contracts—Airtable has both empowered the small staff and made the contracting process much faster than before:

Airtable has enabled those with the information, who are really developing the projects and the scope, to create the contracts, all the input, the emails, and the phone numbers and the conditions of what the project is, and provide that information within the Airtable structure. Then those contracts go to the next step for approval. And then it can seamlessly go to the finance person, who is responsible for a whole other world. Right now they are also responsible for checking vaccinations if it's an in-person engagement versus a virtual, so . . . the finance person doesn't actually need to know the minutia of the project; they just need to be able to respond to what the information is in the Airtable and begin their work. Airtable has streamlined the process, because we also have an extremely high density of independent contractors and projects for an organization our size. Last fiscal year, we worked with 68 artists [as well as] many W-2 employees. Airtable enables us to handle all this efficiently with a 20-hour-a-week finance person. The minutia can happen before it gets to them, and the process happens much quicker.

Having a transparent workflow that empowers people at the program level to take an active role is admirable, but contracting far beyond W-2 employees is true at every performing arts organization. Creating efficiencies in this area frees up more time for high-level strategy and actual program work.

Another activity shared by all performing arts organizations is auditions. Toney highlighted the pivot to Airtable and the successful change in the process for the company's 2021 national auditions. They knew they needed to create a system that allowed for multiple steps: dancers needed to register and upload their materials, including video; those materials needed to be loaded into Airtable; confirmation emails needed to be sent; and multiple internal people needed to be able to access and evaluate the auditions and make notes to be seen by all. Toney made an Airtable form that allows dancers to register their information that generated an automatic email in Mailchimp with a link to a portal for video submissions. Establishing and creating the system took time and thought, but the mostly automated system has saved so much time that they now can't imagine doing it any other way. Figure 1.4 shows a sample audition workflow, and Figure 1.5 shows an events checklist in Kanban view.

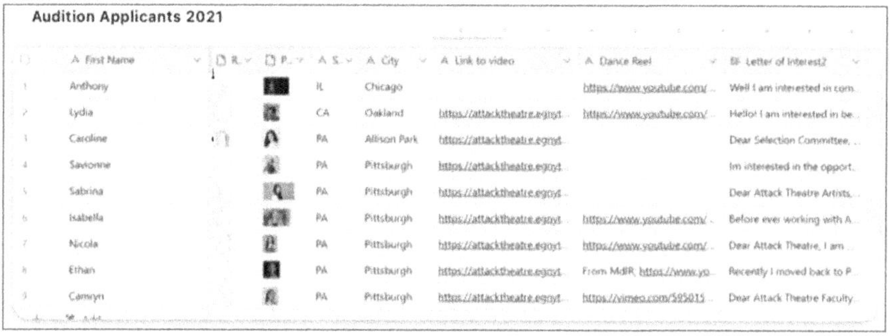

Figure 1.4: Attack Theatre sample audition workflow

Figure 1.5: Attack Theatre sample events checklist and timetable

ArtsVision

Aspen Music Festival (AMF) uses ArtsVision, software designed to support the performing arts industry, for everything except fundraising, marketing, and admissions. To understand how they use it for success, we interviewed the person who manages the ArtsVision software and the operations department: Kate Northfield Lanich, general manager. AMF is both a school and a festival featuring orchestra, chamber, and opera performances. Its mission is as follows:

> *The Aspen Music Festival and School's mission is to be the preeminent summer institution of classical music education, performances, and presentations; to be transformational and inspirational for all involved; to be innovative and a catalyst for change in the world of music, while drawing on and respecting its great traditions.*

AMF operates the 2,050-seat Benedict Music Tent, the 500-seat Joan and Irving Harris Concert Hall, and the 105,000-square-foot education campus that opened in 2016 in honor of Matthew and Carolyn Bucksbaum.

During the off season, the organization works with a slim staff of approximately 35, with only six in operations. However, during the summer, staffing expands to over 100 in operations and more across the other administrative departments. It takes an army of sorts to run a daily performance schedule and rehearsals in an educational environment with approximately 560 students and 80-plus artists. ArtsVision serves as the hub for the season.

ArtsVision is the gospel . . . . It's the culture. Every department uses it and we put everything in it.

Kate Northfield Lanich

Creating a culture for using technology is not automatic. According to Lanich, incorporating the calendar of events forms the spine of the system. From there, she looks at how to use it when new programs expand. She cites as an example:

Our opera program has exploded in the last two years—how do we use ArtsVision for casting and bring that into the orchestra fold? We've started using ArtsVision for our chamber music, so it's all centralized. We've even talked about how to use it for student infractions.

AMF uses Slate for admissions for tracking all student information from audition to registration, but for summer all the information has to move over to ArtsVision. For 2023, AMF developed an application programming interface (API) to get the two systems talking to each other.

A festival's heart is its performances. Similarly, the core of the summer work comes from events. Lanich explains how the production system is driven by events built in Airtable: "The season is in ArtsVision and then each event gets a production form that is completed in Jotform [a drag-and-drop form builder] with specific information we need for every event. That attaches to the event in ArtsVision. There is a weekly production meeting where details in the form are discussed, and decisions and questions asked are tracked. Ultimately, we get out of email communication and go to the exact calendar event to see all the paper-work for that event."

ArtsVision also connects to communications and marketing. For the students, communication happens mostly through email whose content comes from ArtsVision. "Each student gets an individualized email with all the information they need, including an iCal link that syncs to Arts-Vision," Lanich explains. "They also receive daily schedule emails for the opera program." ArtsVision also creates the content for the weekly program inserts, which is then handed over to marketing to complete. The style guide for the performance programs is built into the ArtsVi-sion data, so the organization's standards are kept, such as "O" versus "o" for Opus.

The whole flow is centralized around ArtsVision.

Kate Northfield Lanich

AMF also uses ArtsVision's contracts module. They have three people responsible for contracts: one focuses on staff, another on guest artists, and another on faculty. They put in the employees' personal information, dates, and responsibilities with custom clauses. "ArtsVision gener-ates a [Microsoft] Word document that goes into DocuSign," Lanich explains. "It also autocreates that person in an address book so we have the information in their profile."

The system is different from when Lanich started, but she constantly improves it for efficiency and effectiveness. Ultimately, all incoming staff are charged with significant responsibility at the outset. "ArtsVision allows us to have oversight," she says. "If there were 3 million docu-ments lying around, there would be no way to track it all. ArtsVision allows us to catch things before they become a big crisis."

ArtsVision has grown with the demands of the organization and the users. Early on, Lanich was charged with fixing the practice room booking software system. At first, there was no way to do that within ArtsVision due to its inability to differentiate user permissions for room reservations. So she started using a different system she learned about through her work at The Juilliard School. In 2021, ArtsVision came out with a room scheduling module that AMF tried. "While it isn't perfect yet, the program enables students to log into ArtsVision and see their full schedules," Lanich says. "So anything I had tagged them to, for example, chamber music or their spotlight recitals where they have their own private time demands outside of orchestra performances, they can book the rooms accordingly. Now all of that is on their phone."

Training

Three notable similarities emerged across all interviews and our personal experience:

- None of us were trained to have these jobs or run our work using technology in this fashion.
- We repeatedly relied on modeling as a training method.
- We improved and adapted over time, instead of cementing standard operating procedures around the technology.

In about 2009, Imagination Stage moved from using email chains for setting meetings to training everyone on how to use the Microsoft Office calendar appointment tool. First they started with an all-staff meeting to demonstrate how to use the technology and to discuss the time savings. But the critical move was that when someone emailed to set a meeting, recipients had to answer with an appointment invite, serving as a reminder. After a month or so, all 52 employees were on board.

At AMF, due to the influx of staff each summer, training is standardized. Bringing on 100-plus new employees each season creates a significant training demand. Lanich manages it through a system of who needs to do what in ArtsVision: "I feel like I'm fine-tuning it every year—each team uses it so differently. So the way we have come to do this is that we wrap ArtsVision into our workflow and training sessions for primary orchestra teams. Each orchestra has an orchestra manager, librarian, and stage manager. We have five orchestras, so we get that whole group in the same room on day 2 of them being in Aspen. We talk through the workflow of how to receive their roster of who's in their orchestra, how to do their plots, why we put together a production packet from step 1 through step 15. And then, using that as the trunk of the tree, we talk about ArtsVision. So then they know they're going to receive a roster and how to generate the information to the program book. And so it really kind of ties into the workflow and the timeline that way. Then for each team, I do a follow-up meeting with specialized training. The orchestra managers get specific training, such as how to pull a phone list and how to track attendance, all that kind of thing. Librarians also get specialized training on how to enter new works and how to pull a repertoire tab. For the other trainings, I like to differentiate in terms of who is a creator of information in ArtsVision, who is a report generator, and who's just using it as reference. Since the creator of content [position] in ArtsVision comes [with] a lot of responsibility—because everybody's looking at it and if it's wrong, it's a big deal—I spend a lot of time with that group. The others get put into one group and I train them together to save time."

At the end of the summer, all staff go through an exit interview where the technology used is discussed—what worked, what didn't, and what improvements each employee would suggest. That information is used over the next nine months to make improvements to what exists.

In smaller companies with flatter hierarchies, the improvement process is more ongoing. De la Reza from Attack Theatre says:

> It's an iterative process, just like the creative process if you're really committed to collaboration and the human-centered design approach to everything. There must be a commitment to the dialogue about what [element of the technology] is still relevant and what is still effective.

Training or onboarding staff into an existing technology that the organization has already been using is much easier than getting staff to use something that's new to everyone. In his new work at Pittsburgh Public Theatre as director of finance and administration, Urist discusses their move to Microsoft Teams, underscoring that adopting new technology is really about change management. It is important to begin by testing the technology with early adopters to work out the bigger bugs. Once a system is working well, training can happen with slow onboarding. As Urist explains, "You need people modeling how they are using the system to get others to open it, to get them to use it themselves. That leads to people accepting and using a new system."

The Selection Process

If an artist or organization hasn't begun using these technologies or other tools to improve their work efficiency and effectiveness, what is the process for selecting new tools? The simple answer is matching needs to solutions. The tipping point that inspires looking for new solutions is often the frustration of "18 million different spreadsheets" or dead-end conversations around technology that doesn't work. Bringing together everyone to discuss what doesn't work and what they need it to do is the first step. Consider sending out a digital survey to your staff to start the conversation before scheduling a meeting.

The exact choice of software depends on your budget and the complexity of the collaborative work at your organization. ArtsVision is a custom design for a narrow industry, and the engineers can design specific solutions for your organization. Asana and Airtable are industry-agnostic—both have nonprofit pricing, and you can work with the company's support team to build the most collaborative system to meet your goals. Egnyte is expensive but powerful. Google Drive is a certified nonprofit with Google that can be customized to meet a lot of needs. Slack, owned by Salesforce, has nonprofit pricing, as do many of its communication siblings. The critical factors in selection are identifying your needs, identifying your budget, and considering the change management needed for various technology solutions.

Summary

Performing artists and arts organizations are collaborative in their work. Collaboration in the 21st century is more effective, efficient, and rewarding when technology solutions are implemented for knowledge management, for internal communication, and for workflow management.

Performing arts organizations succeed through the work of people. Research on work cultures (McKinsey & Company, *Harvard Business Review*)[3-5] demonstrates that a supportive and transparent work culture promotes employees' satisfaction, thereby increasing the likelihood of business success. A critical factor to employee satisfaction is clear—consistent and transparent internal communication around the organization operations and worker goals and priorities. The opportunity for technology to support connection, effective collaboration, and clear communication was demonstrated prior to and during the work disruption caused by the COVID pandemic. A deeper understanding and respect for clean, clear technology systems is increasingly needed for success in the 21st century.

Takeaways

- Efficiency and effectiveness are strengthened with intentional implementation of technology systems.

- Codifying and training staff to the systems is critical to success.

- Strong systems require maintenance. Organizations change, people change, technology changes. Think about your technology systems at your home. Get to know what you have, consider what is and isn't working, and tackle one problem at a time while still seeing the big picture. As Lanich noted from AMF notes, "It really does take consistent monitoring and maintenance to . . . maximize how efficient it is. And I think if it just kind of sits, then it has the potential to outdate itself."

- Transparency is the key to employee satisfaction and can be achieved through technology solutions.

- Creating and passing on institutional memory is critical to the future of organizations.

- Hybrid and remote work structures are not required to consider improving or implementing these solutions.

Technology Solutions

The following technology solutions are mentioned throughout this chapter. Remember, this is not a comprehensive list of all the technologies available, but they might help to begin your research.

Knowledge Management

- Egnyte's all-in-one platform makes it simple and easy for IT to manage and control a full spectrum of content risks–from accidental data deletion to data exfiltration, to privacy compliance and much more–all while giving business users the tools they need to work faster and smarter, from any cloud, any device, anywhere (www.egnyte.com).

- Drive by Google provides storage, permission-based collaboration on files and folders, with integration to Google's docs, Sheets, Slides, and other cloud-native tools (`http://drive.google.com`).

Internal Communications

- Slack is a productivity support platform to connect people, and find files, with sophisticated automation (`www.slack.com`).
- Yammer is a communication tool by Microsoft that connects and engages employees across the organization (`www.microsoft.com/en-gb/microsoft-365/yammer/yammer-overview`).
- Matter Most is a secure collaboration and communication tool (`www.mattermost.com`).

Project Management

- Asana is a collaborative project management software for teams of any size or location (`www.asana.com`).
- Airtable is a cloud-based platform that makes it easy to streamline processes, workflows, or projects (`www.airtable.com`).
- Artsvision is a software designed specifically for the performing arts. It manages it all—planning, production, and operations (`https://site.artsvision.net`).

Notes

1. Hansen, Morten T., Nitin Nohria, and Thomas J. Tierney. "What's Your Strategy for Managing Knowledge?" *Harvard Business Review*, March 1, 1999. `https://hbr.org/1999/03/whats-your-strategy-for-managing-knowledge`.

2. Asana. "Anatomy of Work 2023 - Rise of the Connected Enterprise." Asana. Accessed May 22, 2023. `https://asana.com/resources/anatomy-of-work`.

3. Hansen, Morten T., Nitin Nohria, and Thomas J. Tierney. "What's Your Strategy for Managing Knowledge?" *Harvard Business Review*, March 1, 1999. https://hbr.org/1999/03/whats-your-strategy-for-managing-knowledge.

4. "How Companies Can Turn the Great Resignation into the Great Attraction | McKinsey." Accessed May 22, 2023. www.mckinsey.com/capabilities/people-and-organizational-performance/our-insights/great-attrition-or-great-attraction-the-choice-is-yours.

5. "People & Organizational Performance | McKinsey & Company." Accessed May 22, 2023. www.mckinsey.com/capabilities/people-and-organizational-performance/our-insights.

Keeping Track of Everyone

Patron/Donor Management + Everything Else

Knowing your customers and tracking their data is critical to success in any 21st-century business. In fact, having reliable and valid data can give you a superpower. In the performing arts, our customers are not as product-defined as those in retail or other business sectors. Understanding how people engage with performing arts organizations and experiences is a longitudinal process with a desire for multiple points of engagement that increase over time. An idealized journey for a customer becoming a subscriber and then a donor and eventual advocate is sometimes called the "ladder of engagement" (see Figure 2.1).

Individuals may be audience members or only donors; some may have children who have taken an education class with your organization, whereas others might hold another position of interest that is worthy of keeping a record, such as programs officer in a foundation, board members, volunteers, or local politicians. Since the 1980s and '90s, tracking all the information needed to maintain these relationships has become easier with customer relationship management (CRM) or customer relationship management system (CMS) software, also known as ticketing software, donor software, point-of-sales software, or a nonspecific general database like Microsoft Access. Tracking and using customers' histories and connected relationships is what makes databases so powerful and far superior to simple spreadsheets—recognizing that in business, spreadsheets do have a role in data analysis and visualization.

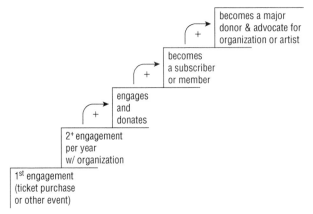

Figure 2.1: Sample ladder of engagement

Business can become quickly complicated when systems are not unified, synchronized, or singular. If an organization runs ticketing software donor software *and* has a separate point-of-sale system for its food service or restaurant, it is difficult to see a full customer data profile (CDP). See Figure 2.2.

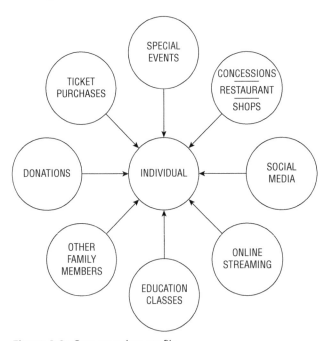

Figure 2.2: Customer data profile

Without having a clear understanding of the full experience of a customer, missteps are easily made that create distrust in future engagement. These missteps create an emotional impact that disconnects customers from your organization and work. It is not uncommon to feel disappointed when, after purchasing a ticket to a show, you receive a continued series of emails asking you to buy versus thanking you for purchasing. Or customers might have a feeling of frustration when receiving a "Thank you for supporting our campaign" email when they know that they didn't this time. The same emotional distancing results from a lack of personalization—for example, a "Dear Patron" salutation for a donor appeal. A lack of personalization creates a feeling of "Don't you know me?," which does not increase the desire to engage with an organization—or worse, it pushes patrons and donors away.

Managing all this information is, however, not easy. Success relies on effective system design, data processes, and maintenance. Data reliability and validity are necessary to fully achieve organizational success. As Katina White, Tessitura Support Administrator at the Pittsburgh Cultural Trust, noted in her interview, "Garbage in, garbage out." This is increasingly true as the technology environment demands greater privacy controls for customers. If you want to have audiences and donors who engage with you frequently and deeply, collecting reliable data and using it responsibly is a must.

CRMs have two distinct perspectives. Each person should be represented as an individual with unique needs, and each person's (customer, donor, volunteer) data should reside in a single database that is accessible to all elements of the organization that have contact with the customer. Centering knowledge requires buy-in and organizational change for some. Success comes from understanding customers and building relationships with them.

This chapter explains how to design and maintain a CRM system to collect the best data to achieve and measure organizational goals. There is no perfect list of what data to collect, but we offer strategies to identify what you need for your organization. Interviewees share how they maintain and use their data for greater business success. You'll learn how to use data, whether for board meeting visualizations and grant reporting or for strategic decision-making. A good database drives successful engagement with audiences, donors, students, and so forth. All of this takes training and buy-in from users.

Finally, this chapter recognizes that as technology changes or organizations grow, data systems must adjust as well. We present a simple framework for selecting and designing a CRM system that meets all your customer data profile needs to achieve your mission.

Structuring the System

One of the ideas that repeated in the interviews for this chapter was to consider the two sides of the system. The user interface needs to work for the staff member, the fundraising manager or the marketing team, and meet the needs of the largest income-producing arm of the organization, whether that's education sales, ticket sales, or donors. There is no perfect system. When we interviewed Matt Morgan, founder of Concrete Consulting, he explained, "You're always going to make some compromise when selecting a system. We go into these big projects with a vision of what we want. And then we look at the available products. And we see the checkboxes and see what features they have and what they do, and what they don't do. But we have no real experience of using them."

Morgan began as an IT consultant and went on to head the IT department at the Curtis Institute of Music. In his opinion, the key to system success is "internalizing the desires and goals of the organization and matching the technology to those goals." At Curtis, the overarching goal was integrating systems as much as possible to allow for a holistic view. Curtis, as a music and education organization, earns 10 percent via tickets and 90 percent through admissions and fundraising. Morgan noted that Curtis functions more like a cause-based nonprofit, prioritizing fundraising over tickets. Thus, the solution had to meet these two major needs. They developed a mostly integrated system using Blackbaud's Raiser's Edge, Financial Edge, and the Student Information System. External integrations came from their email provider, ShowClix, for concert tickets, and ASIMUT for class and room scheduling.

For Morgan, a successful CRM system is achieved when users are able to do their job easily: "I mean, ... from my perspective as IT director or CTO, when I can see them doing it without asking me a lot of questions, I know that moved the institution forward. Basically, when we've gotten it to the point where we have technology that's usable by regular people to do their jobs."

Yet being able to use the system is not the same as using it to the best of its ability. We spoke with Justin Gilmore, a nonprofit professional with experience in technology consulting, selling, and implementation, who works for a major technology company and has also worked as an employee for arts organizations, advocacy, and food assistance organizations. Gilmore has a lifelong passion for using data for good. In his words, "Data is worthless without values and context." Hence, looking down just one silo of data offers a lackluster understanding of customers. He explains, "A common implementation pitfall is thinking of your types of individuals as a single-pick list instead of a multi-pick list." For example, Jordyn Smith isn't just a donor or an audience member; they are a donor, audience member, and frequent purchaser of pre-show and intermission concessions or drinks. You don't want to send one email, then another, then a third in a promotion campaign. To be successful, you must design the system holistically for future use.

Size is not a determinator of success. Attack Theatre uses data throughout its processes (`https://attacktheatre.com`). As a dance and education company with a $1.2 million budget, their work includes arts education in schools, theatrical performances, tours, community programs, and partner programs. Artistic Executive Director Michele de la Reza explained that they use Little Green Light (LGL) for their CRM. It connects with their email, ticketing, and donor pathways as well as their work management system, Airtable. But LGL is the hub. According to de la Reza:

> The CRM is definitely the nerve center of our organization. AT's earned income does not follow a traditional dance company model of ticket sales and/or school fees. The smallest percentage of our earned income comes from ticket sales, and the rest is from arts education fees, commissions, and some touring. Communicating effectively with these different constituents requires a customized system of labeling and tagging. With thorough records, we can communicate the presence of new programs. For example, collecting information that answers "Are you a symphony who interacted with us in the past? Did you know L'Histoire du Soldat is back in rep? Are you an educator who saw us perform at your school or had us in your classroom? Did you know we are now offering Act 48 credit for our summer educator intensive or that we have funding to underwrite two artist residencies in rural communities?'"

Attack Theatre integrates LGL with Stripe to process donations, with TicketSpice for ticket sales, and with RegFox for class and event registrations.

Understanding all the touchpoints of your audience across your activities contributes to success. Attack Theatre offers a unique success story as an organization with multiple audiences. They have created a system for how to track these differences, particularly those who have contact with the organization but have not participated in a program. Ultimately, these points of contact indicate the possibility for the individual to have a future engagement. De la Reza explains:

> An important aspect of our tagging system that we've created doesn't necessarily track participation but tracks possibility. For example, it might be a group for educators (sending them emails about upcoming education opportunities), a group for former staff and board (sending them an email to be a part of a big anniversary or going away party), a group for families.

Good systems are a work in progress, solving problems one at a time. Large organizations have more money and people to work on CRM systems. Another scaling opportunity for multiple organizations to gain the power of a larger organization is to form a consortium of organizations that share a system. One model is offered by the Pittsburgh Cultural Trust in Pittsburgh, Pennsylvania (`http://trustarts.org`). The Trust manages the downtown cultural district, a 14-block arts and entertainment neighborhood, one of the largest areas curated by a single nonprofit. Operating within a unique public-private partnership model, the Trust is a national model for urban redevelopment. The Trust hosts a shared installation of Tessitura that serves them; their resident companies that perform in their spaces, like the Pittsburgh Ballet Theatre, Pittsburgh Public Theater, and Pittsburgh Opera; as well as organizations in the Cultural District in downtown Pittsburgh and other neighborhoods. Organizations' sizes range from $2 million to $60 million, so working together lifts all ships.

The Trust's shared Tessitura system was one of the first and remains one of the best, examples in the United States. This is perhaps because of the Trust's unique history. At the Pittsburgh Cultural Trust, they built a shared Tessitura as an IT addition to an existing shared services model. Katrina White explains:

> Since Pittsburgh arts organizations were already implementing a resource-sharing model for things like health insurance and ad sales, a new department was created in response to a need for a shared CRM. This department [Information Strategy and Technology Services, or ISTS] services 10 organizations that participate in a consortium utilizing Tessitura and a shared e-commerce platform.

Christine Wingenfeld, Partnership Manager and Data Analyst at the Trust, adds:

> We are a department of the Pittsburgh Cultural Trust, but we
> work with all the consortium partners, and a lot of what we were
> founded on came out of the concepts through shared services
> since it had existed before us, which helped the shared data-
> base come together since relationships with other organizations
> already existed.

Tessitura is one of the most popular systems used in the performing arts, according to the 2015 National Ticketing Software Survey, and the shared installation is increasingly common, allowing for a strong IT hub to serve many organizations.[1] Wingenfeld offers an explanation for its dominance in the market:

> Tessitura is designed to understand your patron very holistically,
> so you're not just looking at their donation information or their
> ticket history, but you can see across the whole so when your
> development associates are on the phone with a patron they can
> see the shows they're coming to and how much they have given.
> Perhaps there's a patron who has invested thousands of dollars
> over the years through their ticket purchases. The system enables
> you to identify them as this person is also high value, but they're
> investing in us in tickets, not donations.

Ultimately all the patron's information is in one place. This removes errors that result from siloed information. It means that anything out-of-system, like community-event attendance, must be input into the system to ensure a full picture is maintained.

Gathering + Cleaning

CRM systems are only as valuable as the data entered in them. And, as noted earlier, there is no such thing as perfect. You can't buy a system and expect it to run seamlessly forever. Much like any form of technology, it requires consistent maintenance to be reliable. Take for example, a car. If you own a car, you have to add gas, change the oil, rotate the tires, and wash and wax regularly. CRM systems require significant attention to run well. Staying with the car metaphor, they are more like a high-performance racecar with fancy transmissions than a standard car.

CRM systems have inputs and outputs. The inputs must be as clean as possible to ensure the most reliable output. But, as Morgan notes, the complexity of integrating systems is imperfect: "The challenge I almost always find is getting data from system A to system B. Consider email marketing and fundraising systems; each is a four-dimensional database that includes a lot of history of activity." Integrations can never be perfect because there's no way to fully capture their history.

Furthermore, singularity is lost. There is no single user ID. Morgan notes that at Curtis perfect integration couldn't happen because, in each separate system, separate user IDs were generated for each individual constituent. "They were linked rather than actually integrated."

As noted by Morgan, CRM data typically has multiple inputs that are automated from transactions and online engagement, as well as input by humans at box office windows and donor record updates with checks or other donations. The complexity breeds imperfection, so scheduled cleaning is necessary. The good news is that there are many ways to input, clean, and maintain data to increase the likelihood that your organization will have reliable and valid data to use. As Wingenfeld notes, at the Trust, "Leadership understands that we have all this data and want us to use it better. A big piece is having clean data."

The good news is that most CRM systems have tools and procedures that can deduplicate and do basic data cleaning; of course, the process does require oversight. At large organizations or those with shared systems, data cleaning is managed by an IT department and done regularly. At the Trust, the IT department manages cleaning with a weekly procedure and quarterly national change of address (NCOA) updating. Wingenfeld explains:

We have a procedure that runs every week, and it cleans up some of those duplicates with certain criteria we define. It can catch if "lane" is spelled out or abbreviated and the like. As long as the name matches and the address matches, there's a merge process that helps clean that up.

External data appends can also be used to support a robust data ecosystem. Andrea Newby has been using robust data appends for most of her career. In the last 16 years, she has worked at both the North Carolina Symphony (www.ncsymphony.org) and TheatreSquared (https://theatre2.org).

Located in Raleigh, North Carolina, the symphony holds more than 300 concerts, education programs, and community engagement offerings that reach adults and schoolchildren in all 100 North Carolina counties. At the Symphony, Newby used Archtics from Ticketmaster.

While Ticketmaster is known for its work with popular music concerts, it was an early vendor in the field and continues to support organizations today. Newby notes that:

> **At the symphony, we became one of the most sophisticated users within the arts with a holistic view. Everywhere I've worked, we've had a holistic CRM, which is really helpful because as my time went along, I worked both in the marketing and fundraising departments, so a holistic view helped with my role as director of patron loyalty.**

Newby has a natural intuition for working with data. Recognizing that data does not always come in perfect, Newby ran both data cleaning protocols and data appends. For her, it was a way to get the most out of the data and save money in the long run. Clean data means high-impact contacts:

> **At the symphony it was really fun working with our own data. So, we used zero-party data [data customers have voluntarily provided to the organization][2] and then we would append it with some first party data [behavioral data collected from customers' interactions with websites, products, apps, social media using IP addresses and logins to help marketing teams create customer segments based on interests, topics, products, and demographics] as well as use third-party data. We would, of course, use their transactional history, and we appended demographics and psychographics as well. It was a lot of data hygiene, but it kept costs down. It was essential, especially in 2008, when we were incredibly lean.**

Newby joined TheatreSquared as director of marketing and communication in February 2020 and by fall 2020 her marketing feats were heralded at the National Arts Marketing Conference for creatively connecting to communities throughout the lockdown. TheatreSquared, located in Fayetteville, Arkansas, performs bold new plays in an intimate setting and has grown to become the state's largest theater, welcoming more than 80,000 community members to 350 performances and events each year. The organization uses Tessitura. There Newby currently appends information to her CRM using data from Melissa (www.melissa.com).

This sounds almost too perfect, but proper data cleaning can't be done without some manual labor. Even with robust automated sweeps for deduping, appending, and cleaning data, individual attention is necessary to ensure your data is as reliable as possible.

People's Light Theatre in Malvern, Pennsylvania, is known for its resident company of actors, and it's one of the largest nonprofit professional theaters in Pennsylvania, serving over 80,000 (www.peopleslight.org).

It is located on a seven-acre campus that includes two black box theaters, scenic shops, rehearsal halls, classrooms, a restored 18th-century farmhouse to house guest artists, the Bistro restaurant, and The Farmhouse banquet and catering facility. People's Light is part of a Tessitura consortium in Philadelphia. While the team at the consortium does regular data deduplications and cleaning, Director of Patron Experience Eve Trojanov tackles more detailed work:

> **We really do a lot of the data scrubbing. A lot of that also comes from my interaction with our team, who have more tight customer service and sales representatives. They'll let me know because they've directly reported to me if they've come across a lot of really bad data. And then, I will give it to my team because I have the numbers on my side because we have about six apprentices and three full-time people as well. I will give it to them as a project and be like, can you go through and clean.**

An example of a heavy but important data-cleaning project is something Trojanov has been working on for the theater's upcoming 50th anniversary. After shifting operations during the pandemic, People's Light Theatre lost touch with some of the subscribers, some of whom began subscribing in the first year of operation. To highlight these high-engagement supporters, they want to include all who are able. Trojanov has her team making and tracking individual contact with those subscribers who have dropped off so they can determine who just changed addresses versus who have aged out or are unable to make it to the theater anymore. While this process is labor intensive, the data will be highly valid and reliable when they need it to be.

At smaller organizations like Attack Theatre, data is still a priority. They train all program officers and staff on basic input and reports from LGL. But they need a consistent cleaning system, and de la Reza notes, "We are considering investing in a 5–8-hour/week contractor who can live anywhere and is solely responsible for maintaining CRM and producing reports. This would help mitigate the changing of staff."

Using Data Analytics for Strategy + Planning

Data should only be collected if you plan to use it. It is best to track what you need, not everything, as the more extraneous data you order, the harder it is to maintain its integrity, even with regular cleaning. Transaction and attendance data for performances and donations are obvious, important, and useful, but the goal is to use data for evaluation and planning. Measuring what matters is cliché but true. And different users may want different reports from the same data to answer different questions. Again, at the consortium level, an IT professional may be serving many organizations and users with many different needs. In today's world of data, this is an exciting opportunity, not a bad thing. Wingenfeld is a data evangelist. In doing strategic data analysis for the Trust and all the consortium users, she notes, "I am reaching over 40 users and 1,800 dashboards."

Of course, data analytics is her job and her passion. "My focus is on the dashboard analysis side of things. Just a couple of years ago, Tessitura released an analytics tool that is built into the system and part of the agreement. It's through a company called Sisense which is similar to something like Tableau." This moves the concept of creating a report into creating a dashboard, the difference being that no export is necessary. Wingenfeld offers this example: "We used to run this performance audit every week. But instead of somebody having to pull that out and dump it into a spreadsheet manually, we just have a dashboard, and magically, the numbers update."

Wingenfeld has been doing this for a while and has a system for success: "I start everybody with a set of templates; all they have to do is change the filters. From there, users can copy the sample to use as a template for their organization. So instead of starting from a big scary blank dashboard, you're starting from something that's in there." This encourages users to explore the system. But playing with numbers and data doesn't get you across the finish line. Knowing the system is there doesn't help you know which questions to ask. To solve that problem, Wingenfeld explains: "I created a series of internally built and maintained dashboards to answer things from my experience with the ballet that I recognized as frequently asked questions. These dashboards are designed as a series of questions, for example, How did that show do? How did that campaign do? How did that promo code do?" See samples Figures 2.3 and 2.4.

Tessitura is not alone in moving from reports to dynamic dashboards. They are critical to linking job actions to data in many ways. Morgan notes that as a consultant:

> Some of my philosophy as a tech person working to move nonprofit organizations forward technologically, is that it happens more from the ground up than from the top down. So, you can say that you've got a strategy to integrate your CRM data and leverage it better. Still, at the ground level, that depends almost entirely on the ability of the actual fundraisers to use the data themselves and know how to use it themselves.

Morgan, like Wingenfeld, believes that users have to drive their own success by empowering them to create their own dashboards:

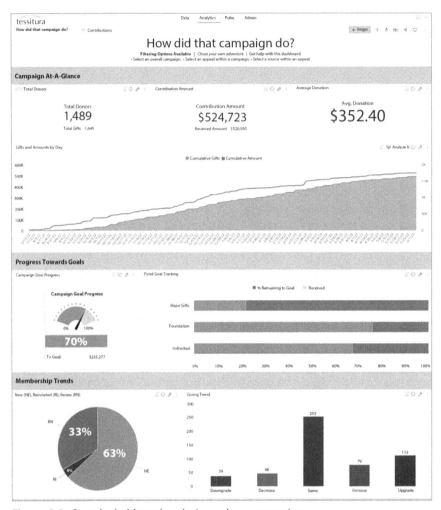

Figure 2.3: Sample dashboard analyzing a donor campaign

Created by Christine Wingenfeld

I focus more on if I'm going to build a dashboard, I want it to be a dashboard that the fundraiser can build and use because I so often build dashboards that are not the actual information that they use to do their jobs, but it's really hard to get good information about what they need. But one nice thing about Raiser's Edge XT, the new one, is they can control their dashboards themselves.

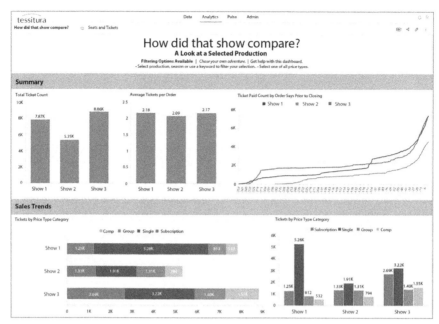

Figure 2.4: Sample dashboard to compare show attendance
Created by Christine Wingenfeld

As managing director for People's Light Theatre, Erica Ezold wants to use data to predict the future. They are trying to map patrons' overall engagement across both development and marketing: "We are thinking about who and what data we can pull so that we can track when, specifically, patrons are engaging for like three times in a season. Because we think that has an impact on when they really become a stakeholder in the organization. They have full buy-in."

Ezold is also looking holistically across the organization and considering how all stakeholders might offer opportunities for future programs, from education customers to commercial engagements at the restaurant or Farm House. And she knows that times have changed:

> Prior to the pandemic, we had very good, reliable data analysis that we would do in terms of being able to track single ticket sales based on prior patterns. And so right now where we are setting up, what are the new patterns? What are the marketing strategies that we need to change because of that? What are the new things we need to track against?

Data is there to inform decisions. As Ezold notes, "We want to use the data to create the changes we want to make."

Data-Forward Company Culture

Just moving to using a CRM system does not magically create a data-oriented, successful business. Having a data-curious or data-forward company culture creates success. This requires staff buy-in and organizational commitment. To do this, everyone needs to understand the impact of data on their work with training to empower them to accomplish their jobs. The organization supports this work by implementing a strategy and goal-based CRM system following some of the recommended better practices, best expressed as "Success is not defined by on time and on budget"—meaning that interdepartmental understanding and action around meaningful customer behavior must be tracked and measured.[3]

User Training + Onboarding

Data only serves a purpose if people are using it effectively and efficiently. That might be scrubbing data, integrating new tools, or creating dashboards for decision-making. If no one is using the technology, it isn't solving the problems it was purchased to solve. Organizations that are truly data-forward hire and train to meet current and emerging technology needs. However, all these organizations must create staff buy-in and train to their specific systems. This becomes particularly important when new technologies are added to an organization and staff workflow. Karen Graham, a nonprofit consultant and coach specializing in leadership and technology strategy, noted in a recent article[4] that in her 22 years of supporting nonprofits in choosing and implementing technology solutions, this has been a consistent theme. "Organizations of all sizes and levels of digital maturity seem to trip over user adoption, really using the system." She explains that it isn't a technology issue—it's a change management issue.

In our conversation, Graham explained how user adoption affects technology success: "I don't think that organizations are lagging, or, you know, not being as successful as they could with technology, because of lack of tools. I just don't think that's the case. But I do see organizations really challenged by user adoption, that comes up over and over when I do training."

While training users individually is essential, change management starts earlier. Graham recommends starting when you begin thinking about making a technology investment or change:

It really starts right when you're even considering making some kind of technology investment by involving the right people, articulating the reasons for the decision, getting people on board before you've even started to shop for products. And making sure that you're designing the whole thing around the needs of users and what's going to really work for the organization.

Essentially leaders must solicit buy-in from all users. Graham recommends finding means to allow users to have quick wins because they use the technology:

A quick win is always great. A common pain point for staff, I think, is that they don't have as much time as they would like. Where if you can just automate a process if you can find some productivity gain, that gives them back 10 minutes a day, those are 10 minutes that they can use doing something that's much more meaningful to them. And that feels like it's advancing the mission of the organization in a more salient way. Not that technology stuff doesn't advance the mission of the organization, but it's just not as tangible to people. And so little productivity gains early on are really important.

Many organizations do standard training provided by the CRM provider. However, once the training is complete, users must practice and continue to learn by working in the system. At People's Light Theatre, Trojanov implemented a living document system for the user handbook/manual using Guru. This allows staff who are feeling lost to get quick how-to instructions on cards.

At the Trust, Wingenfeld does this by creating small wins with dashboards as she is onboarding new users to the data analysis end of the process. She has created a best-practice lesson plan for others to use.

RECOMMENDED TRAINING PROCESSES FROM CHRISTINE WINGENFELD

Lesson 1: Create Templates for Frequently Asked Questions

Every organization has its "FAQs"—"How did that show do?" or "How did that campaign compare?" These make great starting points for getting new users onboard with a data analytics tool. A simpler dashboard with additional notes and explanations for how to use the filters can guide them through getting comfortable with the system. They can be reassured that they won't break anything or change anything for anyone else if they adjust filters to look at the show or campaign they have in mind.

Lesson 2: Introduce a Three-Level Process for Getting Started

The goal is never to start someone from the big-scary-blank-dashboard. From the first level, as view-only for the templates, users are introduced to ideas and options for creating their dashboard. Then, they can copy one of those templates and adjust it to their needs. Maybe instead of the total number of tickets, they just want to look at paid tickets. Or maybe there's a widget they want to remove or replace with something else. From here, the third level begins with a blank dashboard, but users can copy in their favorite widgets from the templates.

Lesson 3: Be Available Consistently

It takes time to get data analytics as a focus in people's schedules, especially at smaller organizations or during busy times of the year. By having consistent sessions, it gets people's minds on data analytics and time blocked on their calendars as available to work on building or reviewing dashboards. Some days may be a larger group with many questions, while others may be just you and one other person working on projects quietly. Having a mix of sessions also drives some interest and intentionality—alternating featured topics with open-ended time while mixing in a few intro overviews throughout the year.

Lesson 4: Create a Local Community

Use your local knowledge or communication systems, Google, Slack, Microsoft Teams, or others, as a place to share tips, questions, or data puns. Maybe include more general data literacy lessons for those who are both active dashboard builders and those who are just viewers to learn how to better interpret and understand the data. Be sure to celebrate everyone's progress and invite them to present on a topic, create a dashboard showcase, or just give shout-outs for victories of all sizes.

A component of change management that is sometimes forgotten is the emotional component of change. Graham has written on the subject and shared perspectives on the emotional undercurrents that need to be addressed:

It's so emotional when people have to change the way they work, learn some new products. A staff member or leader is used to being in many environments, often the smartest person in the room. And then they have to learn this new technology that just throws them off balance. And they feel embarrassed to admit in front of their peers that they don't know how to use it yet. And it slows them down. And it's just frustrating. And maybe they feel some loss of control because they used to know all the work-arounds to get the old system to work. And now, they're not as useful anymore because their problem has been solved. You know, there's just like, all these, these emotional things that come up with change.

Ultimately the change at hand is a cultural change that needs to be supported from the top. Graham explains that while finance doesn't make the most compelling argument for leaders, "I think speaking to their heart and helping them make the link between technological change and mission effectiveness is the key to doing that."

Graham's last piece of advice is to "mind your infrastructure." Be sure that whatever technology you are planning to use can be used. Graham explains, "I think there are lots of organizations out there that are excited about jumping ahead to technology that will help them do their work better. But then maybe they leapfrog over some of the basics, including good Internet connection, up-to-date operating system and computers, and security." Indeed, security is increasingly a critical piece of an organization's infrastructure.

Privacy, Security + Legal Compliance

Changes in public policy are impacting various technologies run by organizations, including how they collect and use data. In the early 2000s, organizations in the United States had to meet credit card security through payment card industry (PCI) compliance and credit card encryption.[5] More recently, public policies have been enacted that affect organizations and their collection, storage, and use of personal data. Three significant policies are noted here, but keep in mind that it's important to work with vendors to stay on top of changes. It is also important to note that while these laws may not be created by the United States or in the specific state in which an organization operates, they often still affect business practices.

The *General Data Protection Regulation (GDPR)* is a comprehensive data protection law that sets out guidelines for the collection, processing, and storage of personal data within the European Union (EU) and European Economic Area (EEA). While the scope of the law applies to organizations, regardless of original location, that handle the personal data of individuals residing in the EU, websites cross borders without an organization's knowledge. GDPR requires that individuals provide informed and unambiguous consent for collecting or processing data (hence the pop-up prompting about cookies on almost every website). It also gives individuals the right to access their data, correct inaccurate data, erase data, and the right to object to the use of data in particular ways. It also requires organizations to notify individuals if their data was leaked during a breach within 72 hours.

In the United States, after GDPR's implementation, the state of California passed two data protection laws that provide many of the same protections covered in GDPR, including the *California Consumer Privacy Act (CCPA)* and the *California Privacy Rights Act (CPRA)*. Both the CCPA and CPRA are designed to enhance consumer privacy rights, provide greater transparency, provide control over personal information, and impose obligations on businesses to protect consumer data. While California has a history of creating stricter protective laws than the United States overall, its actions still have an impact more broadly.

These policies affect internal operations as they affect data available to organizations, particularly from outside entities like Google Ads or Google Analytics. The result is a greater need for exceptional first-party data, as third-party data will be less available. As Ezold notes, at People's Light Theatre, "more people have to really be opting in as we move from a third party to first-party data."

As organizations and artists continually adapt to new policy landscapes, staying engaged with their technology partners is important. To comply with current and upcoming policies, Gilmore recommends "understanding who you are working with and who they are working with. If you're choosing the right technology and the right company, they should be providing those things for you. It should be included in the roadmap, and you should be able to see the changes they've made over the past few years, like two-factor authentication."

Graham agrees and offers questions for organizations to consider when assessing risks involving ransomware and crises out of the organization's control. "It's just something . . . to ask . . . about because if they have a ransomware attack, or if their vendor does, then what happens? Like what's the recovery plan for that? What's the potential damage to them? And just kind of business continuity concerns, I think those are good questions to ask your vendor, like, what's your history of downtime? If our system goes down? In the middle of a busy time of ticket purchases, or whatever, what happens? What's the backup plan?" Ezold notes new entrants into these areas of risk: "Of course, there is now cyber-insurance."

At the organizational level, digital literacy is critical to security. Gilmore notes that "the biggest vulnerability is having someone steal a user's name and password." Morgan echoes the concern around local breaches and passwords. He explains, "The most important thing they can do, the single most important thing they can do to keep themselves secure, is never to use the same password twice." He acknowledges that that is difficult in a day of software-as-a-service and a multitude of logins required just to accomplish a day's work. Thus, his solution is to use a password manager, which makes it more convenient and encrypts all passwords. Furthermore, Morgan recommends testing and training employees. At Curtis, they used KnowB4. At Curtis, emails are sent to individuals to see if they take the bait and click or download. If they do, the staff follows up with a training opportunity. At Curtis, the vast majority passed the test, and those who didn't pass were offered training. According to Morgan, staff improved markedly over time.

When asked about password protection and security, Graham noted that solutions like LastPass or other encrypted password solutions are good, but that single sign-on, also known as two-factor authentication, is the more secure solution: "Single sign-on is probably the direction to go. Eventually, but I think a password vault can be a steppingstone to that. And it's certainly much better than just like having a spreadsheet of your passwords saved on your desktop or drive."

Smaller organizations can lean on technology partners to provide security and even some training for increased digital literacy. According to de la Reza:

> Egnyte is very focused on security and continues to provide seminars and updates. Internally, there are lots of safeguards we have in place related to folder permissions, etc. We also have a cyber security module on Paylocity that we will require employees to attend. We've instituted two-factor authentication for LastPass. I know there was a breach, but I love it. It has changed the world of managing passwords. We only shifted to this two years ago. We also have two-factor authentication for QuickBooks and other software containing sensitive info. Everyone has password-protected logins to the server/Egnyte. Externally we rely on Egnyte continually updating their security systems.

Morgan notes that to address security concerns, organizations often restrict computers at the user level and how the employee can install or use software to accomplish their job. In his opinion, security can get in the way of mission impact and staff effectiveness. Staff must have a sense of ownership of their technology tools. This involves an element of trust from the organizations. Morgan feels strongly that organizations must trust in their staff and recognize that self-reliance is critical to an effective workforce:

I believe that making the updates automatic is a must. They are best practices. But I still have people telling me that staff shouldn't be admins on their own computers. But that's out of date. People are creative; creative people need to be able to do what they need to do with their computers. And if they must stop to ask you for permission every time, they're not doing their jobs.

Ultimately, instead of limiting staff autonomy, it is more effective to use password encryption and security training for staff.

Finally, our infrastructure and security concerns continue to our physical campuses. For People's Light's seven-acre campus, securing facilities is essential. While many of us have found solutions with key cards, they are moving to more mobile solutions to allow for more seamless access dissemination as production teams change. Ezold notes that overall, the company is working on upgrading its infrastructure by outsourcing that side of IT. It is "helping us with infrastructure upgrades and data security, like all sorts of things like that . . . our security system for the buildings is now able to be accessed with a key card or the app on your phone." Similar solutions can be used for virtual call boards and other stage operations.

Artificial Intelligence: Automation, Machine Learning, + Chatbots

The future of CRMs will be driven by artificial intelligence (AI), and the future is here. All the major companies serving the performing arts have incorporated access via plug-ins or app exchanges to many forms of AI, from automation to machine learning. Machine learning can support decision-making in two directions: future predictions and evaluation of past performance. The key is understanding what you want to know from the data. Predictive machine learning uses the past to predict a future outcome. It can be used to support making a decision, but it is potentially harmful because it is looking backward through time and includes the social context that may no longer be relevant. Machine learning can use the same data but simply analyze it to answer questions, such as "By applying this promo code on this date did we increase new audiences or lose money to our usual audience?"

Organizations will likely provide some level of customer service using chatbots. A chatbot is a computer program that uses AI to understand customer questions and automate responses to them, simulating human conversation.[6] For example, consider the abandoned cart syndrome—whether the cart contained a donation or a ticket sale. A chatbot can be trained to recognize behavior and then intercede along the purchasing journey to support the sale or donation. Further personalization can occur if the system can identify the customer via a login and engage according to past behaviors. For example, if the chatbot sees that this person tends to buy tickets in pairs or as group tickets, it can prompt the customer with, "Would you like the link to group sales or individual tickets for our upcoming show?"

Simple automation might also be considered a form of AI. As Gilmore noted, automation "doesn't take your hand off the wheel. A good automation system should schedule tasks and prompt staff to engage with the individual at the right moment and in the right way." This aligns with greater personalization within a data-use path. Gilmore provided an example from a family-oriented performing arts organization and using automated dynamic content. "If I'm attending dance performances, then I should see a picture of a dancer in a donor appeal."

Automation can support all levels of organizations, perhaps offering greater opportunities to smaller organizations. At Attack Theatre, they are increasingly enacting automation to save time and prevent data errors. De la Reza explains that:

> One of the challenges of capturing all this data is that somebody needs to enter it. The person keeping LGL up to date is not part of the program team that is interacting with all the people. One system we are piloting is automation in our Accounts Receivable/ Accounts Payable Airtable. There is a click box for "Add to LGL." The person who is entering something to pay an artist or invoice an organization or a school can click that box. It will go to the integration queue in LGL and be entered.

Attack Theatre has also found automation valuable for tracking participation and reporting on appropriate grants. De la Reza explains:

> Most importantly, we created this same automation from our Participation Logs. Our logs track all our engagements that reach over 20,000 people of all ages each year. It is a lot of data. It is broken down by department, program, in-person or virtual, free or paid, number of youth, number of adults, school district, etc. This is the place most used for gathering data for grants or board reports. It does not rely on income but on participation.

The contact point is used for tracking individuals over time. "If there is a human coordinating the engagement, that is the person we want to keep track of. Did they then become a ticket buyer? A donor? A board member? This is only possible if we can efficiently bring them into CRM and follow their life cycle with AT."

While not a form of artificial intelligence, statistical modeling can help us understand past and predict future engagement. The for-profit sector uses statistical modeling to predict future sales patterns, and these tools are increasingly available to the arts. Examples existing in the field are tools like Wealth Engine that predict the likelihood of donation. Another example would be how a fundraising manager can predict which of your new ticket buyers will react to your organization's annual appeal by using a statistical model generated in real time as you create the mailing list. These tools should support decision-making by answering four questions:

1. What happened?
2. Why did it happen?
3. What will happen?
4. How can I improve?

Selecting + Designing a CRM with a Robust CDP

Performing arts organizations are frequently approached by sales teams from CRM systems explaining how their system will solve all the problems the current system has. If the system costs more, they will argue that their system has efficiencies that will pay off in the long run. However, from our experience, the key to creating or maintaining, or improving upon a current system is, as Morgan explains from Concrete Computing, focusing on the purpose of your database as related to the mission and work of the organization, the required data to answer the questions and purposes, the relationships between various tables and data inputs, rules, likely queries, and reports. The key is to understand how employees, the users, will be using the data, including how that data will be used to inform decision-making.

Additionally, it is important to understand that for-profit CRM systems, like Salesforce, are often used in nonprofit settings. However, the core purposes and outputs differ. Hence, leaning in on the systems designed for nonprofit performing arts organizations or utilizing nonprofit packages, like Salesforce's, is critical. Ultimately performing arts organizations working as nonprofit organizations have different structures, cultures, and data streams, for example, tracking information about donors and tickets. For-profit businesses don't need the donor relationship as it isn't a part of their business.

Conducting a thorough needs assessment and creating a request for proposal (RFP) with identified selection criteria is always recommended. And, while there are hundreds of donors and ticketing solutions on the marketplace, the performing arts require an increasingly broad range of data management capabilities. In addition to standard tasks such as seat mapping, subscriptions, and sales reports, many systems have significant CRM functionality. Used correctly, these systems can not only present a more complete picture of individual or family's relationships with your organization, including ticket sales, donations, and interactions with customer service, but also their engagement across social media as well as a diversity of communication pathways and preferences.

Once all this is done, Gilmore's biggest piece of advice in this process is "define your problems in such a way that you are *not* unique. You don't want to be in a market of just one." While nonprofit performing arts organizations and artists are trained to think of their work as unique, particularly from a grant-writing perspective, ultimately, the data problems have more overlaps than differences. He also recommends moving past "conceiving of the database as an archive and defining the processes around the certainty of particular pieces of information rather than seeing them as a transaction record for future engagement." One good strategy is to ask the salesperson, "Who is your ideal customer for your product?"

Takeaways

Picking a CRM system is complicated and should take consideration and time. In the 21st century, working closely with vendors and specialists is essential, particularly with respect to changing policies for data security and privacy. All stakeholders in the system should be engaged in the process because they all must work with the system once it's implemented. This work will be emotional and will take time to cultivate buy-in from both leaders and staff. Using templates and automation creates opportunities for staff to find quick wins for continued growth. Having a staff excited about working with data to help support and inform their work to achieve your mission is exactly why data can be a superpower for your organization or career success.

The 2015 Survey of Ticketing Software conducted by the Artrs Management and Technology Laboratory at Carnegie Mellon University suggested general high satisfaction with ticketing and larger CRM systems across the board; selection can still be a daunting process. The following is adapted from the survey's findings and offers a five-step process emphasizing first taking the time to understand organizational needs and then specifically seeking out a vendor that matches these criteria.

1. **Determine Needs**

   a. Taking the time to reflect on your organization and articulate specific needs and priorities is a very important and often overlooked step. Most modern ticketing systems have integrated CRM elements, so it is very important to include all relevant departments in the decision-making process. When preparing for such a major decision, a multidepartmental task force, including staff and board members, may be a good idea. Deploying a new system may mean significant changes in the everyday workflows of your staff members. While goals for an implementation will include providing a more positive experience for your patrons and more data in the hands of your staff, a poorly planned and implemented deployment can be very painful.

   b. First, it makes sense to consider the general environment in which the system will be deployed. Here is a list of issues that you may wish to prioritize.

      i. Organizational Priorities

         1. Ease of use by your patrons and on what devices?

         2. Sufficient staff training

         3. Price for transition and annual maintenance

         4. Desired level of customization

         5. Specific functions and features (see below)

         6. Brand recognition (this is assumed at this point)

         7. Recommendations from colleagues in relevant industries

         8. Customer service (vendor support)

      9. Integration or replacement of existing systems

    10. Required by a venue agreement

- Next, consider the specific needs you might consider in making your decision.

ii. Specific Needs

    1. Credit card processing

    2. Online sales

    3. Seat mapping/reserved ticketing

    4. General admission ticketing

    5. Subscriptions/season ticket capability

    6. Multiuser (multiple sellers can be logged in at once)

    7. At-home ticket printing for customers

    8. Security features (ticket forgery prevention)

    9. Barcodes/QR codes/gate control

    10. Customer support/tech support for our staff

    11. Subscription sales/discount packages

    12. Group sales

    13. Automated sales reports

    14. Customizable sales reports

    15. Ability to print images or logos on ticket

    16. Ability to add a suggested donation

    17. Integrates with any separate systems

    18. Includes a membership management module

    19. Includes a customer relationship/donor management module

    20. Mobile integration

    21. Social media integration

    22. Demand-based pricing capability

2. **Identify Vendors**

a. Armed with a ranked list of needs, you will have the necessary information to identify systems that may be a good fit for your organization. A good first step would be to begin with the systems commonly used by organizations within your budget category. Visit each system's website, speak to peers using their products to learn the differences between each, and compare the vendors to the checklist of needs identified in step 1.

3. **Contact Vendors**

   a. Once you have decided on your finalists, it is time to contact the vendors directly and begin evaluating the competitiveness of their offerings and how willing they are to accommodate your specific needs. You may consider asking about the following:

   b. Opportunities for a hands-on demonstration, allowing you to experience the system for yourself.

   c. A list of client references matching your discipline and budget size. You can then contact these organizations about their experiences.

   d. Request a list of client's websites, allowing you to note specifically how the system can integrate with their platform and how it handles transactions and other functions such as donations, if applicable.

   e. Sample Questions

      i. *Customer/Tech Support*

         1. What type of support is available? (e.g., online, phone)

         2. Is there 24-hour support? If not, what options are available in the event of an after-hours emergency?

         3. What is the average response time to support requests?

         4. Is there a support fee? If so, how much does it cost, and what exactly does it cover?

      ii. *Data Integration*

         1. Can the system handle both online and internal sales? If not, does the vendor partner with another ticketing software vendor to provide complementary services?

         2. What software does your organization currently use, and what capacity does the ticketing software have to integrate with your current software?

         3. What is the time frame for migrating data from the current system to the new system?

         4. What is the capacity to export data from the system, and in what format can it be exported? (e.g., Excel file, CSV)

5. Does this system include integrated functions (donor management, class registration, etc.) that could replace any of your current software? What fees are attached?

6. Does this system have mobile solutions to sell tickets on all types of devices?

7. Will this system be able to integrate email delivery or social media data? Can it integrate with other providers offering these services? (Mailchimp, One Cause, etc.)

8. How does the system parse subscriptions with or without reserved seating?

iii. **Data Security and Storage**

1. Does the system provide PCI compliance?

2. Is the data stored with the vendor or on the organization's servers?

3. What security protections and encryptions are in place?

4. What are data loss statistics or up-time histories?

iv. *Infrastructure*

1. Is the software hosted online, or will your organization need a server to host it?

2. If the software has cloud functionality, which features (if any) can your staff members access from their mobile devices?

3. Is it purely cloud-based, or if local instances are required, what are the compatibility and system requirements?

4. Will the system require your organization to rent or purchase ticket-printing equipment?

5. If the system uses barcodes/QR codes, will your organization need to rent or purchase specialized scanners?

6. Does the system provide at-home printing?

v. **Price**

1. What is the setup fee?

2. Is there an annual license or maintenance fee?

3. Are there any additional fees for your organization? (credit card processing fees, per-ticket fees, customer service, etc.)

       4. What fees are charged to the customer? How much control will your organization have over setting those fees?

   vi. Reports + Dashboards

       1. What transactional data do you want to be able to analyze?

       2. What automated reports come with the system?

       3. Can you create custom reports on the fly?

       4. If the vendor will build custom reports for your organization, what is the customization process, cost, and turnaround time?

       5. How does the system track the source of the sale?

   vii. Staff Access

       1. How many user accounts are provided and at what cost? (e.g., how many people should be able to log into the system at the same time?)

       2. How many user accounts come with the system?

       3. How do you add user accounts if your organization grows? How much do additional accounts cost?

       4. Can you customize the information or functions that individual users can access?

       5. What information can you draw from each user account? (daily sales activity, relationships across programs and family members, etc.)

       6. If the software is web-based, can the staff access it from the browsers (and browser versions) currently installed on their computers?

   viii. User-Friendliness

       1. Are hands-on demonstrations available online?

       2. Are demos available once your data is in the new system to train new employees?

       3. How much staff time can you expect to spend setting up events? Selling season tickets? Pulling reports?

       4. How easy is this system for online customers to navigate?

       5. Is the web portal mobile adaptive? (Can your users easily purchase tickets on mobile devices and computers?)

4. **Make Your Decision**

   a. After speaking with vendors and other users of your top ticketing systems, revisit your list of priorities once more to evaluate which system best meets your needs. If you initially convened a cross-departmental team or staff and board task force to create this list of desires, this would be an appropriate phase of the selection process to reengage these key stakeholders. A new ticketing system can provide your organization with significant benefits, but a successful rollout depends on broad buy-in.

5. **Prepare for Installation**

   a. Rolling out the new ticketing system is a major organizational change, so it's important to manage the process efficiently and transparently. You may wish to consider the following factors:

      i. Does your chosen vendor offer any training?

         1. If so, consider providing multiple opportunities for staff members to take advantage of these educational materials. A workshop several months before they can begin using the system is likely to do little except provide them with basic familiarity. Proper reference materials can be important to users before, during, and after the new system's rollout.

         2. Think about how long it will take to train users on the new system as part of a deployment timeline. Ensuring that they have the proper time and support to adjust to their new workflow will prevent setbacks later.

      ii. How long will it take to transfer your data into the new system?

         1. Migrating and "cleaning" old data can require significant time. Communicate with your chosen vendor about how much of this cleaning and migration they can oversee and how much your staff will be responsible for.

         2. Ensure that after the data has been migrated to the new system that records are intact and flagged appropriately. Especially in a modern system that is likely to have integrated CRM functionality, ensuring that accounts aren't duplicated and that all fields are populating correctly is important when trying to create a full picture of a constituent's relationship with your organization.

iii. Who will be responsible for creating usernames for staff and configuring their profiles?

    1. Division of IT responsibility between the vendor and your IT staff (or the individual responsible for maintaining the system) should be settled before a system is selected. Ensure you know who oversees account management and that processes for adding and managing users are in place.

    2. Ensuring your staff members have timely and full access to the new system will give them time to familiarize themselves at their own pace, even if the planned transition is slated to take place at some later date.

iv. How close are you to starting a new season?

    1. Carefully consider when your system will be rolled out. If, for example, your organization is dark during the summer, then you might consider that time frame as an ideal window.

    2. Although data transitioning and initial system setup may certainly occur during your regular production time frame, the disruptive and possibly chaotic transition itself is best scheduled for a time of the year when it will disrupt the core of your business as little as possible.

    3. If possible, try not to have multiple systems operating simultaneously for longer than necessary. The presence of an old familiar option is likely to be attractive to staff members and may inhibit their full adoption of the new system.

Technology Solutions

The following technology solutions are mentioned throughout this chapter. Remember, this is not a comprehensive list of all the technologies available, but they might help you begin your research.

Structuring the System

For structuring your system:

- Blackbaud (www.blackbaud.com) is a software company fueling social good with multiple products, from Raiser's Edge NXT, its signature CRM system with data intelligence, to fuel fundraising, to K–12 learning management systems. A demo with an on-site visit is typical of the process.

- ShowClix (`www.showclix.com`) is a full-service ticketing solution. The price begins at a fee per ticket.

- ASIMUT (`https://asimut.com`) is a scheduling, room booking, and event management software serving academies and faculties in fine and performing arts. A demo with an on-site visit is typical of the process.

- Little Green Light (`www.littlegreenlight.com`) is a constituent management software that focuses on donor relationships. In addition to expected CRM features, it can accept donations, send acknowledgments, and send customized mailings if you don't integrate an external email program.

- Stripe (`https://stripe.com`) is a credit card processing service.

- RegFox (`www.regfox.com`) is a registration and event management tool.

- TicketSpice (`www.ticketspice.com`) is an online ticketing software.

- Airtable (`www.airtable.com`) is an online management tool that creates critical and unique workflows for managing programs to marketing.

- The Tessitura Network (`www.tessituranetwork.com`) is a unified system designed for arts and cultural institutions with ticketing and admissions, fundraising, memberships, marketing, business insights, education, online, mobile, and more.

Gathering + Cleaning

Archtics by Ticketmaster (`https://business.ticketmaster.com`) is one of many solutions offered by the company. Whether for local arts and cultural nonprofits or Coachella, Archtics is used for live performing arts.

User Training + Onboarding

Guru (`www.getguru.com`) describes itself as a wiki that can be used as an intranet to support company knowledge sharing. It is organized as a collection of cards that employees search to answer questions like "How do I refund a ticket purchase?"

Privacy, Security, + Legal Compliance

KnowBe4 (`www.knowbe4.com`) offers security awareness and training solutions and enables your employees to make smarter security decisions every day. From phishing awareness to government security and risk compliance, they have multiple products to meet different business needs.

Notes

1. Crawford, "2015 National Ticketing Software Satisfaction Survey."
2. "Zero-Party Data vs. First-Party Data."
3. Petersen, "Best Practices and Customer Relationship Management (CRM)."
4. "(16) Why User Adoption Keeps Tripping Us Up, and How Your Nonprofit Can Do It Better | LinkedIn."
5. "What Is PCI Compliance? Everything You Need To Know – Forbes Advisor."
6. "What Is a Chatbot?"

3

Growing Audiences + Donors: Tools + Tactics

Performing artists and organizations exist and succeed because they have created art that connects with their audiences and they have financial strategies that keep the business alive and thriving. Financial strategies should evolve from an organization's mission and programs offered. Some programs easily translate to selling tickets, merchandise, and concessions (earned income), whereas others are funded through donations (contributed income).

There are five core components to success in the performing arts business:

- Defining the mission, vision, and values of your enterprise.

- Understanding your position in your marketplace. For example, are you the fifth Shakespeare Theatre in a 20-mile radius or the first?

- Understanding your audience's interests, wants, and needs. For example, they may be interested, but need show times that start early in the evening.

- Creating products or experiences of value to your audience with pricing and packaging at levels at the intersection of your mission and your audience needs. For example, if you want to share music with everyone, you might offer some free experiences that are funded through sponsorships or donations.

■ Communicating these products or experiences to your audiences in the places and ways they want to hear about them.

Organizations that clearly understand themselves, their community, and their audience have greater success when establishing strategic plans and goals. These strategies begin with understanding how finances need to be stacked and how digital technologies can provide pathways. Some organizations operate well at 70 percent earned income, whereas others might operate similarly at as small as 10 percent earned income. Some artists actively use customer relationship platforms like Patreon; others depend on social media and email subscriptions.

Chapter 2, "Keeping Track of Everyone," clarified ways to track everyone engaged with your organization and your work. But a CMS or CRM database won't generate money unless you have trained staff with goals, a plan, a timeline, and tools to integrate actions from the CRM to make it work. Underpinning success in converting data into actions is a golden brand. We cover branding extensively in Chapter 5, "Defining Who You Are," but to provide context here, a strong brand delivers on the promise of the organization or artists' work. The words and images align with the mission, vision, values, and work. In this chapter, we focus on using your data for action and using technology tools and tactics to develop relationships that can help create strong earned and contributed income streams.

Marketing + Communications

Marketing is a term used in many different ways. This chapter includes all points of contact and communication between an artist or organization and their community or audience, with a nod to advertising. Performing arts organizations are unique in that their marketing cycles are typically organized around a season of shows with scheduled donor appeals and other engagement opportunities, from corporate sponsorships, to space rentals, to education programs. The seasonal structure overlays the workflow. This structure creates an opportunity. It allows audiences to develop habits of engagement and can give organizations the opportunity to learn what works with their marketing plans.

Brand strategist Julii Oh works with clients that include San Francisco Ballet, Detroit Symphony Orchestra, and The Cleveland Orchestra. Before creating her consultancy, she worked full-time as chief marketing officer with Miami City Ballet and was vice president of marketing and customer service for the New York Philharmonic.

Explaining the unique qualities of the nonprofit performing arts, she said. At the New York Philharmonic, I quickly realized that it's completely cyclical. You're marketing and selling a classical season every single year. Sure, the works change, but it's still the same product. Rather than taking on a rote formulaic approach year after year, it affords you the opportunity for a rich, fertile ground for a continuous learning model where you can run an enormous number of tests within a season, measure, and gain actionable insights—both short and long term. And this model allows the entire [marketing team] to adopt this iterative approach, which is how an innovative department or organization works.

Oh is passionate about marketing and believes innovation is at its core:

> **This way of thinking, testing, measuring, and iterating is required within today's modern marketing team. And how failure is perceived as an opportunity to learn and iterate. It's also what builds a team with agility and rigor to navigate through these incredibly unprecedented times of change.**

She also recommends that organizations have a clear marketing tech stack, including a digital asset management system for content files:

Arts organizations route a massive number of marketing materials across the organization to review and get approved. There is now a tool that should be part of the marketing tech stack that really pulls that work into a system so it's no longer someone manually emailing it around and marketing and consolidating all the changes. It easily delivers ROI on time saved across the staff alone by easily 50 percent or more. And if you factor in the sheer volume of assets that are trafficked, it's a multiplier effect of time saved.

She iterates how automation and personalization within the right CMS can also increase impact and save time. "There's also marketing automation that replaces the need for someone to build emails and create content to add in. Rather, you can use automation tools to also customize the content to a particular user that may have visited the web and send them related information or like content that they viewed."

Oh notes two other components to a powerful tech stack: project management tools (discussed in depth in Chapter 1, "Getting on the Same Page") and digital asset management systems (DAMSs). "Project management truly helps teams collaborate, streamline communication, build in team accountability, time savings, and automation on various tasks. There are DAMSs (digital asset management systems) that help metatag the many creative assets so that the organization has access to the same set so it reduces redundancy and manages resources much more effectively and efficiently than ever before. Your teams definitely need this so that your assets are strategically leveraged."

The Customer Journey + User Experience Design

While organizations want to take audiences and donors through the marketing funnel quickly (see Figure 3.1), the key to success is understanding that different customers have different needs, wants, and journeys. For example, subscribers have different needs, emotions, and touchpoints than first-time ticket buyers. Additional factors such as age, education, and lifestyle can also significantly impact the journey (see Figure 3.2).

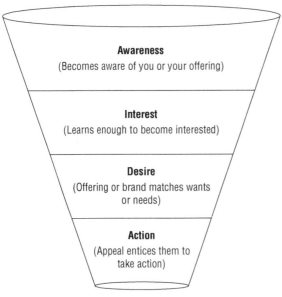

Figure 3.1: The marketing funnel has four stages: Awareness, Interest, Desire, and Action (AIDA).

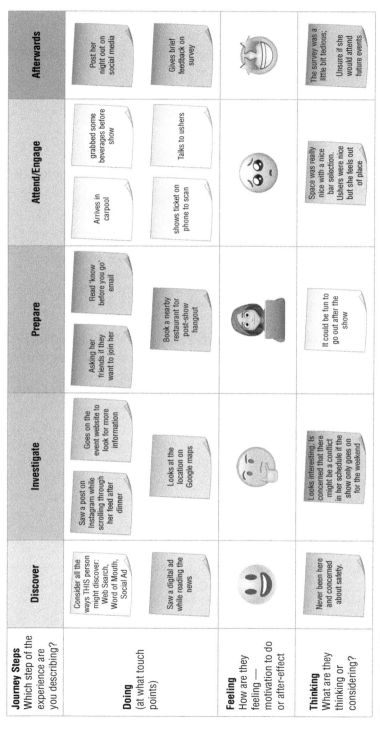

Journey Steps Which step of the experience are you describing?	Discover	Investigate	Prepare	Attend/Engage	Afterwards
Doing (at what touch points)	Consider all the ways THIS person might discover: Web Search, Word of Mouth, Social Ad Saw a digital ad while reading the news	Saw a post on Instagram while scrolling through her feed after dinner Goes on the event website to look for more information Looks at the location on Google maps	Asking her friends if they want to join her Read 'know before you go' email Book a nearby restaurant for post-show hangout	Arrives in carpool grabbed some beverages before show shows ticket on phone to scan Talks to ushers	Post her night out on social media Gives brief feedback on survey
Feeling How are they feeling — motivation to do or after-effect					
Thinking What are they thinking or considering?	Never been here and concerned about safety.	Looks interesting. Is concerned that there might be a conflict in her schedule if the show only goes on for the weekend	It could be fun to go out after the show	Space was really nice with a nice bar selection. Ushers were nice but she feels out of place	The survey was a little bit tedious; Unsure if she would attend future events

Figure 3.2: Taking time to map your core customers' journeys focuses your messaging, increases efficiencies. and saves money.

Part of this information comes from data—some exists in your CMS, and some needs to be accessed from available external sources. But data tells only part of the story. User experience design has to be part of the discovery process.

Aubrey Bergauer is the CEO and founder of Changing the Narrative, a company that serves organizations and individuals who want to make money and grow their customer, audience, and donor base. Her background comes from working in classical music. Her work as the executive director at the California Symphony (`www.californiasymphony.org`) led her to understand the significance of using both data and conversation to understand current and potential audiences and donors:

To do this right, data hygiene was the top priority because we knew if we didn't have that right, we couldn't communicate with the different segments. Data hygiene is everything so you can actually know what people's behaviors are. And [for] the stuff we can't get because it's not a transaction, we talked to them.

Bergauer created the Long Haul Audience Development Model at the California Symphony, which focuses on patron retention across marketing and development departments, eliminating traditional silos that were isolated to one system, process, or platform. During her tenure, single ticket sales increased by 97 percent, the subscriber base grew by 46 percent, and concerts were added to support audience demand. Individual giving increased by 52 percent, with nearly four times as many donors. To accomplish this change, she relied on user experience design, data hygiene, tight segmenting, and automation. Bergauer explains, "New ticket buyers and new donors need to be on their own communication pathway. Nationwide, the statistic from the Association for Fundraising Professionals is that first-year donor renewal rate is 19 percent. That's across all nonprofits."

She acknowledges that some people push back at the idea that segmenting works. To them, it's not worth the time or effort. That's when getting comfortable with automation plays a role. "We have to be segmented. We have to be savvy about this. Some people say, "I've read about all these efforts for first-timers, inviting them to come back again. That's a lot." My reply is that even if you have to import your new first-time buyers after every concert into a system like MailChimp, you can then have your next four emails automated that go to those people. It doesn't matter if you are dealing with 100 people in a particular segment or 10,000 people, the automated process is the same. The process is what we need to think through."

Ultimately you simply cannot do business as one size fits all. That's where the tech stack can help us.

People's Light

Director of Patron Engagement, Eve Trojanov, uses technology to segment audience data to better understand their patrons at People's Light (`www.peopleslight.org`), a professional theater located in Malvern, Pennsylvania. People's Light use Tessitura for their CMS, and she uses Airtable to collect information about patrons' user experience.

Trojanov explains that they moved past the standard practice of sending an email post-performance because it wasn't getting the full picture of all types of attendees—guests of those purchasing the ticket, the ticket buyer, and the subscriber. They still send an email, but they expanded their reach significantly by adding QR codes in the space for those who want to complete the survey digitally in the moment and paper forms on-site at the theater that are completed by the patron and then entered by hand into Airtable for analysis (see Figure 3.3). "We needed to figure out how to get the people who are not receiving those emails, if they're coming with their friends or family or a group, and give them easy access to responding at the lobby level as they exit the theater. We've been using Airtable to get that feedback. When people turn in those paper surveys, our apprentices type them into Airtable. We also put out a QR code if people don't want to fill out a paper where they can answer all the questions directly in a form."

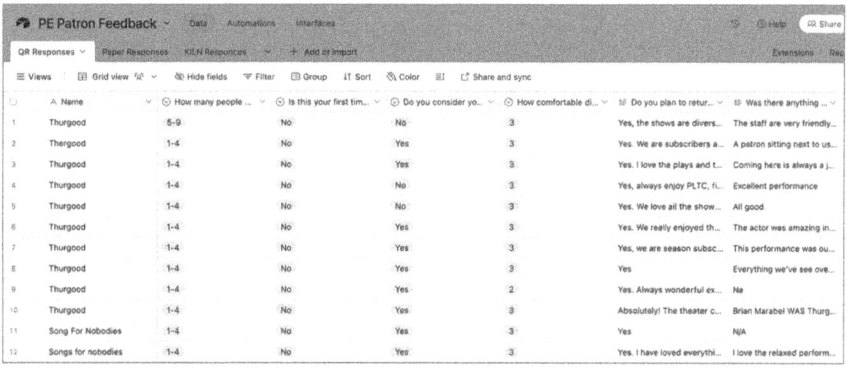

	Name	How many people ...	Is this your first tim...	Do you consider yo...	How comfortable di...	Do you plan to retur...	Was there anything ...
1	Thurgood	5-9	No	No	3	Yes, the shows are divers...	The staff are very friendly...
2	Thergood	1-4	No	Yes	3	Yes. We are subscribers a...	A patron sitting next to us...
3	Thurgood	1-4	No	Yes	3	Yes. I love the plays and t...	Coming here is always a j...
4	Thurgood	1-4	No	No	3	Yes, always enjoy PLTC, fi...	Excellent performance
5	Thurgood	1-4	No	No	3	Yes. We love all the show...	All good
6	Thurgood	1-4	No	Yes	3	Yes. We really enjoyed th...	The actor was amazing in...
7	Thurgood	1-4	No	Yes	3	Yes, we are season subsc...	This performance was ou...
8	Thurgood	1-4	No	Yes	3	Yes	Everything we've see ove...
9	Thurgood	1-4	No	Yes	2	Yes. Always wonderful ex...	Na
10	Thurgood	1-4	No	Yes	3	Absolutely! The theater c...	Brian Marabel WAS Thurg...
11	Song For Nobodies	1-4	No	Yes	3	Yes	N/A
12	Songs for nobodies	1-4	No	Yes	3	Yes. I have loved everythi...	I love the relaxed perform...

Figure 3.3: This image shows how Airtable can be used for surveys. This image shows a sample section of the patron feedback survey used at People's Light.

They are not asking for personal information or trying to align to the individual. The questions are experiential. "We really need to ask ourselves why we're asking these questions and what we're trying to get out of it. We are trying to ask better questions. We are trying to understand how many people were in your party, so to make it easy for the patron, we have categories: one to four, five to nine, or 10 plus. From this, we can figure out if they were single ticket buyers, potentially subscribers, or if they were Group Sales."

This also helped uncover hidden first-time visitors and potentially capture their information. It has been really interesting because the thing that we don't get in the retention survey emails is a sense of how many people in the audience were first-time visitors. When we only send an email, a lot of those people said no, this wasn't my first time. But there were people in their group that it was their first time. At one of our shows recently, it was kind of a 50/50 split, first time versus not their first time.

Frequency and churn are also important. "We are starting to ask people if they consider themselves a frequent theater-goer because we're trying to figure out the magic number to lock people into our orbit and get them to continue to return. And we're seeing that three times is really that number. We also ask: Do you plan to return in the next 12 months based on your experience today? Was there anything that made your experience at the performance particularly satisfying or unsatisfying? What emotions did you feel?"

People's Light is a 7-acre campus with unique spaces. The experience in these spaces is also important:

Because we're trying to make our spaces feel accessible, welcoming, inviting, we're also trying to ask people on a scale of one to three, how welcome did you feel and how comfortable did you feel navigating the space? Especially because while we're not a super old theater, we operate out of an older space.

The subscriber experience is different than that of a newcomer, so subscribers get different questions:

We know that we can count on them for in-depth feedback. The feedback they tell us comes from someone in-the-know. "I really feel like they should have moved stage left during this part of this song." It feels like they're experts. They are our evangelists and know us best. Is this our best work?

Data and Automation

Understanding how to segment to meet the core customer journeys in your organization takes a savvy use of data. Automation makes implementing it with a small staff possible.

TheatreSquared

Andrea Newby, director of marketing and communications at TheatreSquared (www.theatre2.org) in Fayetteville, Arkansas, has used data and automation to grow audiences and donors. The first step is to understand your audience's data and the second is to determine where you want to make change.

With the knowledge that a 2 percent increase in audience retention equals a 10 percent decrease in operational costs, Newby analyzed TheatreSquared's situation and decided to begin reaching out to each single-ticket buyer in their first year seeing her organization. "I really focused on getting them back at the second [year as a] single ticket buyer and then becoming multi-single ticket buyers."

Keeping data clean is a high priority. While data appending missing details such as contact information, preferences, and demographics is one key to her success (discussed extensively in Chapter 2), it is an essential step in data hygiene to get conversions. For example, at TheatreSquared, they use a tele-funding and a telemarketing team. "Having clean data, we could see the lift," said Newby. "They were getting pick-ups, not hang-ups, and conversations. Even in 2020, they sold $50,000 in streaming subscriptions for us."

Newby also uses data to identify subscribers who are at risk:

> If they were utilizing less than 75 percent of their tickets, that's a red flag, and we have a subscription sales specialist who does outreach. It's a blend of high tech and high touch. Both of those are working in tandem, which is really helpful.

TheatreSquared uses Prospect2 for email combined with Tessitura. Prospect2 allows for complex processes and automated communications tied to customer types. Newby notes, "We have automated performance reminders and flows."

Google Analytics has offered particularly useful insights from community partners. She explains that in the years after the pandemic lockdown. "I've really been focusing on marketing the shows and rebuilding the audience, but I use our Google Analytics and have a heatmap by channel and the number of tickets sold. I can see our referrals with that report. I can see that in our specific experience, Fayetteville partners refer a lot of traffic to our site through their calendar. So, we intentionally met with our partners and talked more about the calendar and more ways we can partner. Now we also do social media giveaways. All of it helps build our list. But without that Google Analytics information, we might never have known."

Automation across platforms is complex but incredibly useful. Newby notes that Prospect 2 also provides a bridge between Facebook, YouTube, Instagram, and Tessitura. She has set up specific automations and systems:

I can load lists and add tags through Tessitura that are assigned to an automation that if this tag is added, they are added to this Facebook audience. In this automation, it has part one, where you tell it when you would like it to begin. Then you can create a part two that says, once they've entered this and purchased a ticket, they're leaving that tagged Facebook audience.

We have used other automation work for our posts and performance reminders. [At] the end of our fiscal year, we worked with our development team and identified those who are new to file and gave them a specific message, versus those who were unrenewed donors, versus those who have been subscribers for a long time. So being able to be specific with those groups is important because we all need different things along that journey. I also do a special automation if they're unrenewed subscribers, depending on the time of year. It's a great branch logic system.

Team, Tools, + Tactics

How one defines the word "team" in a performing arts organization varies. We regard marketing as part of everyone's work, even if it is simply having an elevator pitch in mind for a chance meeting with a future audience member, donor, or board member.

Michael Troutman, director of marketing at People's Light notes. "Marketing works across an organization and its myriad of teams when it comes to technology, from people who interact with various facets of technology on a ground level, from a data collection standpoint, from a patron agent standpoint, from an accessibility standpoint, from those who are neurodivergent, and from others with various degrees of visual or auditory impairment."

Website

The coordination across the organization must also be echoed across the technology tools used. Websites are the core hub of information and transactions for most organizations and artists.

People's Light

At People's Light, the website (`https://peopleslight.org`) provides information and clear actions for the user through intentional analysis and design. Troutman explained.

> **The biggest thing for us is utilizing our website for connecting to the community. One of the ways that we're utilizing our website is through SEO [search engine optimization]. It has become a big facet of the company. We want people in Chester County to realize they have a neighborhood theater that can bring them professional theater, outreach, and art education. With that being said, if we're easily found and have a strong online presence and footprint, when they're looking for entertainment or for a cultural and civic center in Chester County, People's Light will come first to mind.**

In addition to strong SEO, People's Light is a Google nonprofit with a Google Ads grant (`www.google.com/nonprofits`). As they are focused on the Chester County area, Troutman notes that the company uses geo-targeting as a component of their advertising, whether with Google Ads or other digital opportunities. "Using data that we can assess, we identify zip codes that have the highest level of donors, the highest level of single-ticket buyers, and the highest level of subscribers." See Figure 3.4 for sample ad.

Troutman notes that it can be helpful to work with consultants for digital marketing. People's Light works with Capacity Interactive (`www.capacityinteractive.com`). Troutman explains:

It's been very useful to understand trigger-based actions using one of their tools called the behavior infuser. It's activated actions that users take on our website. That kind of insight contributes to how we can modify our website to make it more user-friendly. It has prompted us to reach out to some board members who are like our internal focus group in terms of how we're messaging and how user-friendly certain pages are. That ensures that we take special care on those pages that are more highly sequenced than others. "Understanding and knowing website

Figure 3.4: This is an example of a geo-targeted ad. It is for the Barrymore Award–winning "Lettie" in the *Philadelphia Inquirer* digital campaign.

Image provided by Troutman.

behaviors enables us to send certain types of messaging via email, which is our bread and butter in terms of how we communicate and sell."

Video

For the performing arts, video offers the most direct path to help patrons and donors understand your work. Video has been demonstrated to be a decision-maker for purchases, particularly by those audiences and donors who are a little unsure. Video can be used on websites, embedded in emails, and is a core aspect of most social media.

Black Ensemble Theater

Lyle Miller, marketing manager and IT coordinator at Black Ensemble Theater (`https://blackensembletheater.org`) in Chicago, uses video on social media, but he explains that video is also used in their performance space for deepening the audience experience:

Social media's probably the fastest and most widespread way to get a message out. But even on-site, we have monitors playing media and history. We do a lot of musicals about the lives of famous performers. And in that, we show history, their lives, and educational things that [patrons] wouldn't have known about, as well as showing their perseverance and how they got through certain situations. Especially for young people who come to the theater, we want them to see the origins of this great music they're listening to.

Video is a significant connector for Black Ensemble Theater's audiences and not a new add-on. Miller has been editing videos for over 25 years. Currently, they use Adobe Premiere and After Effects. The key to editing for Miller is telling a story:

When you're editing, for me especially, you try to tell a story with the material, as opposed to just throwing up some clips with the score playing. Don't be lazy about it. If a critic said the show will make you feel great, there should be an image of somebody feeling great at that time on screen, for example. I think that's more important than the tools and even the footage. [Understand] your story before you get started.

At Black Ensemble Theater, each show gets a trailer for marketing and advertising. During previews, they interview audience members and add that to the trailer. This model, Miller claims, creates "a twofold effect because people will share the trailer because they're in it. And when they come to the theater next time, they'll be easier to solicit for comments."

Social Media

Social media feels natural as a user but managing it as part of your career as an artist or as a professional arts marketer for an organization takes considerable thought and effort. Chun Wai Chan, principal dancer with the New York City Ballet, has found that it has definitely helped his career, but "it requires a lot of time and attention to create content, but it benefits you to think about how to market yourself and connect to people around the world."

Social media management takes effort and intention. You need to identify the social media channels that align with your current and future audiences and donors. Bergauer of Changing the Narrative explains, "Pick a few things, decide to be excellent at those things instead of being mediocre at a lot of things." Being excellent includes taking the time to craft content that aligns with your brand, connects to your audience, and creates the actions you want. This includes staying engaged with your team, your artists, and your followers.

Emmet Cohen

Whether you do it yourself or engage a team, artists know that social media is critical to their careers. Jazz pianist and composer Emmet Cohen (`https://emmetcohen.com`) has a small team that helps him maintain a presence on his social media channels. He emphasizes the importance of consistency to maximize the impact on the algorithms that create the feeds:

I was looking for consistency, showing up on people's feeds with consistency. Social media really is all about consistency— consistency over quality or quantity. That's what YouTube rewards, consistent uploading. If you're uploading three times a week, four times a week, it's going to give you some more traction than it would for someone who uploads once a month. That's the algorithm. Thinking about it all as being as consistent as possible with all the forms of social media and trying just to keep it on a slow simmer.

People's Light

For People's Light, Troutman says they've done research among their patrons and peers. He notes that. "[Our] biggest outreach is with Facebook, second is Instagram, third is with YouTube. That's where we see the most depth. There is a higher watch time on YouTube, but our users engage with us most frequently on Facebook. I believe that with the advent of TikTok, that is probably going to be the next wave when we are focusing on younger audiences."

There is a difference, however, between engagement of existing followers and getting leads to new people: "Instagram gives us a chance to do more lead generation. And then the other social media platform that we're going to be growing from a business development standpoint is LinkedIn." In fact, LinkedIn has been particularly good for developing relationships for rentals, corporate support, and volunteers:

> It's also been a good tool for us to engage corporate support for volunteers. Because a lot of volunteers will look to organizations like People's Light for skill-building and team-building initiatives within their organizations or departments, or affinity groups. And there's also the opportunity for them to also have corporate functions and or similar events that we can do at our award-winning event space, the Farmhouse.

Troutman uses a combination of social media ads and organic posts to achieve his goals. He explains:

I always like to say that marketing is not just about selling and telling. It's more so about relationship building. You need to leverage your advertising or your promotions, you're selling and telling, to open the door for a relationship. But then you still have to follow up with a conversation. So how can you lead people that have at least a basic level of interest into a deeper conversation?

How can we make this introduction via flyer via organic posts via display ads, to get you to give us a call, or stop by our box office, or send us an email, or join us for a meeting—that's where the relationship is going to be built from. And I would add not to be afraid to have that conversation online. That means sometimes you have to get into the comments. You have to get into direct messaging, which is almost like emailing, but through that social media platform. That's where the relationship is valid. They saw our ad, and we have high impressions—that doesn't mean anything. We want conversion. The only way you can convert is if we have a conversation.

Having conversations on social media takes time and attention. At People's Light, some of this work happens with the patron services team. Troutman's colleague Trojanov explains:

Patron services answers questions on our socials, as they know the most about the details of the shows, like the running time. We had a couple of apprentices who really wanted to work in marketing. Since they weren't in the marketing department, we said they could do some work in social media while in the box office. As they answer questions on social media, they can identify something that is coming up a lot on Facebook, something we need to tell marketing to include in a "know before you go" email or make it clear on our website. So, it does open up the opportunity to work more symbiotically with marketing as well.

PARA.MAR Dance

Social media also offers a path for working directly with artists as a company. Founder and Director of PARA.MAR Dance, Stephanie Martinez, notes how they used social media as a tool to recruit dancers. For her, it is a way to have greater accessibility, as a lot of people can't fly in just for a single audition:

> We were offering a couple of scholarships to the Carmel Dance Festival, where two of our dancers would go there to dance. We had them audition on social media. We taught a phrase, and then we had them learn it and email us a link to the video as their audition. We create the opportunity on a social media platform, they submit online, and I can go through and look and choose. It seems to be successful.

Email

The secret to email is to do the right amount with the right content at the right time. Email is a permission-based marketing system, and the goal is to have people want to open and read your content, not unsubscribe from being emailed too much.

Black Ensemble Theater

Black Ensemble Theater sends out a weekly email and a robust monthly newsletter. Miller notes that the newsletter can be tricky because "you have to have content, and contributors need to be consistent." Their email program is Robly, which is disconnected from their CMS. Email is a digital form of direct mail.

People's Light

People's Light notes that email is their bread and butter. They use email to customize the user experience by using segmenting. Troutman explains:

> Email is why the relationship building is so important because, once we know that you want to hear from us, then we can tailor our messaging around what it is that you want to hear from us, because some people want more than what's going on behind the scenes, some people want just the place, some people just want special effects. They want to know about our annual golf outing. So whatever people's points of entry are, that enables us to customize the user experience.

Erica Ezold, managing director at People's Light, emphasizes the importance of segmenting audiences and emailing to each segment's wants and needs:

We're really needing to lean into the data tools that we have and get more out of them. We need to be cultivating a single-ticket-buying audience and repeat single-ticket-buying audience more than a subscription. So really, the tools we're using now have to do with segmentation and thinking about who we are approaching with what message.

Troutman's main tools are Tessitura and WordFly. Troutman explains that the technology is simply a tool for strategic implementation. "What is driving our success is what we funnel into our emails, and we're able to do that because we're able to generate promo codes. The promo codes help us in a number of ways. One is leveraging the right pricing model to engage an audience, particularly a new audience member. That will also enable us to segment, at the onset, what productions are of interest and how we acquired that new prospect. Then, once they're in our database, we can communicate with them through targeted email."

Emmet Cohen

Artists find email valuable as well. Jazz pianist Emmet Cohen notes:

> My newsletter is one of the most important parts of my business. You know, people buying tickets to hear jazz concerts as part of a season—the market segment for people who will spend that kind of money will be mostly older from [ages] 50 to 80. Some young people will learn about it from social media, but I think email is good for my particular market segment.

This self-marketing opportunity came out of the pivot he made during the pandemic lockdown:

I collected email addresses and had almost 5,000 people on my email newsletter that don't all come to gigs or follow what we do. So, I send out a monthly newsletter with where we're playing and what we're up to.

Subscriptions Are Not Dead

The usual purchase options for a show in the performing arts are single tickets, group tickets, and subscriptions, be they standard, part-season, or flex passes. In the glory days of the 1970s, documented in Danny

Newman's *Subscribe Now!* (Theatre Communications Group; 3rd ed., 1981), it was not unusual to have the majority of tickets sold as subscriptions. As our organizations have matured, demographics have shifted, and additional leisure time options have emerged in the 21st century; many arts organizations have seen shrinking subscriptions and increased single and group ticket purchases. Some organizations, like Phoenix Theatre, are experimenting with new models for long-term engagement that align with the Netflix monthly model. The traditional subscription exists and can succeed on its own when organizations use data combined with conversation.

Savannah Philharmonic

A recent subscription success story can be found with Savannah Philharmonic Orchestra and Chorus (SPOC; `https://savannahphilharmonic.org`). They completely sold out their 2023–2024 season subscriptions by late spring of 2023. When speaking with executive director, Dr. Amy Williams, she noted that they limited subscriptions to 80 percent of capacity so that single tickets could still be offered to those just learning about the organization or who couldn't purchase a subscription this year.

The secret to their success was a strategic blend of data analytics, data collection, and relationship building. They started with data from 2018–2020 to get a sense of the previous trends. Like many in the classical music industry, SPOC was far from selling at full capacity. Of more immediate concern was the need to sort and understand disconnected data with ticket sale information coming from the venue's ticketing system at the Savannah College of Art and Design and the organization's donor database, Virtuous. The two systems didn't communicate, and the information wasn't synthesized.

The first job was to find someone on the team who works well with data who could manually clean and analyze the data, practically row by row, in Excel. They quickly saw that only two zip codes in the city supported the organization out of the entire Savannah, Georgia region, even with one of the fastest-growing counties in the country nearby.

Another key to success is learning about the community. While the data was being cleaned and analyzed, Williams went into the neighborhoods and talked with people:

When I came in, I started looking at things and talking to community members. I realized we had a significant branding problem—people did not know who we were. They did not know we existed. And worse, they didn't know they could come [to our concerts].

Looking at the data and listening to the community uncovered some truths about the organization's current state:

This allowed us as a staff and board to have the hard conversation that people did not know who we were. So, in the 2022–2023 season, we knew we were out of COVID [and that] we had to make a change because the couple of concerts that we did weren't selling well. We realized that when we were talking about the organization, we were talking to ourselves. We were talking in our own bubble.

To solve the problem, SPOC launched the Phil the Neighborhood Series:

We would bring a small group—three, four, or five [musicians] and a sound engineer. We asked the neighborhood to help us advertise. And we had a caveat that we had to be able to go on the local TV news and announce that we were doing these concerts.

They also made online announcements through community partners and called their current single-ticket buyers who lived in a neighborhood where they planned a concert to help forge their connections.

As noted earlier, user experience data comes from listening. Williams notes, "Before each neighborhood concert, we also did a focus group with the neighborhood association or whoever was the one that answered the phone for the first call to pull people together—the movers and the shakers of that neighborhood." They let the community lead the hyper-local marketing and had to be comfortable with letting go of some control.

For the nine neighborhood events in September 2022, neighborhoods were chosen by analyzing zip code data and identifying those that had the capacity to buy tickets but had not been buying them. The events were used to forge a human connection. Williams explained:

What we learned in that process was that we were more powerful through individual connection than in a large blast of communications. Word of mouth is better advertising than anything else. Our metric of success at each event was 50 to 100 people. Instead, we saw between 300 to 400 people at each one. And then we watched ticket sales jump drastically. It launched into the 2022–2023 season, and every concert was sold out. Once we announced one concert was sold out, there'd be a frenzy to buy the others.

People who attended the events and listened to the music signed up with their emails to receive more information—the data capture was significant (see Figure 3.5 and Figure 3.6). SPOC immediately sent an email

Figure 3.5: At an outdoor concert at Hull Park, people signed up to receive information from the SPOC.

Credit: Bailey Davidson.

Figure 3.6: SPOC's performances at Hull Park demonstrate the power of going where people are to grow audiences.

Credit: Bailey Davidson.

to welcome them to the organization, explained Williams, "So, it's not like they were just sitting, waiting for a sale—they got a special email."

The key was creating curiosity and desire. At the concert announcing the 2023–2024 season, all current subscribers had a renewal packet in a little orange bag waiting for them on their seats. According to Williams:

Because of what we'd learned, we knew our personal approach is much stronger than the big media blasts. It took off like fire. It blew up the phone lines from people calling to renew their subscriptions. From there, we slowly put subscriptions out to people who wanted to know how they could be involved. We had a small [printed] brochure planned for May, but we didn't even do that because we had no subscriptions left. We [sent] one sheet of paper explaining what a subscription was with the form—that's all they needed. Our [marketing] costs were much lower than anything I've ever spent before.

Another key component was hiring a telemarketing firm. Initially, they used the 2018–2019 subscriber and single ticket lists for the telemarketers to call anyone who had dropped off since then. Williams said, "Because I can't afford to pay someone to sit in our office and make those sales, I can have the telemarketing firm that I just pay when they make a sale. So that's been a huge converter, too."

But the key is integrated marketing, Williams believes:

While we do use phone calls, we know we have to have all those other channels aligned as well—social media, e-blasts, direct mail, and PR. Everything has to have a timing point to it for when it hits in order to keep the momentum going.

It may be surprising that SPOC relied heavily on phone calls as the transaction point. That's because the existing venue software didn't provide a clean, easy ticketing path for subscriptions. The venue is moving to a new software soon, hopefully making the online salespoint seamless.

Williams notes that for SPOC there are two strong communication paths: Facebook events and targeted emails. She explained:

We can't ignore good ol' Facebook events and asking people to start sharing them—then it suddenly just goes through. I would say with our emails, we have to really target specific emails for specific purposes to certain people.

They use Constant Contact for emails since it works well with their core CRM, Virtuous. SPOC has 6,000 followers on Facebook.

Now that their data is clean, Williams focuses on keeping it clean and using it wisely. She partners with a firm called Peachtree to help identify potential donors: "We've run [our contact lists] through Peachtree to tell us their median household income, their net worth, and all these pieces that help for donations."

They also use data by targeting key zip codes and sending "new mover cards" to invite people moving to the area to a concert. They purchase the list through their marketing partner, Enertex:

We saw 60 percent of those invites come and convert to subscribers. This broke my original thought process that you should never [try to] sell a subscription to someone who's only come to one concert, but they're coming and converting to become subscribers.

The magic is in the data and having candid conversations about it. Williams advises, "Understand your data and [help] the board to understand." She recommends ignoring most data from 2020 to 2022 from during the pandemic. "It doesn't matter. Look at the data before then, because when organizations say people are not coming back because of COVID, I always ask, did they come before COVID? Organizations struggle with that. It's a hard question to ask and an uncomfortable internal conversation that an organization must have because they might see that they weren't doing it right to begin with."

While knowing your data is important, perspective is also important. Williams recommends, "Look at your data and compare it to the community's data. Does it match?" She also notes that you don't need a fancy data analytics software. "I've watched so many data migrations—organizations get overwhelmed. When all else fails, just use [Microsoft] Excel."

Remember the customer experience. Williams recommends listening to people, particularly those who aren't showing up in your spaces:

Just listening to people, you can gain a lot of information. We made hard changes organizationally. The orchestra is no longer in tuxedos. We are thinking about the entire process of walking up to the hall—are you welcomed in? What are you allowed to wear in the hall? It's the whole journey. When are you allowed to clap? We've tried to pull down a lot of that. And yes, we've angered some people along the way. But to the people who we've frustrated along the way, my statement is always the same. If they ask why can't the orchestra be in tuxedos? People love dressing up! My immediate response is that I agree with you. But if someone comes in slacks and a polo shirt, I do not want them to feel that they are judged because that might be the best thing they own.

Artists

Subscriptions are not limited to organizations. Artists have found the subscription platform, Patreon, to be of value for creating a stable flow of income through its premium model. Ballet Dancer, Chun Wie Chan, finds that Patreon (`www.patreon.com/Chunner`) has been very helpful as an alternative to YouTube as a place to share dance classes, conversations, and trailers with interested fans.

After building a strong following of YouTube followers and email subscriptions, Emmet Cohen developed a Patreon-like membership model on his own website (`https://emmetcohen.com`) where member-only content is provided. "Emmet Cohen Exclusive offers four tiers of support," Cohen explained. "Each membership tier includes limited-edition personal gifts as they are produced. Members are the first to receive all new CDs and vinyl records before they become available commercially." Cohen goes beyond the subscription model of Netflix or Spotify and points out that it is a one-to-one relationship with him. His website states, "I hope you will consider deepening your relationship with me, my music, and our community. Join us further in exploring the genre and securing its legacy by becoming a member of this private community of supporters." To create the membership site, Cohen uses Squarespace for his website, where the commerce bundle allows for a membership portal, a sales point for the membership, and a standard shop.

Artificial Intelligence—Now + the Future

Technology changes rapidly, and savvy leaders and artists are aware of the opportunities and risks available to their organizations. As noted in Chapter 2, CMSs increasingly offer machine learning, predictive modeling, and other forms of artificial intelligence (AI) for analyzing data and tools for segmenting, personalization, and targeting communication. Furthermore, large language models (LLMs), such as OpenAI's ChatGPT, are increasingly being used as plug-ins to standard fundraising and marketing software tools and individual practices. OpenAI has launched an enterprise-level option that keeps your business's data private. It's important to note that while these tools are valuable assets, they are not a substitute for human interaction. Additionally, the output from LLMs must be checked. LLMs are best used as inspiration and as a starting point, as they can "hallucinate" and provide misinformation. Also, some chatbots running LLMs can be hacked. Therefore, use them to save time and offer inspiration, and check their work.

Julii Oh notes from her perspective as a brand specialist and consultant that while generative AI, particularly ChatGPT, has been quickly adopted, leaders need to use it with training and strategy:

I would strongly encourage leaders to resist just tacking AI on because there is pressure or buzz to get on it. Firstly, there has to be training on prompt usage (that is, how to ask it questions to result in the best answers), as well as an understanding around the shortcomings.

Once training and strategy are in place, Oh articulates the technology win available: "In short, ChatGPT can help support teams as an efficiency booster, time saver, skill enhancer, and workload manager, and provide learning and development."

Many fundraising and marketing professionals use AI tools to support their work in myriad ways:

- Creating custom emails for donation appeals
- Drafting custom communications for segmented audiences
- Creating language to promote events and encourage registration or ticket sales
- Create social media posts

AI is already able to support your digital advertising. For example, when placing an ad with Meta, you can upload a selection of text and images and let the system run multiple a/b tests for you.

Oh notes that AI is predicted to be a significant part of customer service in the future. It is already available through chatbots in most e-commerce industries. "Customer relations (CR) is your front line, but during peak time, that team is stretched beyond its bandwidth," Oh said.

Oh offers questions to consider when making sure your CR team is set up for success including:

- Is the team operating with very little change—how it's always been done in the past?
- Are they, at a minimum, on a phone system that provides voice over Internet Protocol (VoIP) like RingCentral and Ooma Office?
- Are their emails running through a ticketing system that centralizes all inbound inquiries (no matter what channel but minimally emails) so that the next open rep can address it and also so that the inquiry has been fully addressed and "closed out"?
- Has the CR department been updated as a full customer contact center outfitted to field inquiries via every communication channel from a chatbot, social media DM, email, and text?

- Do they have the necessary tools to field calls and handle the multiple channels that exist today with a consistent level of service that meets your bar?

"This [last point] may be the area that is primed for innovation in a profound way by AI. There is the rapidly evolving Chatbot 2.0 with its generative AI capabilities," Oh suggested.

It's just a matter of time when this expands from just the big corporations to being able to build a generative AI-based chatbot that allows for conversational style service that can address more complicated inquiries than is currently available now through chatbots. It will be much more common and thus, expected from the customers.

Artists are also using AI. Cohen is using ChatGPT and sees it as a tool to help artists in their careers in various capacities. For example, he has used it to help craft his newsletters or to scour the Internet for information:

If I'm low on time, I can ask it to write a newsletter in a certain style, have it include the venues we'll be appearing at, and make sure it knows I'm grateful for the opportunities. It spits out something that still needs to be edited but can be an important technological tool that allows me to spend more time at the piano, and less at the computer. We even recently asked it to tell us to list all hip-hop music between 1990 to 1995 that used jazz samples, and it gave us an extensive list. I think AI will be an important tool in artists' lives in more ways than we can currently imagine, and I'm one to embrace new technology.

Donations Adapt: Apps, Taps, Codes, + NFTs

There are many pathways for donating to artists and organizations. The standard donate button should be a part of your websites and Facebook pages. Donation campaigns and appeals are communicated across all forms of communication—from mail to telemarketing. However, digital fundraising opportunities have expanded as the web, software, and our personal devices have become more sophisticated. New pathways for special events, from golfing to wine tasting to galas, are a pillar of many fundraising plans and offer an additional ask to corporations and individuals to engage and donate. Silent and live auctions are also common online or in-person elements of these events. As smartphones became popular, mobile apps have been designed to bring the auction to your patrons' palms.

Black Ensemble Theater uses the BidPal app during their annual gala's silent auction. In addition to automation around bidding, they could also live stream the event. According to Miller, "We were able to register potential donors on the site, and patrons could buy their tickets seamlessly, totally virtual. That allowed them to see a live stream and donate as the performance was going on."

While apps that allow for engagement during special events or performances are increasingly well-known and incorporated by most leading CMS used to build and update an organization's website, other digital tools also allow for seamless giving. These include Square, Clover Go, SumUp Plus, and Helcium.

DipJar

DipJar, an emerging fundraising device that's gaining momentum, was founded in 2020 and offers Classic and Pro levels. It's a quick credit card donation point you can use at events or a venue, replacing the acrylic donation or tip box used at the bar or information table.

"A lot of organizations have something like Square or just a credit card reader. That's very transactional," pointed out Melissa Smith, vice president of sales at DipJar. "It's really as simple as somebody pulls out their credit card, dips it in the machine, and it makes a noise and lights up, giving them a fun donor experience."

While DipJar Classic doesn't capture complete donor information, DipJar Pro adds features, including a QR code for the donor to use for a receipt and to provide your organization with contact information. When asked if the QR code was a stumbling block, Smith gave an example of a recent event she attended: "We had a lot of older-generation [guests] who were not tech savvy. No one had a problem. Everyone pulled out their phones [and said], 'Oh, that's so cool.'"

In addition, Smith explained how she has seen DipJars used in cross-promotional events with local businesses:

A lot of small businesses used to do donation days for organizations with 10 percent of sales going back to your organization. Due to inflation and other factors, businesses often now say, "We don't have profits to give back—we're struggling ourselves." With DipJar, the business can get cross-marketing, and you are not asking for any money [from] the owner. You and the business can give shoutouts on social media saying "Our DipJars are at East End Brewery, go grab a beer and donate," or vice versa. You're getting that good relationship with the business because you're sending

> **them some customers, and it's good [for you] if any people grabbing a beer make a $5 DipJar donation.**

Pittsburgh Ballet Theatre started using DipJar Classic in 2020 when they launched Open Air: A Series in Celebration of the Performing Arts. While they made performances free to the public during the pandemic in 2020, they wanted a safe, touchless way to accept donations for people who wanted to support them. They had one unit at the registration table and roving volunteers with DipJars — the volunteers walking around the park for anyone who was getting ready to watch the series was by far the most effective. They also gave branded stickers to every person who donated. They now take DipJars to all their events and put them in the theater lobby at performances (see Figure 3.7).

Figure 3.7: The PBT's DipJar and accompanying marketing.
Photo provided by Melissa Smith.

Ballet RI began using DipJar at their 2023 gala, setting donation levels at $2,500 with descending amounts. Director Kathleen Breen Coombs explained how they leveraged the technology. "We didn't do a live auction, we just [asked for] a gift from the heart at the gala. Everyone who gave got a blinking heart [with] the hope that everybody in the room would have a blinking heart by the end of the evening. And it worked."

They now use the DipJars at smaller appearances and events as well as in the theater lobby during performances. Dylan Giles, Ballet RI's marketing director, explains that in the past, they tucked a donation envelope in the program with little success:

Now we can say [during the curtain speech], it's just a super simple thing. If you want to donate, there's a DipJar in the lobby—it'll take you 10 seconds. It's set to $20, and if you want to give $40 do it twice. I've heard that speech at other theaters that have them in the area, and it's just so simple. [The DipJar] has lights and it kind of does a little motion at the transaction. It's just that little level of interaction, while taking away so much of the red tape.

QR Codes

QR codes were invented in 1994 and gained traction as the new, cool tech in the United States in the early 2010s, but quickly lost favor as they were cumbersome to scan and connect to assets. In 2020, however, they made a comeback due to upgrades in mobile technology that automatically recognized codes and the need for touchless transactions during the early years of the COVID-19 pandemic. Today, they are part of many, if not all, commerce experiences. Ordering by QR codes is common in bars and restaurants, and arts organizations use QR codes to link to more information within their space.

Black Ensemble Theater includes a QR in their printed programs and postcards with links to their donation and ticketing web pages. The success rate for use of the QR codes is about 10 percent of patrons. Although that might not seem significant, it allows users to access the material the way they liked in a frictionless manner. That is a win for any organization.

Attack Theatre, a dance company in Pittsburgh (http://attacktheatre.com), began incorporating QR codes at events and performances. The company posts a QR code by their ticket table and on the café tables where the audience sat to grow donations on-site. Those codes linked to Venmo—a quick pathway to donation for a younger or more tech-friendly crowd (see Figure 3.8).

Figure 3.8: Setting up a QR code for a Venmo donation is easy.

Photo by Brett Ashley Crawford.

NFTs

Non-fungible tokens (NFTs) exist as digital drawings, music, or other creative pieces, sort of like digital trading cards that people purchase that exist on a blockchain. NFTs have created new ways for artists and organizations to sell work and engage with their community. They can also be sold by organizations as memorabilia or in unlimited editions as part of a fundraising appeal. NFTs often include smart contracts that become an avatar for membership in virtual communities.

Emmet Cohen, who uses Nifty Gateway, SuperRare, and OpenSea NFT marketplaces, notes that NFTs can be another way to connect with fans or buyers:

> **It is a separate marketplace, with different collectors/supporters. NFTs can also be a used as a way of creating a membership, to own a part of something. I think that the technology is in its infancy and will likely change many things for artists in particular.**

Takeaways

The marketplace is always in motion. Understanding your environment and your current audience and donors is critical to success. While personal connections are key, data-informed work is essential in a 21st-century performing arts business.

Repeatedly, our interviewees noted the importance of data and data hygiene. Understanding your patrons' and donors' habits and preferences increases and deepens your potential to build a deeper relationship with them. Clean data allows for effective segmenting to communicate in ways that match your varied customer journeys. Using external data offers perspective and a view for potential audiences and donors. We recommend that you follow national and global organizations that track trends and patterns for all of us. These include:

- Nonprofit Tech for Good Report, an annual global study of digital marketing and fundraising (www.nptechforgood.com/2023/02/01/announcing-the-2023-nonprofit-tech-for-good-report)
- The annual Benchmarks Study by M+R (http://MRSS.com), with a focus on fundraising
- The annual Nonprofit Communications Trends Report published by the Nonprofit Marketing Guide (http://nonprofitmarketingguide.com)
- The Nonprofit Email Report by Neon One (http://neonone.com)
- The Charitable Giving Report, published annually by Blackbaud (http://blackbaud.com)
- The Nonprofit Trends Report, published annually by Salesforce (http://salesforce.com)
- Capacity Interactive's annual report on digital marketing (http://capacityinteractive.com)

Understanding your user experience by listening and engaging in real conversations is important with your existing customers and people who aren't engaged with your business. Once you understand their needs, wants, and values, you can better adapt your offerings and communications to what they need.

Savvy tech stacks allow for efficient and effective practices. Using project management tools to integrate systems or a simple virtual phone solution can save time and money. Automation requires stopping and thinking through the processes that happen and how you want them to occur. Whether automating approval sequences for content or email flows, it is more efficient and reliable.

Seamless pathways for your customers to learn and engage is non-negotiable. Having outside perspectives and using analytics can tell you where your donors and audiences are confused or if they simply drop off the intended path.

Artificial intelligence is here to stay. Consider how you want to use it, learn how to do it, then let it help you get your work done—whether it is using machine learning for trend analysis or an LLM for advertising copy.

Finally, technology is always changing. It has and will continue to change marketing, fundraising, and event work practically on a daily basis. Doing the work well means being ready to adapt and learn.

Technology Solutions

The following technology solutions are mentioned throughout this chapter. Remember, this is not a comprehensive list of all the technologies available, but they might help you begin your research.

Video

- Adobe Premiere (http://adobe.com) is a timeline-based and non-linear video editing software.
- Adobe After Effects (www.adobe.com/products/aftereffects.html) is a digital visual effects, motion graphics, and compositing application used in post-production for film, video, and TV.

Project Management

- Airtable (http://airtable.com) is a collaborative project management platform.

- Monday (http://Monday.com) is a tool for collaborative project and task management.

Special Events

- Bidpal/OneCause (http://onecause.com) is a platform with an app that puts the attendee experience in their own hands.
- DipJar (http://dipjar.com) is a fundraising device that offers a cashless, seamless solution for events or organizations.

Artificial Intelligence

- ChatGPT (http://openai.com) is an LLM-based chatbot developed by OpenAI.

Email

- Constant Contact (http://constantcontact.com) is an online marketing company focusing on email marketing to build customer relationships.
- Prospect 2 (http://prospect2.com) integrates with Tessitura and uses easy drag-and-drop editors across campaigns, automations, forms, and pages. The goal is to use data to build and adapt customer journeys for a better customer experience.
- Robly (http://robly.com) is an email service provider designed for businesses of all sizes, specializing in supporting charities, nonprofits, education, and religious organizations.

Data Analysis for Marketing

- Enertex Marketing (www.enertexmarketing.com) provides direct marketing campaign planning and execution, data processing, list brokerage, and list management services.
- Peachtree (www.peachtreedata.com) works with organizations to keep their mailing lists clean and up-to-date with a full range of hygiene services, from address validation, household address change updates, email validation, removal of duplicate records, and much more.

Subscription

- Patreon (`http://patreon.org`) is a subscription-based membership platform for creatives and artists.

Customer Management Systems

- Virtuous (`https://virtuous.org`) is a nonprofit CRM providing fundraising, volunteer, and marketing tools to create more responsive donor experiences.
- Tessiturta (`http://tessituranetwork.com`) is a unified system for arts and cultural organizations.

Project Management + Surveys

- Airtable (`http://airtable.com`) is a cloud collaboration service used for project management, surveys, and much more.

Making Magic: Enhancing Artistic Productions

When all the production elements of any performance come together to enrich storytelling, the experience is magical and exciting. The set, props, lighting, projections, sound, and costumes are all beautifully in sync, and no one element stands out above the others. Of course, the performers are also part of the magic, but there are already numerous books about that craft. This chapter is about the technology used all around them.

Each of the professional designers, artists, and production staff members interviewed here are passionate about creating art and equally thrilled with the tools that technology offers to help them keep on schedule and budget, and to sometimes help them create something entirely new. Interviewees also mentioned the importance of making sure the technologies they used aided in the storytelling. Unless technology itself was part of the story being told, not one of them wanted their work to distract from the whole.

This chapter covers ways technology can help flesh out creative ideas, as well as ways to help different production areas work together. The software, hardware and web-based programs referenced in this chapter are pulled together at the end for easy reference. As everyone interviewed pointed out, technology is changing constantly, so the specific tech solutions mentioned may be out-of-date by the time you read this. Instead, consider paying attention to the ways people use technology to problem-solve and to grow their artistic product. A quick online search will help you find similar or updated versions of technologies currently available.

From budget-friendly ideas to over-the-top aspirational projects, this chapter has something for everyone. No matter the size of your budget or organization, you'll find elements that you'll be able to use to breathe fresh life into your own productions.

Set Design

The set, including furniture and props handled by the performers, is the foundation of creating the illusion of the performance happening in a particular place. Whether that's a realistic single room, several locations that require many moving parts, or a minimalist series of platforms, the work of the set designer is the first visual step in creating the world of a production.

We've highlighted the set designers and production teams of two 2023 regional shows: a co-production of *Clue* and an outdoor production of Shakespeare's *The Merry Wives of Windsor*. While we follow the process for designing those specific productions, we also delve into the way they work with technology in general and use it to solve specific design challenges.

Czerton Lim, Freelance Set Designer for *Clue* at Indiana Repertory Theatre (IRT) and Syracuse Stage

For the co-production of *Clue*, Lim had to make sure the set fit well in both venues. "That added a layer of complexity," Lim explained, "because Syracuse Stage is much smaller backstage. Using digital renderings absolutely made for a streamlined comparison. We overlaid the Syracuse Stage and IRT backstage areas onto our designs to make sure we were respecting the architecture—that we didn't assume we had an extra 3 feet, or that an actor could still exit out a narrow alleyway that only existed at IRT, but not at Syracuse Stage." See Figure 4.1.

"And of course, most of the [moving set pieces] were designed within an inch of their lives to allow for them to fit offstage at Syracuse, but also to maximize their effect onstage," Lim added. "It was a gentle balance."

"I am still completely old school in terms of my approach to drafting," Lim admitted. He prefers to create first drafts by hand on paper. For *Clue*, he passed his initial set drawings to an associate to scan and turn

into digital images. With those, Lim worked with the artistic and production teams at IRT to make needed adjustments. "I can manipulate a
simple scan in Photoshop and be able to create different options quickly
to share with the director and say, 'Okay, here are five options—which
one are you feeling good about?'" When the basic look and functionality
of the set design was agreed to by all, his associate created 3D digital
files using Vectorworks.

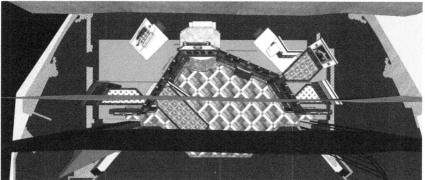

Figure 4.1: Top: Digital 3D set rendering with a transparent area to show how pieces fit
together; Bottom: Overhead digital 3D rendering showing how the set fit backstage in
both theaters.

Digital renderings by Donnie Woodard, associate scenic designer.

"Communication lines and being absolutely open to adjustments is
crucial," added Lim. Working with the show's production team and
scene shop, Lim used several iterations of the virtual 3D renderings for
Clue to have important conversations about how elements would fit
together, any needed revisions, and how they'd be built.

"Honestly, there's a love/hate relationship for me with Vectorworks, AutoCAD, and Adobe Creative Cloud," Lim said. "They are such fantastic tools, yet they're prohibitively expensive and limited in terms of access for young designers and some theaters."

Lim knew audience members at *Clue* might remember the original film and board game. So, for fun he used Photoshop to create a face inspired by a certain actor from the movie in each of the painterly portraits he created. "In the dining room scene, there was a very large painting of a version of *The Last Supper* I created to which I added the faces of every character, including the murdered and murder suspects," Lim described.

IRT sent Lim's files for the paintings to a large local printer to have them output on canvas. "I was really hesitant," Lim admitted, "but from 10 feet away, they looked like they were hand painted, brushstrokes visible and all. Three, four years ago, I would have considered that would have to have been someone [in the scene shop] executing a painting. So, being able to print large format has been another fantastic resource."

The set for *Clue* was built in IRT's scene shop because it appeared there before moving to Syracuse Stage. According to IRT production manager Malia Argüello, working with Lim's digital renderings was a game changer: "We had certainly received 3D set renderings before, but that was the first time we worked with 3D storyboarding—[Lim] rendered every scene in 3D so we could see exactly how everything fit together. That gave us the ability to look from above and from every angle. We talked about what we could do, even before we got into the space."

For extremely detailed set elements like grills on a gate or other decorative elements, IRT sends digital files to an outside shop that specializes in laser cutting and can get the job done in one day. "When labor is such an issue in the theater, it's faster to do laser cutting than to have to try to find someone to do the hand cutting. That precision work will take someone maybe two weeks to sit and cut," Argüello explained. "As audiences now love a more intimate space, that means detail work. We also invite our audience onstage on opening night to tour the set, so we want it to look realistic and to tell the story—laser cutting gives that precision."

Laser cutting machines range greatly, depending on the size of the table. Be sure to check your area for shops you can outsource the work to. If you have the space in your shop and add a lot of detail work to your projects each season and have the needed staff, a purchase may make more sense to your budget.

"Technology has made me a lot faster and a lot less precious about ideas," Lim concluded. "I never fear that time is wasted. Even a bad idea can lead to a better one, or at least I've gotten it out of my system. To be able to archive my process and my steps, I think technology has been a boon even though I haven't completely embraced working digitally."

Scott Penner, Freelance Set Designer for *The Merry Wives of Windsor* at American Players Theatre (APT)

For Brooklyn-based designer Penner's work on APT's *Merry Wives*, he relied on technology and the inventiveness of the theater's staff to create a central set piece. His design called for a bright pink 3' × 2' sculpture of a stag to be mounted high above the actors on a 14'-tall column. To make that happen, the theater asked properties director Nathan Stuber to figure out how to create a sculpture that would have the needed detail, would be weather resistant for their outdoor amphitheater, wouldn't weigh too much for the column, and would survive being handled often as they changed the set for the other shows rotating in repertory throughout their long summer season.

APT purchased a Raise3D Professional Desktop 3D printer, but there are other brands and sizes for smaller budgets. Alternatively, consider outsourcing specific projects with businesses that specialize in this area. The vendor can either work with digital files you send or 3D scan a physical item and 3D print it in a lightweight, durable material.

Stuber found his answer with the professional-grade 3D printer APT purchased in 2022. Not only had they already been able to create specific props and decorative elements for sets with the printer, but they had also used it to create needed parts around the property, such as new electric box covers and other facility needs.

Because the stag statue was too large for their 3D printer to produce all at once, Stuber digitally divided Penner's rendering into individual sections (see Figure 4.2).

"I'm a halfway decent fabricator from scratch, but there's no way I could have carved something that looked like that in a reasonable amount of time with all the other work I had to do," said Stuber. "I think I printed it in 18 or 19 pieces, and each of those sections took between 35 and 50 hours. So, it took about a month [in total]. That printer was churning things out all day, overnight, and even on weekends. I just made sure the next file was ready to go and swapped out the filament when it ran out. Then I had two days of labor gluing the pieces together, filling in the gaps, sanding, priming, and painting."

Figure 4.2: APT used a 3D printer to create this stag sculpture designed by Scott Penner for *The Merry Wives of Windsor* set. Because the decorative piece was so large, they printed it in sections.

Photos by Nathan Stuber.

About his general design work, Penner continued, "I'd probably be completely lost if I didn't have all the technology I use. I technically could do any part of my process by hand—I just really don't want to because it takes way too much time."

"Since COVID, I've exclusively used digital 3D set modeling because it's easier and faster," said Penner. "But it's sometimes hard to get directors and other collaborators who are not great with envisioning space to understand that a digital model and a physical model are the same. I usually use SketchUp because it's super user-friendly and compatible with a lot of rendering programs that allow me to take it further."

"Almost all of our [production] meetings are online, so I'm able to take my collaborators through the model online by sharing my screen," Penner explained. "I've had times in a meeting with a director when they wanted to see changes to a design, like adding or removing a wall—I'm able to draw something new in 2 seconds, which allows us to have a constant flow of discovery and we're able to do things in real time."

Artificial intelligence tools are becoming useful in every creative field. "For designing a production of *Charlie and the Chocolate Factory* recently, I dabbled with Midjourney," said Penner. "Some of the things it came up with from what I was asking were fantastic and it was quick. We'll see if [AI] continues to be useful or if it's just a neat gimmick. But it's helpful to speed along the process of brainstorming and seeing a physical object that's stuck in the back of my head somewhere."

"It's helpful when theater scene shops have technologies that allow me to do things that offer more [in my design]," Penner continued. "If a shop has a CNC [computerized numerical control] router for precision pattern or detail cutting, or a 3D printer, or automation that helps scenery move around, it means I have more options as to what I can design because the shop is able to pump those things out faster, and so it costs [their budget] less. So, I think technology in scene shops is helpful and worth theaters investing in."

Costume Design

Whether in dance, theater, or opera, most of the clothing worn onstage is custom made for each performer. Even when there's a large group of people wearing the same thing, say a flock of white swans or a line of Rockettes, each costume is fitted precisely for each body by hand. But technology can still help in several aspects of costume design.

Eric Winterling, Costume Creator

Sometimes, the technology used in production isn't much different from what we use in our everyday lives. Eric Winterling owns and operates a costume studio in New York City. His shop is used by designers for Broadway, opera, ballet, television, movies, and concert tours. He and his team have built many costumes over the years, including for Broadway productions of the play *Leopoldstadt* and the musical *Some Like it Hot,* to the streaming hits *The Gilded Age* and *The Marvelous Mrs. Maisel.*

The technology he uses the most as he's moving around his 8,200-square-foot studio all day is his iPhone. "In the shop, there are desktop computers, but I always have the phone in my hand," he said. See Figure 4.3. "When we think a costume is finished, we send photos to the designer—front, side, and back . . . . We'll get the photographs back with drawings over them and notes like 'This needs to pull back a little bit' or something. And then I spend so much of my time texting and emailing. All my draping, tech and creative work is done on the weekends."

Figure 4.3: Costume maker Eric Winterling's primary piece of technology is his iPhone. Note that his beloved dogs are never far away either, as was true during the interview for this book.

Photo provided by Eric Winterling.

"I don't have anything against working with technology [for costume patterning], I just have my way [of doing things]," Winterling said. "It's a way of checking myself and trusting what I see. In half scale or full scale on paper, I can trust that size and can see if I have the proportions right. I don't think I'm going to know that on a computer screen."

When Winterling does need to use specific technology for the creation of a costume, he outsources the work to shops that specialize in those areas. "I don't have a 3D printer or laser cutter," Winterling admitted. "I mean, I have nothing against them—it's just not where my brain goes when I need a solution. But they can be an incredible thing to use in the right places. Oh, you know where we used 3D printing was on *Funny Girl*. Fanny Brice had this necklace that has a scarab detail built into it for one of her looks."

"Laser cutting is something we use a lot," Winterling continued. "For a gold leather corset that was laser cut with a lattice pattern [for the 2023 Broadway musical *Once Upon a One More Time*], we subcontracted a different company capable of doing the work. Well, I mean, that's fantastic."

Some costumes require more technology than others, such as when they involve light up elements. Winterling explained:

> There's a lot of technology and coordination involved in those. Even though my father was an electrician, I don't do the lights. It really comes down to what the effect is and how we're achieving it. You know, the biggest thing we've ever done was called *Heart and Lights* for the Rockettes. For the 40 jackets, each hole [for a light] had to be in the same place on each jacket. The Rockettes are not all the same size, but each jacket had to have the same number of lights, and there was a map for where each light went into each hole with an invisible zipper in the back of the lining so they could turn the jacket inside out and put the lights in where they were supposed to go.

See the jackets Winterling's shop built for the Rockettes at www .youtube.com/watch?v=L6KWgEPSXDw.

For the 2023 Broadway musical *Once Upon a One More Time*, Winterling was also given two light-up costume designs to build:

> On one garment, we went back to the Rockettes' idea, but the technology had changed. This time the LED lights had to be sewn in, so it's a different way of approaching it and how the costume was made. We had a lot of conversations about what point the costume had to be sent out to have the lights installed, and then when it came back to us, how we'd finish it.
>
> On another costume for that show, we put LED fabric inside a skirt, but we couldn't cut the LED fabric in a triangle, it had to be cut in a rectangle because all the lines go straight for the string that goes into the battery. There's this technique of cutting into the LEDs to get different qualities of twinkle—it's really wonderful.

Scott Penner, Freelance Costume Designer

Penner sometimes also works as a costume designer. "I'm Canadian," Penner said, "and in Canada it's very common to hire designers with multiple disciplines. In the United States, I'm usually hired to design just the sets or just the costumes."

Penner explained:

> I still do most of my costume sketching by hand, but painting is done digitally. Anyone who still paints by hand struggles to keep up with the amount of work, particularly for a musical. And as soon as there's a change or they can't afford the fabric they wanted, they have to repaint. But if it's in Photoshop or a program like that, they can just click and change it out—that is a complete game changer. Technology is still absolutely important in the process, because there's just a lot of work—a lot of changing, a lot of figuring out patterns and color, and how it all fits together.

Lighting Design

The art of stage lighting has a massive impact on any performance. Used to shape an environment, to focus the audience's attention, to set an emotional tone or rhythm, and to add depth and richness to painted backdrops and other scenery, lighting is a powerful tool.

Lighting technology changes frequently, and often in major ways, so we interviewed a lighting designer who works with numerous venues and the production manager at a regional theater about how they keep up with the shifting technology.

Brandon Stirling Baker, Lighting Director for Boston Ballet and Freelance Lighting Designer

In addition to his work with Boston Ballet, Brandon Stirling Baker is best known for his frequent collaborations with director/ choreographer Justin Peck at New York City Ballet and other dance companies around the world.

"Lighting technology is changing monthly," said Baker. "I'm constantly dealing with new sources of light that really change the way I personally think about color, or how I translate color ideas." In addition to designing for new works, Baker often re-creates lighting for older ballets. "I'm almost like a curator—I'm reading old notes, interpreting old ideas that could date back to the 1960s, maybe even earlier, and I'm re-creating with technology of today."

Until recently, stage lighting was almost exclusively created using tungsten incandescent light instruments that closely replicated natural light. They are industrial-size versions of incandescent light bulbs you might use in your home. However, those bulbs are expensive to maintain because they need to be replaced after 1,000–1,500 hours of use, they use a lot of electricity, and they produce a lot of heat. So, theaters began replacing those with LED instruments that last around 50,000 hours, use much less energy, and don't produce any heat at all.

Baker said:

Nearly all of my work is touring all over the place, so it's in my best interest to sort of lean into technology as it changes. For example, a work I designed just as recent as 2017 for New York City Ballet called *The Times Are Racing* with choreographer Justin Peck—that work is already out of date for technology. We completely redesigned the lighting with new LED sources to adapt the same ideas. I'm really excited about it and don't see it as a threatening thing to [my original] design ideas. I see it as a moment to clarify.

Replacing all existing lighting instruments is an expensive, long process for any organization. So, most ballet companies where Baker designs or re-creates his work use combinations of both incandescent and LED lighting. In advance, each company sends Baker their detailed standard lighting plot that lists each type of instrument and technology available. "If they're using technology that's all of a certain era, I tend to lean into that era and try not to add too many different types of lighting fixtures because that can actually complicate my process—color behaves differently from a 2012 fixture versus from a lighting fixture that came out in 2023," explained Baker. "I always send a list of what I'd like to add, why I like the change, and how they'll be used."

Another piece Baker designed with Peck is called *Heatscape*; this time it was for Miami City Ballet in 2015. That piece has gone on to be performed by numerous companies all over the world, including in 2023 in Madrid, Spain. The challenge for Baker was that the tungsten light sources he used in his original design weren't permitted at all there, so once again he had to completely redesign for LED. "I am a huge fan of keeping my eye on the stage instead of looking at the data, the information of what the original light levels were," Baker explained. "So, if a light was at 100 percent intensity in Miami, and it was in a deep blue color, that means something very different [with LED]—perhaps that light is now at 50 percent and it has the same impact and maybe it's even cleaner."

Boston Ballet has embraced moving lights and intelligent lighting, adding 75 moving lights to their basic hanging plot. This allows Baker to save time during the short load-in and when adjusting or correcting lights—there are fewer lights to hang because the moving instruments can be used in different ways and locations on the stage throughout any performance. Baker explained:

> **Flexibility is key when you're creating a work from scratch with a live orchestra with, let's say, three directors. You need to have flexibility at a moment's notice and technology has made that possible. The audience rarely sees them panning or tilting up and down, but they're constantly changing behind the scenes. My roots as a lighting designer who's worked with older technology has allowed me to use the technology of today in a more poetic way, I think. It doesn't have to be constantly in motion, even though the industry is constantly in motion itself.**
>
> **The big thing I'm dealing with right now is follow spots. For the world of ballet, traditional follow spots are slowly disappearing and we're switching to automated. The operators are no longer up in a booth—they're on the stage level in a corner with a little controller that has a camera and is attached to the light itself. That's very cool. Now the follow spot can be [hung] anywhere. They can be directly over the stage or upstage behind dancers so they're backlit. This technology was already common in rock and roll and concert touring, but now it's becoming normal in ballet because the types of choreographers and directors are changing.**

Baker uses Electronic Theatre Controls' Eos console series software and hardware as the main control system for cueing, Vectorworks for drafting, and Lightwright for data management—organizing color inventories, lighting plots, patch and maintenance information. Baker admitted:

> **I don't think [lighting] is an art form that you can ever master. I think it's something that you constantly learn—you're constantly discovering what light is. And you know, we wake up every morning and we feel differently about the sun coming through our window, or no sun is coming through—it's a constant discovery. There's something beautiful about, as a lighting designer, not being a master, but constantly learning.**

See examples of Baker's beautiful lighting at www.stirlingbaker.com.

Indiana Repertory Theatre (IRT) in Indianapolis

When freelance designers send IRT their lighting plots for a show in Vectorworks or AutoCAD, the lighting manager closely reviews them to make sure there are no red flags. "She makes sure that [lighting instruments] are where they need to be and will actually fit in our space and that we have what we need [in our inventory] or that we can get what they want—both in budget and in Indianapolis," explained IRT production manager Malia Argüello. "And she goes through to make sure that it can be hung, gelled and focused in the time allotted—from both budgetary and labor perspectives, which has become so important over the last few years."

Technology requested by lighting designers includes elements such as atmospheric fog haze, special gobos, and moving lights, which IRT rents from a local source. "Moving light technology is changing and advancing so much, it didn't make sense to purchase them because anything would be obsolete in 5 years" said Argüello. "But we've gotten to the point that we want to buy some moving lights now. We're using them enough that it monetarily makes more sense for us to purchase, even if it's going to become obsolete in 5 or 10 years."

In researching the best LED moving light technology to purchase, IRT asked designers which brands they like to work with. They also reviewed each brand's specifications for lumens (brightness), framing, how many gobos each instrument can hold, and color clarity. "We have an ETC light board, so there is a little bit of bias," admitted Argüello. "But MAC Aura certainly can't be ignored. And Chauvet is beginning to come a little bit back into the field—my contacts from education recommended them because they're significantly less expensive."

IRT is also converting to all LED lighting fixtures as their budget allows. "Last year, we purchased 60 LED pars to replace our wash systems. To be honest, I haven't talked to any theater that isn't either in the midst of changing over or planning it," said Argüello. "You can't get the [incandescent] bulbs and they're not making those light instruments anymore. Everything is going to LED, which makes sense."

Video Design

This area of theater technology has grown tremendously over the past 6 years, with rapidly changing technology allowing more types of usage and increasing accessibility to all levels of budgets. Video design is often lumped into either lighting or scenic design categories, but from a practical and artistic standpoint, it's really a category of its own. While the artistry complements lighting and set design, the skillset and technologies are quite different.

We've interviewed video designers who do most of their work on Broadway and with large opera companies, but the smaller organizations interviewed throughout this book have also used projections to enhance their productions. Lastly, the extremely cool work of combining video technology with sociology in our last interview with Lawrence Shea may spur creative ideas for you to use for one of your productions.

Benjamin Pearcy, Chief Technology Officer and Project Director at 59 Productions

59 Productions is a New York– and London-based production company that designs media for special events, artistic installations, Broadway, West End, and touring shows.

During the slow, usually weeklong process of bringing lighting, projections, set. and all other design elements together in the theater as a show gets ready for audiences, Pearcy and his team continue working with a media server called Disguise. With the set designer's drawings, they create a virtual 3D model and add textures using UV mapping, then overlay the projections they're designing for each scene. This allows them to adjust their designs and determine the best angles even before they apply the projections on the actual stage.

"We can see [our designs on the digital set] without seeing what's happening on stage, working in a different location while other things are going on. It's slower to program Disguise, but having the ability to work while we're waiting makes up for that slowness," explained Pearcy.

The first time 59 Productions used Disguise was for *An American in Paris*, for which they won the 2015 Tony Award for the show's Broadway run and a 2018 Laurence Olivier Award when the show ran on London's West End.

Artificial intelligence (AI) can be extremely useful in video design. "AI is an interesting tool in terms of image generation, because very often [we] need to do a fairly straightforward thing," said Pearcy. 59 Productions creates original photos and videos but turns to an AI video enhancer for tasks such as altering speed or resolution. "I might have a video clip of clouds that's 30 seconds long and I want it to last 5 minutes—I have to create all the frames in between, right? Computers already do that," explained Pearcy, "but AI tools generate those frames more effectively and believably because of machine learning. We're always looking for ways to make [our workflow] more efficient, because the path to quality is through many iterations and revisions. The faster we can work, the more iterations we can do, the better."

59 Productions primarily creates video design, but Disguise can also be controlled with a lighting console, which would make for a smooth workflow for anyone designing both lighting and projections.

For each show, the team at 59 Productions must decide if LED screens or video projection will be best. "My background is in lighting design," Pearcy said. "One of the things about projection is I can only add light to what's already there, so we have to work very closely with lighting designers to kind of find that balance. When we're doing video design for a show, light is coming out of either a projector or an LED screen." He explained:

> If we want to be able to apply [video] content to a three-dimensional surface, then it's projectors—right off the bat that rules out LEDs. If it's a backdrop or a flat surface on its own, then there are a few things that go into that decision. Some of it is budget, although they're starting to equalize the costs of very bright projectors versus very high-resolution LED screens, especially in the rental market. So as shops have more inventory, and it's been in an inventory longer, the prices start to come down, although generally LED is more expensive. Then it comes down to the scale at which we might need the surface to be. It's often just a lot less expensive to use projection because I might be able to use two or three projectors to fill an entire full stage backdrop where it would take quite a lot of LED panels to do that. See Figure 4.4.

Figure 4.4: The video design by 59 Productions for the 2023 Broadway revival of *Camelot* at Lincoln Center Theater was nominated for a Tony Award. Because the physical set was minimalist, their projections on the back wall of the stage aided in creating a sense of place. In this photo, a video of falling snow helped set the scene for the opening of the show.

Photo by Rich Baker.

> Generally LED screens are incredibly bright, so that creates challenges we solve in a variety of ways—sometimes we'll put a piece of material or scrim in front of the LED screen that will knock the brightness down quite a bit and smooth out the pixels. We very often have shows that open and close without having any [technical] issues, which wasn't the case not so very long ago. Ultimately, I would say projectors are probably a little more reliable than LED screens. There's just less wiring.

Pearcy summed up, "Ultimately, [our creative] ideas are the thing. All the technologies we use are in service of trying to get those ideas to the stage, closer to what we have in our heads, and that's always the challenge."

Jason H. Thompson and Kaitlyn Pietras, PXT Studio

PXT Studio is a Los Angeles–based firm that fuses art and technology for theater, opera, dance, museums, and immersive environments. Recently, PXT designed three productions that combined live camera feed with fantastical art environments. The performers carried out the action on a green screen set so that the audience could see the reality of what they were doing while they were combined with artistic settings on large screens in the theater at the same time.

In 2018, they designed the green screen elements of *A Trip to the Moon* with the Los Angeles Philharmonic. "We knew we wanted to use LED walls because we wanted them to be green screens some of the time, and other times we wanted them to reflect the actual environment. I've had a lot of experience with LED screens," explained Jason H. Thompson. "I was an associate designer for *Jersey Boys* [on Broadway], and there were a lot of LED walls in that show."

"For *A Trip to the Moon*, we captured live feeds [from the cameras] into our media server WATCHOUT and composited [the footage of the performers] with these retro futuristic backgrounds," continued Thompson. See Figure 4.5.

Also in 2018, they used Cinema 4D for the first time for a green screen production of the opera *Lost Highway* with Oper Frankfurt in Germany. All their projects listed in this chapter were collaborations with director Yuval Sharon. When he proposed a 2022 production of the opera *The Valkyries* for a co-production with the Hollywood Bowl in Los Angeles and the Detroit Opera in Michigan, partners Kaitlyn Pietras and Thompson decided to create their biggest green screen concept while using a video game real-time 3D creation tool, Unreal Engine.

Figure 4.5: Performers moved in front of green screens and were added to artistic backgrounds in real time on the center screen for *A Trip to the Moon* with the Los Angeles Philharmonic at the Walt Disney Concert Hall.

Photo by Kaitlyn Pietras.

Staying on top of emerging technologies is extremely useful for all designers. "Unreal Engine was new technology [to us], which is always scary because you don't know what you don't know. But we love projects like this because we like to file away new technology and wait for the right dramaturgical moment to use it to help tell the story," explained Thompson. "As soon as we started talking about [*The Valkyries*], I was thinking about Unreal Engine." He continued:

> Normally Yuval makes these amazing little pencil sketches of what he imagines, and then we fill in the gaps, and try to enhance things to push it further. But for this show, he couldn't imagine what to do because he didn't know what the world [we had created] looked like. So, he came to our studio and we played the music and gave him an Oculus headset so he could be inside the 3D world of the show. Sharon then gave them directions about what actions specific characters would do and where they'd appear in that

> world throughout every scene of the opera. That was a crazy pro-
> cess. I think we spent a full week just figuring out the beats of the
> show even as we were continuing to finesse [the art].

"Running the whole thing through Unreal Engine was tough," admitted Pietras. "We didn't understand the technology, so we had to rely on other people and explain how theater works. And we had to teach a technical 3D artist how to cue something to live music because they were used to building video games."

Thompson explained that they landed on a complex system using Disguise Media Server as the main foundation: "We were capturing all the video content from five PTZ green screen cameras into Disguise and keying everything out using another piece of software, a plug-in called Notch, and manipulating Unreal Engine in real time. These technologies weren't designed to talk to each other or meant to run a live show that has a couple hundred cues, so it was sort of a fun puzzle."

When Yuval Sharon met with them about a 2023 production of *Proximity*, a trio of new contemporary operas for Lyric Opera of Chicago, he had an interesting vision—an LED halfpipe. Thompson said:

> Yuval's amazing to work with because he'll come to us with a big idea. He knew the space needed to be able to change immediately, to find new ways of showing how the three pieces related to each other, and to create a rhythm that would give the audience time to digest the scenes—from the streets of Chicago, talking about gang violence, and then a wild subway ride that's more psychological than real. I think the audience was able to make unique discoveries they wouldn't have made otherwise. The more we talked about it, we thought it had to be an LED quarter pipe, not a true half pipe.

They used a total of 440 LED screens to create the quarter-pipe design on the massive Civic Opera House stage, covering the entire floor and curving up to create a backdrop of screens. On the floor, they used Black Marble BM4 LED panels. "They're so sturdy and stable that you can drive a car on them, which we did," said Thompson. He continued:

> We originally wanted to make the entire thing to use the same floor panel type. But we had to convince [vendors] to rent this to us at a price the Lyric could afford. When we found the right partner company, ROE Visual, they said they could do the area people would walk on as floor tiles, and then change to lightweight panels that were more of a ceiling product [for the curve and backdrop]. The idea was a little risky, but when we went to Las Vegas and

> looked at the products, we realized we could create a seamless
> curve and that it would be imperceptible that they were different
> panel types to the audience. This wasn't pulled off a shelf—it was
> all specially engineered and designed [for our production]. We had
> a great programmer and the crew at the Lyric was amazing.

As noted earlier, using projections or using LED screens each has artistic and practical advantages. "The beautiful thing about using LED was that as opposed to just projecting onto a curved surface, when it's black, it's truly black," Pietras pointed out. "So, we had moments when we expanded to show the full LED curve, and there were moments when we pulled in and it felt very intimate, like the subway ride Jason mentioned. We played with making the space feel horizontal, vertical, or skewing it in different ways, so we had fun violating that halfpipe shape to what we created."

"The LED also allowed us to play with up lighting [from the floor right under the performers], because we designed the lighting for that production as well," added Thompson. "Positions [for placing lighting instruments] are limited for a show like that, so it was cool to use the LEDs to create that balance and fill things in."

For creating the visual art in *Proximity*, they worked with a 3D technical artist who worked in Unreal Engine. "We had her create different environments according to our inspiration and guidance," explained Pietras. "Then I used her art to create little videos to render out and run through our media server. A lot of the other content I generated in After Effects and Photoshop, so it was a great combination of 2D and 3D content. Then we ran the show through the Disguise Media Server."

"Unreal Engine is so light and nimble when it comes to 3D content creation," Pietras added. "Everyone in the industry has realized that this is a big game changer, and it's everywhere—from film down to the smallest project. It can be a little cumbersome, but it's a fun tool. And it's free, so that's amazing."

Technologies Pietras and Thompson are interested in using for future projects include motion-tracking devices that make the video and lighting responsive to the performers. The basic technology already exists, but the current cost is prohibitive. "I'm also excited about the idea of translucent video panels, or OLED [organic light-emitting diode]," said Thompson, "the idea that you can have windows that become video, but on a much larger scale than the size of a TV. That's something I'm always keeping an eye out for because I know it's producible to a certain scale, but you can't cover a 20-foot area with it yet."

"I would also love to get a live video feed on stage from a completely silent drone that federal aviation regulations would let you fly over an [indoor] audience," added Pietras. "That would be amazing."

Lawrence Shea, Media Architect

Lawrence Shea designs video and media for theatrical visuals, museum exhibitions, and large-scale public works of art, and he is a company member of The Builders Association in New York City. He is also an associate professor of video and media design at Carnegie Mellon University.

While Shea has designed video for numerous traditional shows, during our interview he showed passion for more experimental pieces that combine sociology with technology. He and The Builders Association company members are interested in the effects of technology on the lived experience and looking at how deeply affected we are by technology—how it happens without us being fully aware.

One example of that is a 2015 divisive theater production they created called *The Elements of Oz*. Shea explained:

> We were interested in *The Wizard of Oz*, not to just retell the story, but to tell the story around it. There's a lot of YouTube content about the movie— conspiracy kind of things. We also found interviews with Judy Garland talking when she was older about her experience filming and how awful it was. And she talked about drug addiction and exploitation, so we staged that. There's also a beautiful Salman Rushdie moment when he talks about New York City being Oz—a place for people who don't feel at home anywhere else in the world.

The premise of the show was that a film troupe was interested in the history of the script and in shooting some of the scenes in the order they were filmed for the movie, not the actual final order. Each live-filmed scene was captured at each performance and then edited into the correct final order and shown to the audience at the end of the show.

For *The Elements of Oz*, they decided that the smartphone was Oz. "In contemporary culture, we're wowed by our devices," explained Shea. "We stare at them, we live our lives through them, and they sort of dazzle us while a lot of not-so-great stuff happens." So, audience members' smartphones extended the experience. The company was excited by augmented reality (AR), so they created an app for elements of Amazon Web Services (AWS). "We created these fantastic moments where [the audience's] phones would scan an image target, they'd look up and see the Glinda bubble floating around the theater space above you," explained Shea. "And then it would land on stage and the lights would come up on [an actor] dressed as Glinda, the Good Witch." See Figure 4.6.

Figure 4.6: Audiences at *The Elements of Oz* used an app on their smartphones to see 3D poppies all around them while the scene was being filmed on stage.

Photo by Lawrence Shea.

The theater was opened one hour before curtain to give audience members extra time to take care of the technology and to get acclimated, and they set up phone-charging stations for patrons. Ushers were trained how to help people download the app and to use the QR codes that appeared on an onstage screen for each scene. "[Using QR codes] was kind of clunky," admitted Shea, "so in the later versions we didn't use an image target, we just triggered patrons' phones to vibrate. We told people to leave them on their laps, and when their phones vibrated, to pick them up. We kept changing the technology as we developed the show for ease of use and transportability."

Some patrons either didn't have enough memory on their phones or elected not to download the app, but that became part of the experience as well. "As soon as the play happened, if someone's phone died or they didn't know how to do it, they would just look at the person next to them and it became incredibly social," Shea elaborated. "People were like, 'Oh, well, my phone's working and I'll share it with you.' All of a sudden, they had a sense of pride. People have this very personal relationship with their phones."

To create the interactive smartphone component, Shea and the team designed elements and animated scenes with Autodesk's Maya. Those finished scenes were then pulled into Unity, a cross-platform game engine, where they created a new app, which they submitted for an approval process with Apple and Google.

"I'm really proud of what we did with what we had, but it wasn't easy," admitted Shea. "I wouldn't recommend it to anyone as a template because most of what we did can now be done using web services. You don't have to go through the app approval process, so the authoring of this kind of technology has gotten much easier."

Sound Design + Music Composition

Sound design is part of the storytelling and influences the audience's experience of location, the emotional life of the characters, and the mood of the piece being performed. This can include sound effects, music, building atmosphere, and how the performers are heard. Sound technologies are changing quickly, becoming more robust.

We interviewed a production manager at a regional theater, a sound designer/composer who has years of experience working with theaters across the United States, and the house sound engineer at a large venue where Broadway tours frequently perform.

Indiana Repertory Theatre (IRT), Indianapolis

In real life, many people have access to great audio technology in their homes and in movie theaters with incredible surround-sound systems. "When audiences come to a live theater performance and the sound doesn't wash over them the way it does in those other spaces, when it doesn't surround them and encompass them and tell them the story, they know it," noted IRT's production manager Malia Argüello. "We can't fake that anymore."

In 2023, IRT began installing a new system from Meyer Sound in sections as their budget allowed over time. "Any time you put in a new system, there's always going to be an adjustment period," explained Argüello:

We've not finished purchasing and installing the under-balcony system yet [for the 600-seat mainstage], so we're balancing a new

> overall system with some old technology that's still in place. We have the full new system [for the 300-seat thrust stage], and it's working beautifully. Sound designers who had been here before and come back now that we have a whole new system have had a period of adjustment. In a lot of ways, we're catching up to other theaters. We were smart when we purchased the new system to make sure it was advanced enough and of high quality so it can grow with us. This is something we're hoping to have for the next 15 to 20 years, so flexibility is the key these days.

Most of IRT's productions are plays with music; however, they are beginning to include musicals in their season, which will require body mics. "We haven't traditionally used mics on our casts," said Argüello. "We don't have a setup, a mixing station out in the audience. That's a whole new world for us, and now we're talking about building the infrastructure to be able to do that. So, even though we just got a new sound system, we're going to have to make changes in order to evolve."

Sartje Pickett, Freelance Composer + Sound Designer

Sartje Pickett has worked with numerous theaters across the United States, including Yale Repertory Theater, Guthrie Theater, Dallas Theater Center, and Oregon Shakespeare Festival.

"In many of Shakespeare's plays, there are songs with lyrics that need someone to put to music, and the music needs to fit in with the rest of the design world," Pickett explained. "A good deal of the work that I do is with productions that need songs to be composed for [existing] lyrics. For plays without songs that need music transitions and underscoring, it's sometimes actually cheaper to hire a composer than to pay a licensing fee for all the individual music the theater might use in a show."

Pickett uses various types of technology, depending on what kind of materials she needs to generate:

> I usually use a notation software program called Sibelius to help transcribe what's in my head, and to be able to hear it play back. It's kind of a shorthand for a lot of composers who in the past would have worked with musicians to try out ideas. So, if it's my first time writing for a trombone, for example, I might take some time to use the technology to kind of get there. But then I really need to meet with a trombone player to get a sense of whether what I wrote is going to work for the instrument and how I can write [music] that's better suited.

If a project has too small a budget for live musicians or the material is more contemporary, Pickett sometimes uses virtual instruments. For that sound design, she uses a notation software program to score it and then moves it to a digital audio workstation to complete the work.

Technology can help make sound design a spontaneous process during rehearsals. Pickett explained:

For *Shakespeare's Will* at IRT in 2023, I was improvising [on guitar] with the actor in the rehearsal space because I find that helpful when I'm scoring movement. Sometimes the music comes before the movement, but transitional music or underscoring might come when a need arises. Immediately after rehearsal, I got my phone out and recorded a quick version of what I had been playing. The next day I set up a little recording studio in my hotel room and recorded it with a better microphone. Sometimes you have to get creative when finding a quiet place to record. After I mixed and edited the track on my DAW [digital audio workstation] I went back to the theater and added it to IRT's QLab system.

"We often have QLab set up in the rehearsal room so their sound cues, their music, their atmospherics are part of the rehearsal process—it's another character," noted IRT's Argüello. "That way we're ahead of the game, giving notes and adjustments [before technical rehearsals begin on stage] so that character is more fully developed."

The Benedum Center for the Performing Arts

In addition to the technologies used to create sound for a show, the technology infrastructure in the venue impacts sound design. The Benedum Center for the Performing Arts in Pittsburgh, Pennsylvania (see Figure 4.7) is a 2,800-seat theater that is part of the Pittsburgh Cultural Trust and home to Pittsburgh Ballet Theatre, Pittsburgh Opera, Pittsburgh Civic Light Opera, and touring Broadway productions.

"Touring Broadway sound systems have gone through a significant change," said Christopher M. Evans, house sound engineer. "Their sound systems that they travel with are more complicated, so they often need our support through delay systems or for surround systems."

"In venues like the Benedum around the country, there are specific things they need to do in the way they interface with touring productions," Evans continued, "and a lot of that has to do with communications and the use of digital. We have large Helix and FreeSpeak networks which allow us to interface between touring productions. I also think having scalable systems is very important."

Figure 4.7: Pittsburgh's Benedum Center for the Performing Arts was built in 1928 and was billed as Pittsburgh's Palace of Amusement. Today the building is registered with the National Register of Historic Places.

Photo provided by Christopher M. Evans.

A scalable sound system refers to the ability of the hardware and software to function well when it's changed in size to meet the need of the user. So, this refers to the Benedum's sound system being compatible for touring productions whether they add lots of technology from their own systems or very little.

The Pittsburgh Cultural Trust is fully committed to accessibility for all people, so Evans works closely with guest services and the director of accessibility:

> We use infrared and stream across two different channels—one for audio description and captioning, and one for a newer system called Sennheiser MobileConnect that streams live audio content via Wi-Fi to any iOS or Android phone in the room. We updated our Wi-Fi in early 2020, so now our system can accommodate up to 2,800 people with 100 access points. We're also able to stream audio for people who don't want to use infrared, and for hearing aids, we use a Bluetooth connection.

Playwriting, Directing, + Casting

Technology has numerous tools that can be useful for writing, directing, or helping to create the big vision for a production.

James Still, Playwright and Director

Los Angeles–based James Still has used technology to help his process, and during our interview, he was passionate about ways to highlight how technology and theater can be partners in storytelling. He wrote a multimedia play called *And Then They Came for Me* that included actual filmed interviews with two of Anne Frank's friends who survived the Nazi persecution of World War II. His most produced work to date, the play premiered at George Street Playhouse in New Brunswick, New Jersey in 1999 and continues to be produced each year across the world.

Still created video to allow characters set in the 1940s to talk with their older selves, an interplay between live action and video. "The idea was that actors would play those characters as young people, while the two filmed real-life people were in their late 60s," Still explained. "I wanted that technology to somehow feel like the interview was happening in the moment we were watching the play. So, I filmed with the camera on [the real-life survivors] in a way so that when it was staged, the actor who was playing a young person could look to [the video] and ask, 'What's going to happen to me?' When the rights for the play were made available to theaters and schools, the scripts were originally accompanied by VHS tapes for production. Of course, those were replaced with DVDs and now with digital files."

For a 2017 production of *Dial M for Murder* he directed, Still requested video projections for phone calls:

> I think there were 11 [telephone] calls in total. So, we're talking about either watching a one-sided conversation or hearing a recorded voice. I just didn't think audiences would have the patience for those old-fashioned phone calls on stage, so we filmed them. The set was an interior of a 1950s apartment in London, and the designer added this beautiful [proscenium] all the way around so we could project the calls in different places. When an actor onstage was on the phone, the audience could also see a projection of the character on the other end of the call. Filming those phone calls made the production feel contemporary, while it was still period.

> As a director, I've found Google Jamboard especially useful during casting. When I'm seeing lots of actors, I can put their [digital] headshots on a whiteboard to start assembling the cast. So many auditions are now on Zoom, which means we can see actors from all over the country in a single day and nobody has to fly in. So, people in smaller markets can audition in bigger markets. But that means I've never seen those people live in a room—I'm never getting a feel for that humanity. So [Zoom auditions] have their challenges. However, Jamboard is also useful in trying to record and assemble even the chemistry of the cast. You're just looking at headshots, but you can start to get a vibe that way. And I have found that useful.

Takeaways

Whether you work in theater, music, opera, or dance, any of the ideas shared in this chapter can be adapted to work for your needs. And don't be intimidated by ideas coming from larger organizations with massive budgets—you can learn clever ways of adapting an idea into your budget size.

No matter the area they work in, each interviewee in this chapter mentioned consciously filtering themselves before beginning a new project to make sure the technology they were thinking of using helped add to the storytelling. The lesson here is, don't use technology just to use technology.

Remember that technology is constantly evolving, so do your research before making any purchases. First, define your real needs, goals, and budget. There may be technologies that fit your needs better than others, or that are more budget-friendly.

People interviewed for this chapter suggested:

■ Be realistic about how often you'll use a specific technology, and then consider whether renting or purchasing is a better option for your budget.

■ Look at the long view of how you will use any technology you purchase. Make sure what you select is easily adaptable to meet your changing needs and growth, and that it's high quality to last for many years.

■ For lighting instruments, purchase several at one time if your budget will allow. Because this is an area that's quickly evolving, you'll want to have several with the same brightness and color intensity so they'll balance well. Different generations of lights don't produce the same qualities of light, so designers will have more difficulty, which translates to time, which translates to money.

- For video projection, organizations with any budget size can creatively incorporate the technology into their productions and the technology is almost always rented for each project.

Technology Solutions

These are technology solutions mentioned throughout this chapter. Remember, this is not a comprehensive list of all the technologies available, but the solutions might help you begin your research.

Set Design

- Vectorworks (https://vectorworks.com) is a web-based drafting software for 2D or 3D rendering.
- Autodesk AutoCAD (www.autodesk.com) is a slightly more expensive drafting program used for many design processes with tools for digital precision with measurements and calculations, 3D components, and data sharing.
- Adobe Creative Cloud (www.adobe.com/creativecloud.html) is a bundle of supported design applications that includes Photoshop and Illustrator, among others.
- SketchUp (www.sketchup.com) is a 3D design program. They offer a free basic downloadable and a supported Pro Subscription with a more robust toolset.
- Midjourney (www.midjourney.com) is a generative artificial intelligence (AI) web-based text-to-image program.

Lighting Design

- Electronic Theatre Controls, Inc. (ETC) Extensible Operating System (EOS) (www.etcconnect.com) is an award-winning lighting software and console series that allow lighting designers to write, adjust, and control cues.

- Vectorworks Spotlight (www.vectorworks.net/en-US/spotlight) provides the lighting designer with all the tools necessary to plan and create a light plot and its associated paperwork.

- Lightwright (www.lightwright.com) is lighting device management software that lighting designers and electricians use as part of their workflow from initial design to archiving.

Video Design

- Disguise AI (www.disguise.one/en) integrates a real-time 3D stage visualizer, media playback, and a timeline. It lets you model the stage, view it instantly from any angle, and drop video or still content onto the timeline and play it back onto the stage, without time-consuming re-renders.

- An AI Video Enhancer is a type of software that uses a neural network to enhance the video quality and upscale video from SD to HD (720p or 1080p), to 4K, and up to 8K in one click, with super-resolution upscaling and multi-frame enhancement.

- WATCHOUT (www.dataton.com) is multi-display production and playback software that is optimally run on a WATCHPAX media server.

- Cinema 4D (www.maxon.net/en/cinema-4d) is professional 3D modeling, animation, simulation, and rendering software.

- Unreal Engine (www.unrealengine.com/en-US) is a real-time 3D creation tool created for game developers.

- An Oculus (www.oculus.com/gear-vr) headset allows wearers to see and interact with a 3D digital world and was created for gaming.

- PTZ green screen cameras are pan, tilt, and zoom robotic video cameras that allow an operator to control the camera remotely. PTZ cameras can pan horizontally, tilt vertically, and zoom in on a subject to enhance the image quality without digital pixelation.

- Notch (www.notch.one) is a plug-in software filter for real-time animation editing, compositing, and grading, originally designed for gaming.

- Black Marble (www.roevisual.com/en/products/black-marble-bm4) BM4 LED panels are a sturdy floor system that can support heavy weight.

- Adobe After Effects (www.adobe.com/products/aftereffects .html) is a digital visual effects, motion graphics, and compositing application used in the postproduction process of film making, video games, and television production.

- Maya (www.autodesk.com/maya) is a 3D computer graphics application that runs on Windows, macOS, and Linux, originally developed by Alias and currently owned and developed by Autodesk. It is used to create assets for interactive 3D applications, animated films, TV series, and visual effects.

- Unity (https://unity.com) is a cross-platform game engine used for real-time applications.

Sound Design + Music Composition

- Meyer Sound (https://meyersound.com), a manufacturer of sound systems, offers customized packages of products for customers' needs, training, and support.

- Sibelius (www.avid.com/sibelius) is a music notation program used to write, refine, hear, scan, and print music scores.

- QLab (https://qlab.app) is macOS software for designing and playing back sound, video, light, and show cues.

- Helix (www.clearcom.com/Products/Products-by-Name/HelixNet) is an Ethernet networking playback system.

- FreeSpeak (www.clearcom.com/Products/Products-by-Name/ FreeSpeak-Wireless) is a multi-channel wireless intercom system.

- Sennheiser MobileConnect (https://en-us.sennheiser.com/ mobileconnect-smartphone-hearing-system-app) is a smartphone-based audio accessibility system that works through a Wi-Fi network.

Playwriting, Directing, + Casting

• Google Jamboard (www.google.com/jamboard) is a free digital white-board collaboration tool that works in real time through Google Workspace with a web browser or mobile app.

5

Defining Who You Are: Branding, Rebranding, + Residencies

A good brand can communicate many things about you as an artist or organization, including what to expect from you, the value in what you offer, and your place in your community and industry. Your branding should also be in alignment with your organization's mission statement and values, as well as offer a vision for what you seek to achieve. Every aspect of your brand should be carefully considered, from your logo, colors, images, to the tone of the language and tone you use to communicate.

While there are many nuanced elements to any brand, we've included a graph for a basic understanding of the three primary areas—how you want to be perceived, the way you present your brand, and the way patrons perceive your brand (see Figure 5.1). Note that your community's perception in the far right of the graph is perhaps the most important of all. Consider making sure that your branding and marketing efforts reflect the customer and community experience.

Numerous technologies and systems are available to help in the process of defining and refining your brand:

- **Branding**—Online research, digital or in-person meetings with stakeholders in and outside your organization

- **Brand Identity**—Design programs such as Gravit Designer, Canva, Sketch, or Adobe Creative Cloud

- **Brand**—Metrics and interactions on social media, ticket purchase and donation data, website traffic, or surveys through SurveyMonkey or features available through your CMS or email system

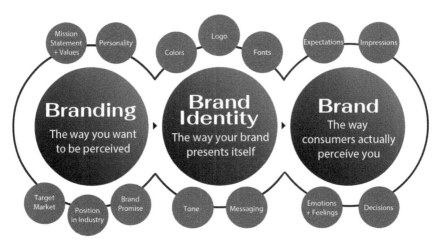

Figure 5.1: This graph offers a clear explanation of the basic elements of a brand.

Graph provided by Paul Hansen.

To protect your brand, not only is being thoughtful about everything you create important, but closely monitoring everywhere you or your organization appears online is crucial.

- Monitor what appears about you or your organization online by setting up a Google Alert that will let you know when it finds web pages, newspaper articles, or blogs that mention you or your organization.

- Monitor how event calendars describe you and your performances. This includes your home-base market and those in markets where you tour or have a residency.

- Keep updated photos, logos, and short biographies available on your website. People often grab stock photos or use AI to promote you rather than ask for materials.

AI has presented new challenges, especially when working with presenters or venues. AI "hallucinations" such as fake biographical details and mashed-up identities—caused by pulling from all online information about you whether it's true or false—can impact your brand. If people use an AI chatbot to write a description about you, it could be completely false.

Brand Style Guide

Presenting a consistent, cohesive brand is crucial to creating a sense of cohesion and trust with patrons, donors, students, and anyone who interacts with an organization. This includes font usage; tone of verbiage; approved versions of a logo; and ancillary art, colors, and anything else that is wrapped into a brand.

The goal is that every piece of communication from an organization has the same look and tone, no matter which department it's from. This includes emails, website, social media, print pieces, signage, and promotional products. Of course, there will be variables, such as new ancillary art for each season or a specific production. But even that should blend well with the existing brand.

In order to keep all staff, interns, and outside designers on the same page, having a concise brand style guide is crucial. This can include a PDF of the information listed earlier and files with the approved logos and art pieces. Programs such as Canva have brand identity controls similar to website CSS.

Brand strategist Julii Oh suggests making a review of the brand style guide mandatory for existing employees and anyone working with your organization:

> The common way of sharing has been to put it in a shared drive for the organization; however, it's passive. New employees won't intuitively know where to find it, and new or freelance designers need to be onboarded.

To be accessible to all employees, the brand style guide can live inside the navigating tool on your internal network or project management platform. If you don't work with those, the guide can live in a shared drive folder on Microsoft or Google. According to Oh:

> It's so much easier now than ever to provide access to this guide and the parameters to using it that everyone should know about. In fact, these days you could even create a video to provide further guidance around what your brand is so there is a richer, deeper meaning and understanding about your organization.

Branding Through Social Media

There's little question that social media has become one of the primary marketing and branding tools for the performing arts. While the algorithms and popularity of various platforms are ever-changing, social media remains a cost-effective way to promote the performing arts, to interact with and grow audiences and donors, and to humanize organizations and artists.

Whether arts organizations have a one-person marketing department or a large team with a designated social media manager, most already harness Facebook, Instagram, and other platforms to define and refine their brands. Through organic posts that include behind-the-scenes activities such as rehearsals, tantalizing photos and video clips from performances, or interviews with artists or patrons, they build excitement and understanding about their performances and art forms. Examples of organizations that excel at this include New York City Ballet, Chicago Shakespeare Theater, and Seattle Symphony. Chapter 3, "Growing Audiences + Donors," offers several examples of large and small departments working effectively on different platforms.

To create the most compelling content, they closely monitor analytics for their posts and paid ads on social media platforms to see what types of content their followers react to. They even monitor related ticket sales and donations that were timed with specific posts. That information helps them understand what type of future content followers want from them and will interact with.

Some performing artists use their personal social media accounts to help define their own brands and to connect with followers and fans in a relatable way. One gold standard example is jazz pianist Emmet Cohen, who's featured in other chapters of this book. He successfully uses social media for his worldwide following and to monetize additional content.

For this chapter, we've interviewed four artists who are prominent in their fields and who use social media well to expand their brands. See Figure 5.2.

Jane Monheit, Jazz Singer

Based in Los Angeles, California, award-winning jazz singer Jane Monheit tours the world and has numerous solo albums. She uses technology to not only promote her brand, but also to streamline expenses.

Figure 5.2: Jazz singer Jane Monheit (upper left; photo by Jeremy Ryan); New York City Ballet principal dancer Chun Wai Chan (upper right; photo by Liunian Wang); opera singer Nina Yoshida Nelsen (bottom left; photo by Icarus Photography); and choreographer, artistic director Stephanie Martinez (lower right; photo by Todd Rosenberg)

Monheit presents a brand that is as warm and personable as her rich singing voice:

> **If I were to describe my personal brand, the first word I'd use is relatable. It's deeply important for me to find common ground and to share my real life with my listeners.**

Her posts on Instagram and Facebook include everything from album release announcements, tour dates and venue information, advice to younger vocalists just starting out, and photos of her pets and family.

To have control over how she's branded and to save on expenditures, Monheit and her husband have taken over much of the work formerly done by a manager:

> **You know, we don't make a lot of money, so any expense we can cut makes a huge difference to our lives. Through technology, [musicians] don't really need to pay a large team of people. And that makes a difference for artists like me who are in these very, very small music genres.**

However, Monheit continues to work with an agent to book appearances and to handle contracts.

In addition to the informative posts on social media, she uses the platforms to sell merchandise. Her Facebook page has a Shop Now button that allows her followers to purchase autographed albums and branded merchandise such as T-shirts and mugs. On Instagram, her Linktree includes buttons for everything from booking cameo appearances, signing up for her email list, and purchasing and downloading her recordings. Monheit's website (`http://janemonheitonline.com`) includes all that information but receives much less traffic than her social media accounts. The major benefit of keeping a website is that numerous other sites and organizations pull tour dates for their markets to include in their own listings of upcoming music events and things to do. Monheit's husband manages the back end of the site with Squarespace.

Venues around the world that book Monheit appreciate when she promotes the appearance dates on her personal social media pages, but sometimes their expectations become too much. She's cautious about how often she posts about a specific club or city so as not to annoy followers who are not in that area.

Certain venues and music festivals send Monheit graphics they've created as part of a promotional campaign and may request a video from her to post on their own website. "When a venue wants to collaborate on a promotion, that's the greatest," she said.

"I always work as a producer on my own albums, but I'm not always credited," Monheit explains. She controls every aspect of her branding, promotional materials, and album covers: "I don't want somebody else to choose a font for me. It's also nice to have much more control over our own images."

Monheit frequently uses her iPhone and desktop for meetings and to teach voice lessons. She said:

I do all my business on my iPhone, which makes touring a completely different situation. My life is streamlined because of it.

Teaching is an important part of our tradition as artists—to pass on knowledge, and Zoom has been life changing because I've been able to work with students from all over the world. It would be great if that kind of technology improved so there was no lag. For instance, during a lesson with a student earlier today, I was trying to explain a certain way to end a song. It would have been easy if I could have sung what I meant along with her accompanist, but because of the slight lag we can't play music together in real time yet.

Chun Wai Chan, Ballet Dancer

When dancer Chun Wai Chan was first hired by Houston Ballet, he had a lot of free time and was heavily into playing games on his phone when not being used in rehearsals. Fellow dancers suggested that he instead "play" social media. "With that [play] mindset, without so much pressure, it was a good way to start social media," Chan explained. "And the more I played, the more time I put in, the more followers I gained."

Chan uses social media to show different sides of himself as an artist and person, as well as the more challenging parts of being a professional dancer. His content topics include showing himself working on specific steps in rehearsal, traveling for appearances in other cities and countries, dealing with injuries and having COVID, strength training and physical therapy, meditation, nutrition and diet for dancers, photos from modeling jobs and articles written about him, and sharing company performance photos and videos.

In addition to his considerable talent and strong work ethic, Chan has been told by fellow dancers that his personal branding on social media helps his career and relationships with the companies that hire him. He was promoted to soloist and then principal dancer in Houston, and then hired as a soloist by New York City Ballet (NYCB). Within a year there, he was promoted to principal dancer. Chan explained:

> By doing social media for myself, it has helped promote the companies' brands. A lot of people [who follow me] come to see me dance, which helps a company sell tickets.

When NYCB and all live performances were shut down during the pandemic, Chan flew back to his native China to appear in several episodes of a wildly popular television program called *Dance Smash*. During that time Chan created an account on the Chinese social media platform Weibo, where he has continued to post about his life and career in the United States. His popularity through the show and on social media have led to numerous guest appearances and modeling contracts in China.

Chan recognizes that social media also allows him to help influence the next generation of dancers:

> Where I grew up, I was the only guy [at my dance school] and most of my teachers were female. I needed male teachers to show me [male dance steps], but I didn't have them. So now I put that online, and [young students] can have some [guidance] from a male teacher.

He posts tutorials, full classes, and other dance career-related videos on his website (`http://chunwaichan.com`) and YouTube channel (`@ChunnerStudio`).

To create video content, Chan uses his iPhone and edits the videos himself. "I used to use a Canon T6 camera and iMovie to edit, but I realized I didn't need that high of quality for good content," Chan explained. "Using my iPhone is easier and I can edit anywhere with an app called CapCut China that has filters, music, and auto subtitles. That helps me save time and money."

As with athletes, dancers' careers can be quite short, depending in part on how well their bodies deal with the physical stresses the profession demands. Many dancers try to develop new skills during their already hectic schedules for their next career step. Chan elaborated:

I have been trying to plant seeds since I was in the corps with Houston Ballet. Because of doing social media, I could be a marketing manager for a dance company because I know how to strategize and to promote a brand—all those things I've learned while branding myself. Because you don't know what's in the future, waiting for you.

Nina Yoshida Nelsen, Opera Singer

Mezzo soprano Nina Yoshida Nelsen regularly performs with opera companies across the United States and Europe. She's also the co-founder and president of the Asian Opera Alliance and serves as an artistic adviser for the Boston Lyric Opera.

She uses her Instagram, LinkedIn, and Facebook accounts to expand her brand as an artist, and to help other artists of Asian descent. She not only shares news about her upcoming performances and concerts, but she also promotes racial equality in opera casting:

The reason I started Asian Opera Alliance is specifically to get away from how people saw me and how I was only seen for what I looked like and pigeonholed me into Madame Butterfly and other Asian-identifying operas. As I've started talking more about what it means to be an Asian American singer, what I try to do [is to communicate the message that] I'm more than just what you see. I don't have to always be seen as this one thing.

In 2021, a non-singer friend asked Yoshida Nelsen how many non-Asian roles she performed in a typical season. "I started counting—I had only sung three non-Asian roles. And it wasn't in one season, but it was in the span of 10 years," she explained. Her friend told her she needed to talk about that on social media—that this was her responsibility because of where she was in her career for all the other artists who aren't there yet and didn't have the platform she has. Her friend asked, "If you don't start writing about it, who will?" Yoshida Nelsen's immediate worries were that speaking up would make her seem ungrateful or might even ruin her career:

> I remember my first post [about the lack of racial diversity in casting operas] in March or April of 2021, right after the shootings [of six Asian American women] in Atlanta. I wrote and rewrote it and went over and over it—am I saying everything I want to say, but saying it in a way that's not horribly polarizing, or not sounding angry? Then I shared it.

Many responses to that initial post were supportive from people who were unaware and surprised that racial diversity in casting was such a problem. "All my advocating that I do now pretty much started from that one post," said Yoshida Nelsen.

Stephanie Martinez, Choreographer + Artistic Director

Stephanie Martinez is a Chicago-based choreographer who has created works for companies across the United States, including Joffrey Ballet, Ballet Hispanico, and Oklahoma City Ballet. In 2020, she founded a new contemporary dance company called PARA.MAR Dance Theatre.

Martinez and her team use separate social media pages and websites for both her work as a choreographer and for the company that link to each other. These include pages on Facebook, Instagram, and LinkedIn:

> I think choreographers can be really effective using social media to establish a recognizable and memorable visual style. We implement strategies to have a consistent visual aesthetic [between the two brands] to create a cohesive and recognizable identity. Whether it's Stephanie Martinez Choreography (http://stephaniemartinezchoreography.com) or PARA.MAR Dance Theatre (http://paramardance.com), font choices, color schemes, and overall design elements remain consistent.

Because they're promoting the art of dance, video is featured prominently throughout all platforms. "Videos that showcase my choreography and the other choreographers for the company are how people get familiar with us," Martinez explained. "We talk deeply about that because it's so important."

To ensure top video quality, Martinez includes in every contract that any company that hires her to choreograph must use a professional videographer to film her work and that she is given permission to use that high-resolution footage to document and promote her work. Those same high standards are also used for filming her own company. For editing video footage, PARA.MAR uses Canva and iMovie.

For more casual social media posts, Martinez relies on the help of her dancers and staff. "I ask them to film rehearsals," she explained. "We go through [what they captured], then they'll cut me a little reel and we'll upload it to social media. They really are my coconspirators and I think they enjoy being part of the process."

When PARA.MAR tours or has a residency, they continue posting about what they're working on and the upcoming performance information in other markets even if they are not self-presenting. "We're always open to helping spread the word about what's going on [to help with] ticket sales and getting people into seats," said Martinez. For a summer 2023 project, Martinez was hired as one of four choreographers to create pieces for a joint project called Moving Arts in Kansas City, Missouri and Cincinnati, Ohio. Martinez not only promoted the event on her personal and company pages, but she used social media to invite several artistic directors from other companies across the United States to attend. "I promoted everybody else on the program, too," she explained. "It's important to share that information so it's not just self-promotion—it's a community activation in the dance world as a whole."

Rebranding

Changing an organization's branding is not to be taken lightly, but technology can help with the numerous elements to consider and projects to be completed at all levels of the process.

We've included two organizations in this chapter that did very well with recent rebrands. For Ballet RI, we included most of their process because they were extremely thorough. They worked with a small budget and the process was managed by the director and one-person marketing department.

To show that the process is similar for a larger organization, we've included highlights from Detroit Opera's rebrand. They had a larger budget, and the process was managed by a large administrative staff. Graphic designers for both organizations used Adobe Creative Cloud.

Ballet RI

Originally called Festival Ballet of Rhode Island when founded in 1978, and later Festival Ballet Providence, the board recognized the need for an updated identity. When Kathleen Breen Combes was appointed the organization's director in 2019, a 5-year rebrand timeline and plans for a budget were created. "A rebrand had been talked about for probably a good 7 years before I joined the company," explained Breen Combes. "There was an understanding that the existing name was a bit antiquated."

When COVID hit in 2020 and general operations ceased during the lockdown, Breen Coombes and the board had time to turn attention to a rebrand sooner than expected. "We carefully considered how to implement this mammoth undertaking," said Breen Combes. She worried about whether the timing of just coming out of a pandemic was dicey, about how audiences would feel about the change of leadership that had taken place, and how they'd respond to a new name for the organization. "You know, this was a risk," she added. "A calculated risk, but a risk nonetheless."

Breen Combes was put in touch with a branding specialist who agreed to work with her pro bono beginning in August 2022. Breen Combes explained:

> [The work] started very much as conversations: Why rebrand? Is renaming the organization the right thing to do? Should we just change the logo? We had weekly conversations for over two months.
>
> She [the branding specialist] had no connection to ballet at all, which I think was good. She was someone outside the bubble to give us a fresh perspective. The reason we decided to do the full rebrand was because we felt the organization was ready, we had a new vision, and we wanted to expand on what we were doing.

They then conducted Zoom discussions with numerous stakeholders, including company artists and staff, other area arts leaders, donors, audience members, parents of children from the company's school, and alumni. "The overall feeling was that everyone agreed that it was time to take the step forward," clarified Breen Combes. Meanwhile, the branding specialist researched recently rebranded dance companies, the industry norm for logos, and companies that had made a resurgence in their marketing and online presence. Marketing Director Dylan Giles explained:

> **Very early on, even before [our new name] was decided, we snapped up two domains:** `balletri.com` **and** `providenceballet.com`**. We agreed to just buy and sit on them. That was one of the savvier moves we made early on. It sounds so simple, but [not having the domain we wanted] would have been a big roadblock.**

They did the same with those names for all social media platforms.

With research completed and after many conversations between the branding specialist, Breen Combes, and Giles about what was important for the new name and logo, they hired a graphic artist to create numerous options for review. Research taught them that the most compelling logos for ballet companies were either black or white. "We wanted something crisp, clean, timeless, and not fussy—something that would still be relevant 20, 30, 40 years from now," explained Breen Combes.

With the name Ballet RI and logo design decided, they hired a photographer for new photos and videos of company dancers to complete the look for their branding. The clean black or white logos allowed for the dancer photos to be the art elements and primary focus (see Figure 5.3).

Giles immediately created a list of additional administrative issues required when giving an organization a new name, including changing the registration with the city and state, Google listing, email addresses, and copyrights. "It was a list of maybe 200 things that needed to be done," he said. They also decided to create an entirely new website, using WordPress.

To help accomplish everything that needed to be done, they hired an IT company and web designer. "They approached the web design, the copywriting, and all of those things from an outsider's perspective and it was quite seamless," said Giles. "It was important that that happened independently of me because we were in the middle of a season—we couldn't sacrifice the current shows and marketing workload."

Giles added:

> **It was also important that we get the new website right and that it looked completely different and striking, so that was one of our biggest challenges. We wanted dance to be the first thing you see, not even our logo.**

Figure 5.3: Ballet RI's brand identity now features their new logo, photos of company dancers, and a graphic element meant to reflect the sea and quirkiness of Rhode Island. Dancers Madeline Glinski and João Alves.

Photo by Ian Travis Barnard. Artwork and logo design by Sage Hill Designs. Image provided by Ballet RI.

The developer and designer worked on making information on the website concise and user-friendly while incorporating the clean new brand identity.

They reviewed the existing website closely and eliminated any repeated or overly long information. This included cutting the events listing on the site and instead sending people directly to Audience View, where they'd not only see the list of performances, but they could immediately purchase tickets. They did the same with their class listing, instead having a link to Dance Studio Manager where people could see the full listing and register (`http://balletri.org`).

To introduce the company's new brand identity to the public, they waited for their fundraising event at the end of the 2022–2023 season. Once a week for 8 weeks, they released new teasers on social media and in emails through Constant Contact to help drive excitement and ticket sales. "We ended up selling out our gala, which we'd never done before," shared Breen Combes. "There were a lot of new faces, and it was the highest grossing gala in the organization's history." The day after the gala, they sent out an email to everyone in their database to reveal the new brand identity, from which they received extremely positive feedback.

"The week of the rebrand was very choreographed," explained Breen Combes. "Thursday evening was our gala. On Friday, the front of the building was painted, the new awning went up, and the new website was up and running. Within 24 hours, the whole [look of our] organization changed."

Ballet RI was able to measure the success of their rebrand campaign in the weeks following the gala through increased attention on social media and subscription sales. "The organic marketing we got from social media was huge right away," said Breen Combes. "And when our 2023-2024 subscriptions went on sale, the first weekend had a 56 percent increase over the previous year with lots of new subscribers. People were paying attention."

Detroit Opera

Originally called Michigan Opera Theatre, the organization's leadership felt the time was right for a rebrand. "The synergy of coming out of the pandemic, celebrating our 50th anniversary, and announcing a new artistic director led us to think about how we could shepherd in a new era for the organization," said Matthew Principe, director of innovation.

Incoming artistic director Yuval Sharon is known for thinking outside the box about what opera can be (Chapter 4, "Making Magic," highlights many of his creative productions in the section about PXT Studio). "So, we thought it was great timing to start thinking about how to reintroduce ourselves to the public," said Principe.

They gave themselves only 8 months to complete the rebrand, which is an extremely tight schedule. Conversations began in August 2021, and the new brand was introduced with a production in early April 2022. Principe admitted, "That was a very quick process, which I believe is an anomaly."

After a board decision to change our name to Detroit Opera (DO), they started working through the aesthetic changes by engaging Detroit-based advertising agency Lafayette American to conduct stakeholder interviews with board members, members of the creative arts in Detroit, single- and season-ticket holders, and staff. The agency also performed a brand audit about where the organization was positioned in the industry, as well as within the Detroit market.

Based on their research and input from the organization, the agency created several options for a new logo and additional creative components for moving forward. "Together, we reviewed the different style options they had created, and we eventually settled on the branding guidelines for Detroit Opera," said Principe (see Figure 5.4). The agency also created videos using the new brand identity with existing footage from the organization's previous productions. With internal staff, Detroit Opera reskinned the existing website with the new style guide, as well as new signage, and all digital and print materials.

Figure 5.4: Detroit Opera's new logo and promotional artwork represent a more dynamic approach to traditional operas that their new artistic director will present. Image provided by Detroit Opera.

After 25 years of having different locations around Detroit for the performances, administrative offices, and rehearsal space, they relocated all areas of the organization to the Detroit Opera House in 1996, which they now own and operate. They also rent the space out when they don't have performances to other organizations such as Broadway Detroit and Detroit Ballet. So the rebrand included everything throughout the large building, from the front awnings to the decorative decals on the windows, and even the stage door sign. Principe explained:

Those were part of our rollout, but we slowly phased them in. We provided new logos and signage to every department and

> iteration of our company around the building, whether it's edu-
> cation development, volunteer association, as well as locations
> within the Detroit Opera House. But it wasn't a 100 percent
> switchover at one moment. So that's the thing I always tell organi-
> zations to be mindful of when they consider a rebrand—the
> financial implications.

Residencies

The Cleveland Orchestra (TCO) is ranked among the top 10 orchestras in the world by numerous publications, including *BBC Music Magazine* and *The New York Times*. The orchestra performs a full season in Ohio, tours nationally and internationally, and has a residency in Miami, Florida each season.

To help increase awareness and attendance for TCO's performances in Miami, they hired Julii Oh to develop strategies that rebuild and grow their audience. After assessing the data and materials, she focused on creative, communication, and sales strategies. Oh explained:

> In looking at the creative strategy for TCO, we needed to make sure
> that we aligned to the core brand pillars and positioning, but to
> figure out how we could resonate in the Miami market. Brand posi-
> tioning remained true and fixed—TCO is one of the world's best
> orchestras, and communicating the story as to why they are con-
> sidered this, what their differentiation was, and how we get this
> message out in a clear way is what I focused on. In [the Cleveland]
> market, some of this perhaps is assumed, but in a market like
> Miami which is neither their home nor where they have consistent
> yearlong presence, establishing those key messages and being
> explicit in all communications is imperative.

When considering changes in how to execute TCO's creative strategy for the Miami market, Oh made certain she understood and respected their key brand positioning pillars. "For TCO, one communication pillar is showing the importance of both their music director and orchestra musicians equitably—this was non-negotiable," Oh explained. "So visually and through the communications (credits, copy blurb), we made sure to visually represent and communicate this."

Where Oh had latitude in the creative was through the use of white space, color, typeface, and clean formatting, making sure to honor TCO's style guide (see Figure 5.5):

Strategically, TCO branding in Miami was where we were able to nuance that by giving it a more contemporized feeling with its lighter, brighter, open, and vibrant vibe. But the core of the product and the way it sounds is still smart and sophisticated while remaining aligned to their brand strategy and guidelines.

Figure 5.5: The Cleveland Orchestra's branding for their annual residency in Miami, Florida uses more white space, color, and a lighter tone than the more traditional marketing used for their home base of Cleveland, Ohio.

Images provided by Julii Oh.

In terms of the communication strategy, Oh stayed true to TCO's core, but made two strategy changes. The first shift was to be explicit about TCO's status by using quotes backed up with proof points, because knowledge about TCO's status and what this meant wasn't necessarily a given in Miami. Oh continued:

At its core, the value proposition [for the Miami market] is the same and this is really the heart of this brand—a stellar world-renowned orchestra with a signature sound that brings a freshness to the old and excitement with the new works. Through this sound, they deliver and promise to move audiences. In effect, the same world-class orchestra, but in the marketing, we represent it with vibrant colors, open air feeling, and lightness—much like Miami feels.

The second shift in communication was to be more straightforward in terms of wording because English is not the first language for many Miami-area households. To be accessible and to showcase the quality experience TCO offers, Oh added QR codes on all printed pieces that connected to music samples for each concert. "There are ways to capture success rates, depending on the site you use for your QR codes," explained Oh. "You can subscribe or pay for QR codes with more features than the freebies, and those typically have stats for whether people used them and how many." Other examples of QR code use can be found in Chapter 3.

For the sales strategy, Oh started by analyzing existing data from TCO's previous seasons in Miami. She reviewed demographics and historical transactional data points to find the story of what was going on with sales:

> **This helped to inform whether we had an optimized scaling in the hall, what we'd need to do to drive demand, to question the pricing strategy for both subscriptions and single tickets, and what tools and triggers we'd need to take as we moved into the season.**

To do this work, Oh partners with the firm AnalytixLive. They provide revenue management software and service that enables insights into supply, demand, and pricing trends. Oh elaborated:

> **A key to these insights is the regression modeling based on an organization's historical sales. This goes beyond simply dynamic pricing—you can zoom in or out on the analysis of the data to understand how you approach your marketing, promotions and pricing decisions to affect the sales outcome even before it's too late to derive enough change.**
>
> **It's a powerful approach, but it's not a fix. This software will not simply tell you what to do. Through predictive analytics modeling, it allows you to adjust marketing strategies and decisions in real time. So with my marketing expertise, I'm able to partner with AnalytixLive, the revenue specialist, make informed decisions that can shift the sales outcome positively.**

Takeaways

Branding should always start with the organization's mission statement and values, and include community and customer impact. Be careful about becoming too self-focused in how you design and position your brand. Marketing that offers patrons and the community ways to be positively affected by interacting with you should be foremost in your branding.

Closely monitor how other venues or organizations present your brand. Presenters and event calendars sometimes grab stock images or use AI chatbots to write information. AI can be guilty of "hallucinations," caused by combining information that appears on the web that may or not be true, or even about you. By registering your name with systems such as Google Alert, you will be notified each time something new appears about you so you can check for accuracy.

Create a brand style guide that shows all the correct logos, colors, graphics, font usage, tone of messaging, and anything else that's important for your brand to be presented correctly. Be sure to update this document as any changes are made to your brand. Keep this document somewhere that's easily accessible to your staff, interns, and outside designers, and consider including a video that will help give a deeper resonance to your brand. Make a review of the brand style guide mandatory for existing staff and outside designers, and part of onboarding for new employees and freelancers.

Social media remains a cost-effective way for performing arts organizations and artists to communicate through their brands. While staying true to your brand, use available analytics to help determine the best type of content to post that your patrons will interact with in meaningful ways. Instagram's Linktree is a great way to provide quick access to more detailed elements of your organization, such as a performance calendar, links to venues in other markets where you will appear, and your website.

Pulling from your personal or organizational brand, social media is an excellent platform to share your values. Opera singer Nina Yoshida Nelsen promotes her appearances with companies all over the world, while interjecting posts about the need for more work in racial equality when casting artists.

Change in your audience, location, or core work requires you to consider rebranding, an involved process with numerous elements to consider and update. While many technologies can aid a rebrand, the most important element is communication with stakeholders in your organization and community. Do the research to make sure you're creating an updated brand that speaks to people in a meaningful way and that connects you to your community.

Presenting yourself or your organization in other markets may present needed adaptations to your brand. Research the market where you will perform to learn what type of visual, written, and spoken marketing they respond to—that could differ greatly from the way you market in your home base. While being certain to retain your brand's core pillars, consider adaptations to colors, fonts, and formatting that will appeal in the other market.

Technology Solutions

The following technology solutions are mentioned throughout this chapter. Remember, this is not a comprehensive list of all the technologies available, but they might help to begin your research.

Introduction

- Adobe Creative Cloud is a set of applications and services that gives subscribers access to software for graphic design, video editing, and web development (`http://adobe.com/creativecloud`).
- Canva is a graphic design platform that has a brand kit available that will store logos, graphics, photos, fonts, and other elements for easy access for those using the program to create branded content (`http://canva.com/pro/brand-kit`).
- Google Alerts is a content change detection and notification service. The service sends emails to the user when it finds new results—such as web pages, newspaper articles, blogs, or scientific research—that match the user's search term (`http://google.com/alerts`).
- Gravit Designer is a graphic design software (`http://softwareadvice.com/graphic-design/gravit-designer-pro-profile`).
- Sketch is a graphic design platform (`http://sketch.com`).
- SurveyMonkey is a free online survey and forms tool (`http://surveymonkey.com`).

Social Media

- CapCut China is a free multimedia app for editing and producing videos (`http://capcut-china.en.softonic.com/android`).

Rebranding

- Audience View is a platform that combines ticketing, CRM, fundraising, and marketing tools (`http://audienceview.com`).

- Dance Studio Manager is software that helps dance studios manage their class schedules, credit card processing, and online registration (`http://dancestudiomanager.com`).

- WordPress is a web content managing system that was originally created as a tool to publish blogs. They have evolved to support publishing traditional websites, mailing lists, media galleries, membership sites, and more (`http://wordpress.com`).

6

Extending the Stage: Digital Content, Education, + Touring

For decades, performing arts organizations have extended their stages through touring, radio, television, and movies. As they seek additional ways to connect with communities and audiences, technology offers new opportunities. While social media, streaming, and podcasting existed before 2020, the pandemic years accelerated digital transformation and changed the way people consume art.

For this chapter, we've interviewed organizations that consistently produce exciting programs and that excel at using innovative technologies to expand their reach. Although some of their efforts began before the 2020 shutdown, everyone interviewed has built on lessons learned during the pandemic. The specific examples here reveal how to strategically build a technology system to maximize your organization's impact. It's also important to note that touring has become more efficient through the use of technology.

Streaming + Simulcasts

Nearly everyone in the performing arts found ways to stream digital content during the pandemic to remain relevant to patrons and donors.

Often, that content was a bit rough around the edges, but it was a time to try new things.

When they were able to return to in-person performances, many organizations stepped away from streaming for reasons that included budget constraints, artistic decisions, or union restrictions. The following organizations have successfully built streaming into their post-pandemic business models, giving new energy and resources for the technology.

Tradition of Capturing Dance at Jacob's Pillow + Hybrid Festival

Jacobs Pillow is home to the longest-running dance festival in the United States and The School at Jacob's Pillow. Each summer since 1933, thousands of people visit the Berkshires in western Massachusetts to attend the Jacob's Pillow Dance Festival, which currently features nine weeks of performances by dance artists from around the world on indoor and outdoor stages, special events, talks, exhibits, parties, and classes.

To preserve history for future generations of dance artists, Jacob's Pillow founder Ted Shawn was committed to capturing dance on film and to collecting photos and other materials. He also conceptualized and appeared in one of the very first silent dance films, Thomas Edison Company's *Dances of the Ages* in 1913.

All the materials Shawn created and collected are included in a vast archive at Jacobs Pillow. "We have the unique privilege of housing not only artifacts, images, and films of Ted Shawn and the work they were doing, but also the work of the artists who have performed on the Jacob's Pillow stages since [the festival's] inception," notes Chief Marketing Officer Jared Fine.

Many of those materials have been digitized and are available for viewing through the "Jacob's Pillow Dance Interactive" portal on their website (www.jacobspillow.org). Materials such as costumes and a large collection of books are available for viewing in-person in the Norton Owen Reading Room at Jacob's Pillow (see Figure 6.1).

"The digital archive is an amazing resource, which also serves scholars, researchers, and students," says Fine. "It provides a deep contextual educational value where you can not only enjoy a piece of art, but you can understand where it sits within the continuum of the past, the present, and the future."

"One thing Jacob's Pillow will never do is stop, which is very exciting," says Fine. When faced with the pandemic shutdown in 2020, Executive and Artistic Director Pamela Tatge decided to proceed with a completely free online digital festival. The Pillow's high standards of capturing live performances enabled Tatge to curate a vibrant season from the archives, supplemented by new onscreen introductions and other contextual information optimized for online engagement.

Figure 6.1: The Norton Owen Reading Room at Jacob's Pillow has monitors for people to watch content from their vast digital archives, as well as costumes, books, and other additional materials.

Photo by Jamie Kraus

Rather than just filming those dance performances in a straightforward way as audiences would experience them on stage, Tatge worked with each group to present what would make sense for that company and that artistic expression in digital output. After investigating several technology options, Jacob's Pillow opted to work with Brightcove for live stream and video on demand, and to work with their Tessitura database for creating access portals for patrons and university partners across the United States.

When they returned to an in-person festival in 2021, Jacob's Pillow decided to create a hybrid 10-week festival on the outdoor stage only, with one company per week. All of those companies' performances were filmed and made available for streaming on demand two weeks later.

> They expected to see a large overlap between audiences who reg-
> ularly attended the in-person festival over the years and those
> who viewed the online festival, but they discovered only an 8 per-
> cent crossover. "There was a greater reach around the country and
> world that was able to access these streams," says Fine. "We also
> saw a large percentage of those new viewers become first-time
> donors."

"The pandemic years changed the way people consume art, and there's a moment here where we see a renaissance of digitally influenced artistic expressions," notes Fine. "Habits continue to change in highly rapid, unpredictable ways. For philanthropy, marketing, artistic projects—it's a new baseline."

New York Philharmonic Media Wall +Digital Archives

The New York Philharmonic (NY Phil) has been at the forefront of every technological innovation, beginning with the first music recordings in 1917. Founded in 1842, they are the oldest major symphony orchestra in the United States and are consistently ranked as one of the top five orchestras in the world.

As part of the recent renovation to David Geffen Hall in New York City's Lincoln Center for the Performing Arts, NY Phil added digital screens measuring 51 feet wide by 8 feet high in the new lobby to simulcast live concerts (see Figure 6.2).

Figure 6.2: NY Phil's Media Wall in the lobby of the David Geffen Hall allows people to watch a free simulcast of a live concert in a coffee shop–like setting.

Photo by Chris Lee

"One of the most exciting things about this space is that anyone can go into the lobby during a concert and watch what's happening on stage for free," explains Gabryel Smith, NY Phil's Director, Archives and Exhibitions. As in a coffee shop, there are sofas, tables, and plugs for peoples' devices.

"If someone wants to dip their toe into experiencing a classical music concert, that's the way to do it," says Smith. "They don't have to stay for the whole thing—no one's going to look at them weirdly if they get up and leave halfway through if they don't have two and a half hours. They can just take in a bite-sized portion."

The wall is capable of up to 16K resolution, and as part of the concert hall renovation, multiple PTZ (pan, tilt, and zoom) cameras were purchased—all with flexible placements. These cameras are capable of up to 4K resolution and are operated via remote control. For any given concert, there are typically no fewer than six and as many as 16 cameras being operated and projected to the wall. Sound for the wall is usually sourced from hanging microphones in the Wu Tsai Theater and fed through an array of ceiling speakers, and there are both analog and Dante network controls in place for times when reinforcing the sound is desired. In the control booth, operators are in place most nights to live-switch between shots to create the experience for the simulcast on the lobby screens. At least one concert per subscription week is also recorded to a rack system of AJA KiPros. These machines are capable of capturing not only the program feed that the audience experiences, but also the individual camera feeds (ISOs) as well as a graphic-free (or "clean") version of the show. This material is archived for future considerations, especially promotional use. "The musicians were very forward-thinking about the simulcast wall," explains Smith about the decision to allow the regular simulcasts.

"We need to think differently about our space," Smith elaborated. **"For instance, right now we're using the media wall in a very traditional sense, but it could be totally different. I'm working on a grant proposal about what it looks like to build out that lobby concert experience to be lots of other things."**

NY Phil is also innovative with technology use for archival purposes. "Our digital archives launched in 2011 before any kind of robust content management system was available, so we had to build our own," Smith explains. Today, they use Cortex by Orange Logic for digital migration and as their content management system (CMS), thanks to a grant from The Leon Levy Foundation and The National Endowment for the Humanities. Cortex is a powerful system now used by several larger organizations, including Carnegie Hall, the Los Angeles Philharmonic, The Kennedy Center, Amazon, BBC, and the United Nations.

Smith and his department staff are in the process of moving all the existing archives from their on-site server onto the new platform in the cloud. At the same time, new content is being uploaded by photographers, videographers, media staff, producers, special event staff, and others.

"Keeping track of all this is a lot of work," Smith shares. "We put it all on a schedule [for public access]. For example performance programs become available immediately as public documents; audio recordings become available on request because that's in our current agreement with the musicians." But NY Phil is working to bridge the gap between digitized and born-digital materials for public access schedules.

Sheet music parts and complete scores with notes are extremely popular in their digital archive collection. "The most energy comes from outside musicians from other orchestras without librarians or from an audition candidate," says Smith. "They go to our site to look up parts marked with bowings, fingerings, and breath marks by NY Phil musicians. The reason we put these things out there is for the intellectual value of the markings themselves—that's really the higher value and what makes these documents unique.

"We don't use iPads [for digital sheet music] on stage yet," Smith continues. "But I'm currently working on a workflow so that we can use our current system for practice parts for the musicians, which is going to be a big expansion of the use of this digital program."

NY Phil's website (`https://nyphil.org`) has numerous links to digital archive materials that are managed by different departments. For example, the Watch & Listen page is managed by the marketing staff. The Archives is currently in the process of migrating all existing media and digital archives files over to the new cloud system. Using Google Analytics, they are able to track which materials and site pages get the most usage and to prioritize them in the workflow.

When we asked what he'd like to offer next in NY Phil's archives, Smith replied, "I don't know how soon in the future this is, but our current media setup and access system is quietly building an archive more complete than ever, with immediate access online. There is immense educational value to the raw stage video recordings—particularly of new or seldom-heard works, of which the NY Phil performs many. These works are also less likely to be chosen for commercial release. With the correct permissions and security infrastructure in place, we can begin to think about how we can make this media safely available via a virtual listening portal, just as it currently is in our reading room."

Second Stage's Journey with Simulcasts

Second Stage Theater is a nonprofit company in New York City that produces revivals and new plays and musicals by living American writers for both on and off Broadway, supporting both established and emerging artists.

For the past several years, they have streamed performances of only part of their seasons. They decide which plays to stream based on several factors, including logistics, financing, and internal bandwidth. "The timing has to be right for us, and we consider what will generate interest," explains General Manager Christopher McGinnis.

Although some writers prefer their new pieces not be streamed, some artists request it. In 2022, actor, rapper, and activist Common starred in their revival of *Between Riverside and Crazy*. "He was very passionate about being able to stream to incarcerated patrons," notes McGinnis. "So that was definitely a focus that we tried to make happen." Serving artists and audiences is important, but some people expect streaming to instantly make money. However, often this is not the reason an organization does it. "Financially, we're certainly not a success story yet," McGinnis says about Second Stage's simulcasts. But their success is more mission driven; he adds, "It's about extending our national footprint. And for our artists and playwrights, giving them the opportunity to have their work shown not just in the 10-block radius of the theater in New York City, but also across the country and across the world."

In fact, the program began through a digital accelerator program that allowed them to take more chances with streaming. "We are part of Bloomberg Philanthropies' digital accelerator program. So that's given us a lot of opportunities, both financially and educationally, to help figure out what we need to do to move forward with streaming," explains McGinnis. "It's certainly cost prohibitive to continue long term, so we're trying to figure out other funding avenues, whether that's contributed income or a decrease of internal expenses to be able to produce virtual performances."

Beyond production costs, further restrictions complicate streaming for Second Stage—the actors' union contract governing Second Stage and many other theaters across the country stipulates that they can only sell as many tickets to each performance as the number of seats in the theater. So, if a theater has 1,000 seats available for a performance and 800 in-person tickets are sold, they are only permitted to sell 200 virtual tickets. "We simulcast the last two weeks of the run, primarily because that gives us a clearer picture of the amount of inventory that we have left and are allowed to sell," explains McGinnis. "Streaming is a way to build back audiences [after the pandemic] and to supplement the income of people that we don't have in the theater right now."

Second Stage believes in protecting the integrity of their shows and the experience of in-person patrons, doing their best not to require any alterations to make shows ready for simulcast. When beginning the design process for productions they plan to stream, the artistic and video teams consider unique needs such as camera placement, lighting, and clear angles.

To handle the virtual ticketing, Second Stage uses Stripe. It creates individual passwords needed to access the simulcasts and integrates well with their CRM, Tessitura. Links for streaming shows are posted on their website (`https://2st.com/history-and-mission`).

They have also chosen to rent all the equipment and to use a third party to handle the technical aspects of producing simulcasts. McGinnis points out the downside of purchasing equipment: "Your technology is going to be out-of-date in three years and you'll be left with cameras that can't do what you want them to do."

Digital Business Model at Boston Baroque

Boston Baroque is North America's first permanent Baroque orchestra. Based in Boston, Massachusetts, they present concerts that bring Baroque and Classical music to life for contemporary audiences, using period instruments and techniques.

Because they have produced commercial recordings since the early 1980s, which have earned them numerous GRAMMY® nominations, branching into streaming seemed a logical next step.

After extensive research about up-front expenses, staffing, technology and streaming partners, contract issues, and potential growth, they chose to invest in working with Boston PBS affiliate GBH Production Group. Their large filming studios, available technologies, and expertise would help them create the best quality product for streaming. They then landed on IDAGIO as the best platform for their music niche, plus some content on Amazon Prime (see Figure 6.3).

As their website notes, Boston Baroque's global reach has expanded since 2020 to include audiences across 55 countries on six continents (North America, South America, Asia, Africa, Europe, and Australia) through its partnership with IDAGIO, the world's leading classical music streaming service. Their 2021–2022 season was the first full season by a Baroque orchestra to stream on the platform (`https://baroque.boston`).

The Promise of Digital

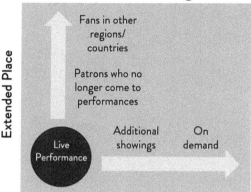

Figure 6.3: A 2023 case study by Advisory Board for the Arts (ABA) highlighted the strengths of Boston Baroque's business plan for streaming. This graph demonstrates the potential audience growth.

Graphic provided by ABA

In order to begin the streaming process, Boston Baroque contacted music artists from existing archival videos to negotiate multiplatform distribution rights. When they launched their flexible digital season in 2020, they promised patrons they would add a new release each month, as well as short interviews with artists.

"The most brilliant thing Boston Baroque did [was] integrating artist union agreements and payments into the annual budget," according to Director of Livestreams and Artistic Planning Matthew Principe. "We'll still talk to the orchestra committee about when we're going to release something, but if you don't have those permissions in line, that can be a problem.

"That's been a financial hurdle and challenge for a lot of arts organizations," he continues. "Thankfully, a lot of those provisions were deferred during the [pandemic] lockdown. Now [those artist expenses and agreements] are something both organizations and their boards must reconcile their priorities about."

As in-person performances were permitted following the pandemic, they decided that any concert they planned to stream would be performed both in the large studio at GBH Studios with a small audience to be filmed, and again at Jordan Hall at the New England Conservatory for a much larger audience. This greatly increased their ticket inventory and potential profits (see Figure 6.4).

Figure 6.4: Boston Baroque works with GBH Production Group's award-winning engineers and technicians at their PBS affiliate television studios in Boston. Senior Director of Production Technology Tim Mangini at GBH notes that they lens with Hitachi high-def cameras and combine manned with robotic cameras. The switched feed is sent through an AJA Helo encoder to Wowza before distributing to IDAGIO. Concert Cue is used for opera captioning.

Photo by Phil Reilly, GBH

"Coming out of the pandemic, many organizations have had growing pains about understanding how best to utilize resources for both in-person performances and a digital atmosphere. Now they have two different avenues, and that's doubling expenses, initiatives, and time," notes Principe. "Understanding all these factors are what arts organizations need to include when planning digital or technological initiatives."

Digital Transformation at SFJAZZ

SFJAZZ is among the world's largest nonprofit jazz presenters. Located in San Francisco, California, the organization was founded in 1983 as a two-day festival. Today, SFJAZZ serves over a quarter of a million fans and students annually through year-round concerts, commissions, education programs, and now a digital platform called SFJAZZ at Home (www.sfjazz.org).

"We have something we're doing and building on, that we've been measuring for a couple years, that we've gotten a lot of data input on, and that we've found an audience for," says Ross Eustis, SFJAZZ's director of digital. "We have an initiative and program to rally behind that's the primary vehicle for how the organization is transforming digitally."

In 2013, they opened the SFJAZZ Center with plans for future streaming needs. In the venue's two performance spaces, they built in lighting, cameras and flexible technology for live-streaming and filming concerts, acoustic speakers in the two spaces, as well as building a control room and all the fittings needed (see Figure 6.5).

Figure 6.5: SFJAZZ included complete video and audio systems and control rooms to enable future live streaming when they built their new venue in 2013. They continued to research how best to proceed and were able to launch the program during the pandemic in 2020 due to the technology already in place and archival recordings of past concerts in the space.

Photos provided by SFJAZZ

The technology stack at the SFJAZZ Center includes Panasonic and Canon PTZ cameras that are robotically controlled and Blackmagic static cameras on the stage, which are all patched to a video suite located on the building's third floor. That room includes several monitors, a switcher console for selecting and fading between shots from specific cameras, and a controller for moving the cameras. A computer is loaded with hardware for the live stream, a software encoder, and vMix software, which allows them to add calls to action and other text overlays over the screen in real time. They also capture each of the video stems for possible future editing of the recording they capture.

In a separate room, they have an audio mixing console. All the microphones on stage have their audio stems and feeds that they put into a Pro Tools session to be mixed and set out live with the video. They also have an Ambisonic microphone that captures the room sound in the main performance space, including applause from the audience.

In early 2020, they hadn't yet begun streaming content in a meaningful way but had used the technology to record the concerts that had taken place in the new venue since 2014. "Our agreements with the artists were just for archival recording, just enough to allow us to capture the concerts without knowing exactly what we were going to do with them yet," Eustis explains.

"When we first started putting our plans together, there weren't a lot of players in the performing arts streaming space," he continues. "One we took a lot of inspiration from was the Metropolitan Opera. They've built the preeminent digital streaming platform for opera called Met Opera on Demand" (`www.metopera.org/season/on-demand`).

Another inspiration was Berlin Philharmonic's Digital Concert Hall, which began in 2008. "It took them 10 years [for the streaming] to become self-sustainable," Eustis says. "I made a connection with Robert Zimmerman, the director of that program who started and built it. He's been a huge mentor and a fan of what we're doing at SFJAZZ" (`www.digitalconcerthall.com`).

When the pandemic hit in March 2020, SFJAZZ was poised to launch a streaming program. They had been doing deep research and development on the workflow, fine-tuning the technology stack, the overall value proposition, and whether there was a market for people paying for quality jazz content while many free platforms existed.

"We took that information and distilled it and put our best foot forward," Eustis shares. "We didn't know how long the lockdown would last, but we decided to create a pilot program for a month to see if our audiences would engage."

SFJAZZ quickly negotiated with the artists from the archive recordings to stream, splitting all donations made from the live streams 50/50 with the artists. Over the first year of the pandemic, SFJAZZ raised $700,000 for artists, and over 15,000 people signed up for the new program.

They distribute digital content through apps powered by Vimeo OTT and their website. SFJAZZ works with Chicago-based Adage Solutions for the custom web platform that sits on top of their CRM, Tessitura. "We've worked with them to build a number of custom digital," according to Eustis. "That's where the paywall happens."

SFJAZZ considered whether to offer the streaming for free, ticketed, or with memberships but landed on charging $5 per month or $50 annually. The service was included as a benefit for existing donors who were already members of SFJAZZ—by logging in on the website, a page unlocking the video player was revealed.

For the streaming schedule, they initially followed Digital Concert Hall's model of live-streaming on demand once a week. SFJAZZ decided on Friday evenings at 5 p.m. Pacific Time (PT). "That's happy hour [on the West Coast], and it works well for the East Coast too," Eustis says. "It was truly a team effort to come up with this series, which we called Fridays at Five."

"The first week was pretty rough compared to what we have now," he admits. "But it was functional, and the paywall worked. That first week was the biggest nail biter—being able to edit [the video], work on the audio, and get it all together remotely. It wasn't perfect by any means."

Several hundred new members signed up for their streaming, and many existing members tuned in. "People really dug it and we saw an incredible potential with it," Eustis reports. "Over the next year as we continued to shelter in place, we did a broadcast every week and it really took off."

When in-person concerts were permitted to begin after the pandemic, they evolved the program to feature its live, in-person concerts as each week's live stream. The platform, which is now called SFJAZZ at Home, features live streams on Fridays at 7:30 p.m. PT, with an encore the next day at 11 a.m. PT. When the concert schedule at the SFJAZZ Center occasionally doesn't work for this schedule, they stream one of the videos from their archives.

"The next big effort we're working on is launching a robust video on demand library." Eustis says. "Members will get access to videos to watch multiple times at whatever time works for them.

"What we've built has been a journey," he continues. "There've been many curveballs along the way, but there's a real opportunity for SFJAZZ to grow this program to become self-sustainable over the next couple years. We've seen very positive signs, but it's definitely not an easy road."

Expanding Content Use at Dallas Symphony Orchestra

The Dallas Symphony Orchestra (DSO), the largest performing arts organization in the southwest United States, is committed to inspiring the broadest possible audience with distinctive classical programs, inventive pops concerts, and innovative multimedia presentations.

Through their website (www.dallassymphony.org), DSO offers access to numerous audio recordings and videos of full concerts through a program called Next Stage via YouTube (see Figure 6.6). "They're made available between two to three weeks after the concert happens, and they're available online for two months for free," explains Denise McGovern, DSO's vice president of communications and media.

"We do radio broadcasts, which is something we've done for a very long time, and we are doing commercial recording again. So, a lot of our digital work is audio-only," continues McGovern. "For streaming video content, we were using Vimeo OTT because it was able to fold into Tessitura, something we had already purchased. But it was actually a very hard integration." So, she moved DSO's content to their YouTube channel because of the platform's increased popularity as a music search engine and ease for patrons.

Figure 6.6: The Dallas Symphony Orchestra captures concerts that are streamed on their website in a series called Next Stage.

"Coming out of the pandemic when we all had to tap dance from week to week, it wasn't until the end of the 2022/2023 season that I felt I could start planning for the future," admits McGovern. "I've had conversations with colleagues from other organizations, and they ask if I would be backing down on how many [digital projects] I was doing. I'm not. Right now, I'm building the strategy for digital content which is starting to become clear."

"Back when I was new to DSO, I went to a symphony league conference and somebody said, capture once, publish everywhere. That stuck with me—we've got this huge bucket of content that we're able to use for so many purposes."

In 2020, DSO CEO Kim Noltemy had a robotic camera system installed in the company's hall to enable concerts to be broadcast live and to increase the quality of the output. With that infrastructure in place, McGovern created a workflow and learned how to script camera angles. "I found two terrific directors from very different backgrounds to help me understand what was needed to capture classical programs," McGovern says. "They helped me find efficiencies and ways to do things that pushed the possibilities of what we could do."

DSO now has seven robotic cameras and two static cameras that enable the director to select shots from many angles. They rent any needed additional equipment, helping to keep costs down. For staffing, McGovern has a team of four freelance camera people as well as two directors who split the season.

With their new technical capabilities, DSO formed a partnership with the Dallas ABC television affiliate as well as PBS and Bloomberg Media, which helped them earn new recognition. "I'm very proud of our Emmy nominations," asserts McGovern.

During the pandemic when all performances were canceled, Noltemy and DSO's music director, Fabio Luisi, organized a joint concert with the musicians from New York's Metropolitan Opera (the Met) and DSO musicians called One Symphony, Two Orchestras. Luisi had previously served as the Met's principal conductor from 2011 to 2017. Since all these musicians were out of work at the time, they offered to pay some of the Met musicians to travel to Dallas to play in the concert. The filmed concert aired on national public television stations (PBS) and garnered a Daytime Emmy nomination for DSO. All profits from the televised concert went to a COVID relief fund for musicians from both orchestras.

In fall 2023, DSO's season included a concert with trumpeter/composer Terence Blanchard. The director responsible for capturing the performance for streaming mentioned to McGovern that it was a shame they only had one outlet. So, she called the Dallas PBS station to see if they would be interested in the project. They were and agreed to pay for production of the interviews and for editing the show together if DSO would pay for capturing the concert and the music editing.

"Management was totally fine to do this project but wanted it to be aired on national PBS," says McGovern. "So, I pitched it to American Public Television, and they agreed to make it available to their syndicate stations. It didn't cost me any more than what it would have cost me to capture it in the first place. Those are the things that I get really excited about—using the content I've already done or augmented just slightly to be able to make it something much, much bigger."

Education, Mentorship, + New Work Development

Numerous performing arts organizations have expansive education programs, from working within schools, to nurturing future artists and projects through education and mentorship programs. We've highlighted three organizations that have exciting programs that use technology well and include lessons learned during the pandemic shutdown.

Converting a Space into a Filming Studio

Attack Theatre, an organization in Pittsburgh, Pennsylvania that has been featured in other chapters of this book, fuses modern dance, original live music, and interdisciplinary art forms to create engaging dance performances and creative education programs (`www.attacktheatre.com`).

When the pandemic shutdown happened in March 2020, they were halfway through a 10-day residency at a local day school with a program called Imagination Station. That multidisciplinary program was designed to involve whatever curriculum the school was teaching at the time. This version involved dancers from Attack Theatre and the school's visual art and language arts teachers.

"We had to quickly rethink the program as a virtual experience from there," explains project and media specialist Dane Toney. "We were able to work out the kinks with that school as a springboard to offer to others. The program morphed to include an in-person option, and a hybrid option with a live stream component—that was definitely because of what we learned during COVID."

During the pandemic, they provided numerous other education programs through Zoom and Google Meet, depending on the platform the schools used. They also created several videos of lessons that teachers could schedule to stream on demand, allowing for much more flexibility.

As more videos were created, Attack Theatre created an interactive menu of lessons that were segmented by age group, grade, and subject matter. They also created supporting lesson plan documents for the teachers.

Attack Theatre's teaching artists created those videos and lesson plans during the pandemic on their own devices from their homes or outside. Then the artistic directors used Adobe Premiere Pro to edit and Adobe Animate to add visual effects, creating the final videos for the program.

These lessons are now assets for current teachers, too. "A number of our teaching artists show the videos while they're in the classroom in person," Toney says. "So, the videos are not only a package for teachers in schools, they're also being utilized by the company." The videos are also valuable for training new teaching artists who join the organization.

When Attack Theatre moved into a new space in late 2020, they made plans to upgrade a large storage room into a studio called The Learning Lab that would be fitted with the equipment needed for filming and live-streaming education and community engagement programs, leaving the existing dance studio open for rehearsals and in-person classes.

To maximize flexibility and future upgradability of the technologies they would invest in, they enlisted the help of Mac Inglis of AudioScribe Pittsburgh. He created a complete proposal list for them to consider purchasing (see Figure 6.7).

Inglis adds, "This list allows for extremely flexible multimedia capabilities capable of local, recorded, broadcast, conferencing, and remote received media to be routed in almost any configuration. While advanced in the capabilities, the end installation should be both easy to use and easy for any future tech operator to understand, upgrade, modify, or improve upon as needed."

Note that the list doesn't include the large-screen television, laptop, desktop computer, or special lighting the space would also need. However, this is a valuable list for any organization considering upgrading their filming and broadcasting capabilities.

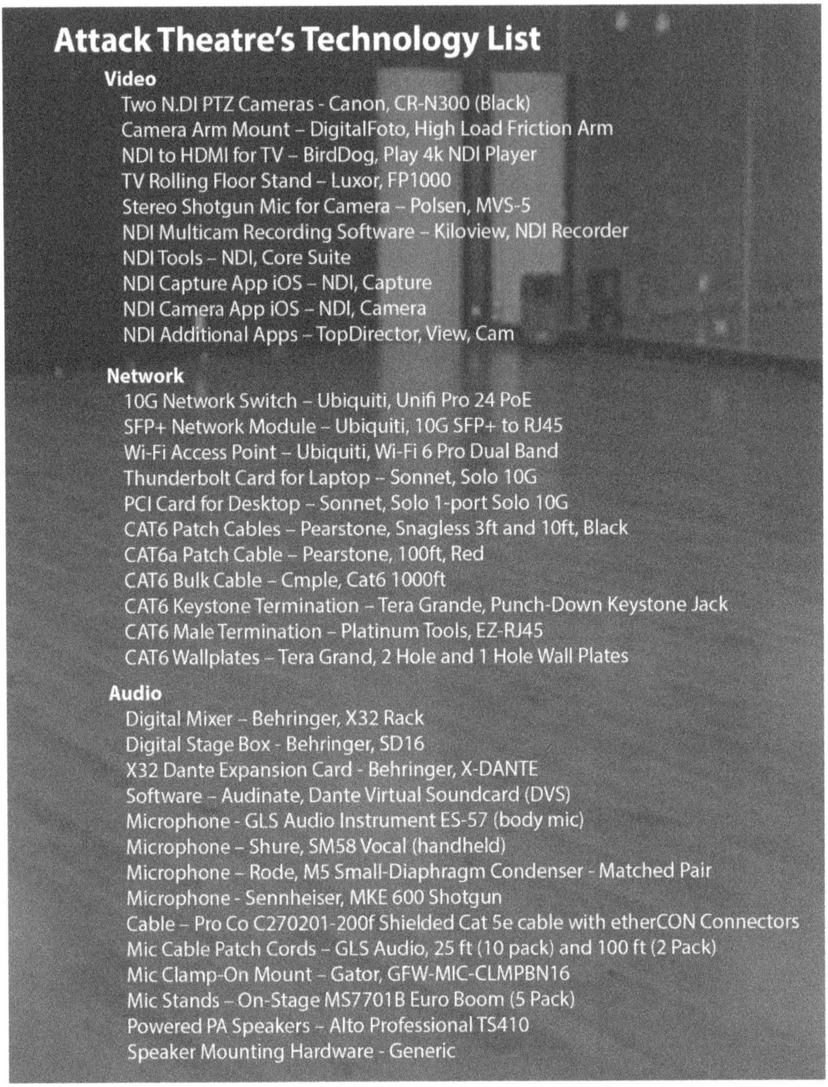

Attack Theatre's Technology List

Video
Two N.DI PTZ Cameras - Canon, CR-N300 (Black)
Camera Arm Mount – DigitalFoto, High Load Friction Arm
NDI to HDMI for TV – BirdDog, Play 4k NDI Player
TV Rolling Floor Stand – Luxor, FP1000
Stereo Shotgun Mic for Camera – Polsen, MVS-5
NDI Multicam Recording Software – Kiloview, NDI Recorder
NDI Tools – NDI, Core Suite
NDI Capture App iOS – NDI, Capture
NDI Camera App iOS – NDI, Camera
NDI Additional Apps – TopDirector, View, Cam

Network
10G Network Switch – Ubiquiti, Unifi Pro 24 PoE
SFP+ Network Module – Ubiquiti, 10G SFP+ to RJ45
Wi-Fi Access Point – Ubiquiti, Wi-Fi 6 Pro Dual Band
Thunderbolt Card for Laptop – Sonnet, Solo 10G
PCI Card for Desktop – Sonnet, Solo 1-port Solo 10G
CAT6 Patch Cables – Pearstone, Snagless 3ft and 10ft, Black
CAT6a Patch Cable – Pearstone, 100ft, Red
CAT6 Bulk Cable – Cmple, Cat6 1000ft
CAT6 Keystone Termination – Tera Grande, Punch-Down Keystone Jack
CAT6 Male Termination – Platinum Tools, EZ-RJ45
CAT6 Wallplates – Tera Grand, 2 Hole and 1 Hole Wall Plates

Audio
Digital Mixer – Behringer, X32 Rack
Digital Stage Box - Behringer, SD16
X32 Dante Expansion Card - Behringer, X-DANTE
Software – Audinate, Dante Virtual Soundcard (DVS)
Microphone - GLS Audio Instrument ES-57 (body mic)
Microphone – Shure, SM58 Vocal (handheld)
Microphone – Rode, M5 Small-Diaphragm Condenser - Matched Pair
Microphone - Sennheiser, MKE 600 Shotgun
Cable – Pro Co C270201-200f Shielded Cat 5e cable with etherCON Connectors
Mic Cable Patch Cords – GLS Audio, 25 ft (10 pack) and 100 ft (2 Pack)
Mic Clamp-On Mount – Gator, GFW-MIC-CLMPBN16
Mic Stands – On-Stage MS7701B Euro Boom (5 Pack)
Powered PA Speakers – Alto Professional TS410
Speaker Mounting Hardware - Generic

Figure 6.7: Attack Theatre shared the proposed list of technology to purchase for fitting a new dance studio as a performance space for creating quality education videos and live streaming. This list doesn't include the flat-screen TV, desktop computer, laptop, or special lighting they also use.

Graphic created by Paul Hansen

PNB Dance Film Festival

Despite initial doubts about the validity of dance on film, Pacific Northwest Ballet (PNB) soloist dancer Price Suddarth created the PNB Dance Film Festival with Artistic Director Peter Boal's approval and now serves as its managing director. "I never saw the relevance of dance on film as far as a piece of classical ballet vocabulary," admits Suddarth.

His opinion began to change in 2017 when he was asked to choreograph a short piece for film as part of a collaboration between PNB and Pixvana, a now-defunct virtual reality tech firm. His piece, *Silent Resonance*, featured two PNB dancers, including his wife, Emma Love Suddarth. Virtual reality (VR) technology used during filming and post-editing created a 360° experience that went on to be featured at the San Francisco Dance Film Festival (`http://youtube.com/watch?v=TStaOhkFrPY`).

When the pandemic hit in 2020, Suddarth was again asked to work digitally with dance.

His friends from the Colburn School in Los Angeles, California asked him to create a film of their students performing a piece he had choreographed for them. He led rehearsals via Zoom, then each student filmed themselves individually on their phones. While many organizations around the world did similar projects during that time, this project was a revelation for Suddarth.

"I was working with younger students, and they were in their houses kicking over kitchen chairs," Suddarth explains. "But I really enjoyed it and found that this was something that could be done—it's not impossible."

Suddarth was then asked to turn another piece he had choreographed into a film for the University of Oklahoma with much higher production values. While he still rehearsed the piece via Zoom from his home in Seattle, Washington, they hired a film crew that used cranes and drones to film the dance in multiple outdoor locations.

"I saw that finished piece and realized that [dance on film] is actually very valuable," he says, "so I ended up doing three films for Kansas City Ballet, and a film series for PNB." In total, Suddarth created 14 dance films in 2020 for organizations that wanted to create streaming content for their patrons and keep their dancers employed and connected with their art.

"A lot [of the projects] were overlapping," according to Suddarth, "but because of the different time zones, I rehearsed the Midwest early in the day for four hours and then switched over to the West Coast companies to work for the rest of the day. It was this incredible chance to work with a bunch of different artists, and the challenge of working over Zoom was actually liberating."

For PNB, Suddarth created *The Intermission Project*, a series of short films that flowed together to create a complete dance experience (see Figure 6.8). PNB's website described the series as:

A nine-part film project presented in three distinct acts, this work aims to capture the complex emotional and cerebral journey we each have found ourselves on this past year. The digital "stage" has offered artists a direct throughway to meet audiences in their homes, right where they sit. With this thought in mind, The Intermission Project has been distilled into nine distinct points, which can be consumed and digested by the viewer at one's own pace and in one's own time—a 4-minute piece here and there, a slightly longer 12-minute act, or the full 35 minutes in one sitting.

Figure 6.8: Price Suddarth created a nine-part film series during the pandemic lockdown for PNB that proved to be an artistic outlet and opportunity for him to develop new skills with technology.

Image provided by Price Suddarth

To create the PNB films, Suddarth realized he needed to work with better technology in order to create something more polished. So he invested in several items, including upgrading to a top-of-the-line MacBook Pro with enough memory to handle the large files.

"PNB has a grant program for their dancers called Second Stage that's generally used for second careers," Suddarth explains. "It's an incredible program that most people use for college courses, but the degree route was not really where I see myself going right now. Because [filming my choreography] is part of my next career, I qualified for the grant and they funded the purchase of the computer."

He also bought a Sony Mirrorless Camera, a Gimbal Camera, reflectors, and a generic panel key light that attached to his camera. "I was on a really tight budget because I had to purchase everything myself," he says. "I could have cut a lot of corners, but this project was really important to me."

To capture more interesting angles, Suddarth purchased a DJI Spark drone camera. He found it easy to drive and the programmable moves helped as he was multitasking as both choreographer and film director.

"I only crashed it once," he admits. While trying to get a shot of the dancers by sending the drone down through a clearing of tall trees on a beach, the drone blades touched a branch, which caused it to immediately turn off and land 40 feet below in the sand. Luckily, Suddarth was able to blow the sand out of the drone's engine, replace the blade, and capture the shot in the next take (www.facebook.com/watch/?v=3621413871309740).

To edit the PNB films, he used a free version of DaVinci Resolve, an industry-standard color-grading application with comprehensive capabilities. Although he loves Adobe Premiere and Final Cut, they were too expensive for his budget. "On those films I was learning as I was going and wasn't necessarily getting paid for these passion projects while we were all hunkered down in our homes," Suddarth states.

The learning curve was steep at first, but he now finds it to be intuitive. "DaVinci Resolve uses a node tree system, which is incredibly confusing when you start," he explains. "Adobe Premiere uses layers, so if you know how to use Photoshop, it makes sense. The nodes are very difficult at first, but once you understand the system, it makes perfect sense and it's quick."

After PNB streamed The Intermission Project in early 2021, Suddarth researched the possibilities of submitting it to dance film festivals. But he knew all nine films needed to be submitted as one series or the arc of the project wouldn't have the same resonance. Between the nine admission fees, the cost of music rights, and fees for the PNB union dancers, the cost was too high for him: "I am a gainfully employed, relatively successful ballet dancer—I am not a starving artist right now. But I don't have money to just throw into this stuff."

While disappointing for him personally, he realized that the high financial burden of applying for film festivals must be a barrier for countless other talented dance film artists. That realization led him to create the PNB Dance Film Festival.

"So, I pitched the idea of launching a film festival that would take away barriers like entry fees to [Artistic Director] Peter Boal," he notes. With the project green-lighted, Suddarth created the plan for the first festival that was announced in late 2021 and took place in March 2022 (see Figure 6.9).

Figure 6.9: The PNB Dance Film Festival began in 2022 and removes financial barriers for filmmakers around the world.

Graphics © Dammiel Cruz-Garrido and Cassandra Lea-Saxton for PNB

"PNB has a huge social media presence, with over a quarter of a million Instagram followers, so we said, if you've got a film, send it to us," Suddarth reports. He created an application using Microsoft Forms on PNB's website where people could include a link to their films. That first year, they received more than 70 submission submissions from over 40 countries, which Suddarth reviewed before sending a group to a panel of judges for potential inclusion in the festival. He also listed the newly formed event on FilmFreeway in 2023, a website for filmmakers to submit their films to hundreds of film festivals globally.

Through sponsorships, PNB was able to award grants to the winners to help them to facilitate creating a new piece that premiered at the 2023 PNB Dance Film Festival. The winner of the full-length category was a contemporary company called Seattle Dance Collective, and the short category winner was Nigerian graphic designer Segun Olamilekan, who had never made a dance film before. "He put together a one-and-a-half-minute dance in the middle of this huge, deserted field on an iPhone," describes Suddarth. "It was genuine, entertaining, and it resonated with everybody who saw it."

The festival takes place each March in a venue in Seattle and is streamed, with 38 countries tuning in. Following the premiere, Suddarth arranges for additional airing for most of the films on the EVRGRN Channel in the Pacific Northwest.

The Reiser Atlanta Artists Lab

In addition to producing quality shows such as the pre-Broadway run of *Water for Elephants: A New Musical*, the Alliance Theatre in Atlanta, Georgia is devoted to mentoring and providing opportunities for artists.

Their website states that they are focused on "expanding hearts and minds on stage and off," which they carry out through an extensive offering of education programs, a national playwrighting competition, the Spelman Internship & Fellowship Program, and a series of podcasts (www.alliancetheatre.org).

To help Atlanta-based theater artists develop new works, the Alliance has an annual program called the Reiser Atlanta Artists Lab. Kay Nilest, BOLDproducing associate at the Alliance, says, "The Reiser Lab came out of a desire to support the local community of artists. Atlanta has a thriving ecology of innovative artists, art makers, producers, and we really wanted to foster not only the development of local work, but the community and collaboration among artists."

The Alliance invited local theater artists to gather in 2012 for a discussion about the types of resources they needed to be able to create and produce their work. Overwhelmingly, the need for funding and a space to gather was at the top of everyone's lists, so the Alliance created the first Reiser Lab in early 2013.

To be accepted in the Lab, a panel of judges selects three project groups, consisting of at least three artists each, to receive $10,000 in grant stipend, as well as a yearlong residency within the theater where they could get artistic mentorship to help support the dramaturgical development of their work. The three groups were given access to a rehearsal hall and other resources, including advising from the Alliance staff in various departments as the artists requested for specific elements of their projects.

There was no expectation from the Alliance for completed projects for a final performance—the Reiser Lab was created to allow for experimentation and development.

"Without restrictions of time or expectations of a specific product, Atlanta artists are able to explore diverse and revolutionary projects that we think will forward all of our collective artmaking," says Nilest.

"This is a reciprocal process and we at Alliance are learning constantly," she adds. "The cadence of the Reiser Lab comes from the needs of the projects and the artists themselves, so we don't dictate what their process looks like. And because of that, we have a lot of opportunity to learn and grow."

The 12-month residency begins each year around the end of May, with a mid-December check-in with the Alliance artistic mentors that may include a presentation of where the project is heading. "We are 100% about process over product," Nilest claims.

"We have a final presentation Festival at the end, which is a public open access opportunity for them to present the culmination of their project, whatever that means to them," she adds. "Each project has a different definition of the final stage for the year. But we invite local producers, directors, and artistic leaders to come and see them with the hope that some of these projects will get picked up for a full production or more development."

Since the pandemic, the use of technology has expanded accessibility and streamlined Alliance's administrative work with the Reiser Lab.

Artists apply online by completing a Jotform located on the Alliance website. In addition to a description of their project, their contact information, and any special requirements the project would need, applicants must attach a 90-second pitch video.

Nilest finds working with Jotform to be extremely helpful and easy to use, allowing her to specify file format and size, which keeps all applications consistent. "I appreciate that it allows me to save all the information in a very manageable way," she says. "I can download an Excel spreadsheet [from Jotform] that has all the information like artist's name, project, etc., and then upload the information to Tessitura, our database." To manage the back end of their website, they use Drupal.

To help artists understand the program and application process, the Alliance has a live Zoom Q&A session as the applications for the next year become available. Led by Artistic Director Tinashe Kajese-Bolden and Nilest, applicants can ask questions through chat about specific elements and hear from current Reiser Lab artists about their experiences. The recorded Q&A is then posted on their website.

To make the final selection of the three projects for the following year, the Alliance hosts an event called the Pitch Party, inviting applicants to gather to briefly describe their proposed projects. "It's meant to be a chance for artists to advocate for themselves directly to the judges, but also it's meant to be a celebration of the artists in general—everybody coming together, networking," explains Nilest.

During the pandemic, the entire Reiser Lab became virtual, as did the pitch event. Post-pandemic, the Alliance decided to keep the video option for artists' pitches. "Many artists were self-conscious about their videography and editing skills, but other artists thrived in that environment," Nilest says. They received feedback that many artists felt more comfortable, better prepared, and better able to articulate themselves as creators through video that they decided to allow artists to opt for either an in-person or prerecorded video pitch. Nilest believes that "it increased not only our accessibility, but it made the process more approachable, which could otherwise be a pretty intimidating experience for some."

"Many of the projects since the pandemic have been multimedia and technology driven. So that's something that is kind of uncharted waters, and we're happy to allow that space and resources for artists to sail," Nilest notes.

One of the few parameters for the Reiser Lab projects is that they must be something that can be presented on a stage, and many applicants have been interested in working with projections. If selected for the program, they schedule meetings with the Alliance electrics and projections and sound teams for support and advice.

As part of a recent project in the program, a storyteller, scenic designer, and quilter used projections in an interesting way. "The largest part of their project was creating quilts that supplemented the scenery and the artistic storytelling," Nilest shares. "They mapped specific projections onto the contours of the fabric—it was fascinating."

So far, three Reiser Lab projects have become full productions in the Alliance's regular season, and several others have been produced at other area theaters. "Atlanta has always been a hub for exciting and revolutionary art makers," Nilest states. "Our goal is to continue bringing local producers and directors into the fold, and we would love to see these projects produced at other theaters across the country."

Touring

When any organization tours, unique challenges and technology solutions become available. To augment what we covered in Chapter 4, "Making Magic," about technology used in venues that host touring organizations, and Chapter 5, "Defining Who You Are" about branding when touring, we interviewed Alvin Ailey American Dance Company because their season is historically about being on the road.

Alvin Ailey American Dance Theater

Founded in 1958, Alvin Ailey American Dance Theater (AAADT) is a modern dance company based in New York City. Their performances feature works created by its founder Alvin Ailey and a host of new choreographers, with a full season at New York's City Center with annual national and frequent international tours.

To build and maintain the AAADT brand worldwide, the company has invested in streaming. According to the company's director of marketing, Larae J. Ferry, "We got validation during COVID of how international we really are. People were watching our digital content in places we hadn't been to in 30 years, including China and South America. So, we've increased our digital footprint. We now have staff in video and editing, and they're shooting everything every day, from classes to performances."

Ferry sees streaming via their website (www.alvinailey.org) and sharing quality content on social media as a way to connect with people in areas where they don't currently tour, or people who have financial barriers to attending their performances. "Our ethos is that we give dance back to the people," she explains. AAADT has broadened the digital content they offer to include everything they do. "We just launched AileyDance for Active Aging, which is for our senior population—one of the most incredibly touching things ever," Ferry says.

Joseph Anthony Gaito, the company's technical director, shared the technologies and human systems they use when the company tours. To keep the dancers, technicians, and administrative staff up-to-date on information while traveling, AAADT uses Microsoft 365's OneDrive and Teams as a portable infrastructure. In addition to managing workflow and file sharing, this is a platform for technical schedules at the theaters, casting changes, programming, information about getting together for casual events, and recommendations about places to explore in new cities for the artists and staff on tour. "Before, we had a black book that was always at the front desk of whatever hotel we were in that had call times, travel times, bus, airport, performances, and vital information like [local] doctors," explains Gaito. "Microsoft Teams is on our phones, it's on our laptops. This has been our information station that answers a lot of questions."

On tour, the company manager coordinates and manages communication among the dancers, technical staff, and the office back in New York, as well as making sure all the travel plans run smoothly. That position also pays bills and works with the venues' stage managers and administrative staff regarding schedules and keeping them aware of any needed changes.

As technical director, Gaito's work in coordinating the company's technical needs with venues is streamlined through CAD files, Vectorworks, and Lightwright. "If I get information from a venue in Switzerland and they say, Hey, Joe, here's the drawing, what do you think? And I say, let me add this, then they bounce it back," explains Gaito. "We can eliminate time in days and possibly weeks

**of back-and-forth—we can do things in two seconds. That has
really changed the game, right?"**

AAADT travels with its own lightboard, lighting instruments, sound-board, and basic tech infrastructure needed for their performances. While they have kept up with advancing technologies available in those areas and updated their equipment, Gaito cautions about the inherent downside. "Our lightboard is an Eos Apex product. Actually, for dance, we're a little over-engineered on it—you could probably set off a rocket right now. It's probably the Maserati of light boards," Gaito describes. "Well, I'm gonna run out of being able to pay people who can manipulate it—[they] have to have a different skill set. So I don't want to get too fancy, because then I won't be able to find someone [at an affordable salary for our budget]. We might take a step backwards to the lightboard that always worked for us. And that's not being negative, it's just making the smart [fiscal] decision."

The company made the decision to rent an entire lighting package from 4Wall Entertainment instead of owning it. "Other [touring dance] companies own their own systems, but that means you need to fix it, you need to upkeep it, you need to buy new," Gaito explains. "Would it be a smart decision for Ailey? In some respects, yes, but overall, no. [When] something breaks [while] we're on the road, in two seconds the support team sends out something new and they troubleshoot. All that comes with the rental."

Gaito also suggests remaining loyal to companies that serve your organization well and that continually provide good service: "We've been with 4Wall since they started, so they lovingly call us the antique road show. We're one of their longest clients, so when we pick up the phone, they answer [no matter where] we are on the planet. That kind of support is priceless."

AAADT also travels with their own sprung floor, backdrops, props, wardrobe, washing machine and dryer, and everything else needed for their productions. When touring internationally, they ship as much as possible by sea. "But I need to make sure we're not performing anything that's going to be in that boat prior to the next time we see it," Gaito cautions. "This summer, we have time to get stuff to our first stop in Edinburgh, so I put [what's needed] on a boat. Sail time is usually at least three weeks, then 21 days to get out of customs, [then time] to get picked up and delivered to the venue. If we were doing performances all the way up to a week before we left for tour, then I'd have to fly everything air cargo and a big [price] is associated with that." To help lower shipping costs, AAADT keeps a duplicate sprung floor, blackout curtains, and other standard items in a storage facility in Germany, and they have everything shipped directly to the first venue of their international tours.

Lastly, Gaito mentions the importance of communication and of honoring systems. The time allocated to loading the technical elements into a theater and then taking them down following performances to load onto trucks to go to the next venue is extremely tight. Everything is scheduled down to the minute, and everyone knows their specific tasks to keep the timeline on schedule.

"We have systems that are in place for a reason," he says. "We've got it down to the minute [with] goals we need to hit every day, every week, every month, every year. If one person goes off script, there's a ripple effect—it's going to affect someone else's department. For example, my prop man was doing something that wasn't within the systems. I [asked him] to stick to the systems because what he had done ruined the electrician's plan, and then that ruined [another technician's] plan. And then we're off schedule. Stick to the plan."

Takeaways

Extending the stage can be many things, from touring to podcasting to live-streaming. Many organizations have also consistently used radio and television partnership opportunities over the years to share their work more broadly. The examples we've discussed provided many lessons learned. The following are a summary of key takeaways for quick inspiration:

- Those who are doing this work successfully have committed to it as a significant part of their business. It is often the most obvious mission-centric solution to reaching a wider audience.

- The art and the people making the art are the heart of the work. Doing work that extends the normal stage appearance requires coordinating the appropriate rights, getting artist permission, and working closely with the relevant unions.

- Invest in a strong, repeatable model for capturing and editing content so that everyone in the organization, from production to media to marketing, knows what to expect.

- Create a digital strategy that aligns with your organization's mission, whether it is for education, archival, or consumer purposes.

Establishing a value for digital in the institution creates broad buy-in of digital initiatives.

▪ Create a capture, edit, store, and release workflow that suits your strategy, budget, staffing, and facility demands. That might mean that you have a hardwired system in your spaces and are doing all the work in-house or that you are outsourcing key elements or equipment. The key is to capture once, use it everywhere—including intersecting with those in marketing, advancement, and other departments across the organization.

▪ But, while systems are needed, experimentation in the face of an ever-changing ecosystem should be encouraged and pursued.

▪ Touring is alive and well and operating even more efficiently with the inclusion of advanced management and production technologies.

Technology Solutions

The following technology solutions are mentioned throughout this chapter. Remember, this is not a comprehensive list of all the technologies available, but they might help to begin your research.

Streaming + Simulcasts

▪ Brightcove is a video-hosting platform (www.brightcove.com).

▪ Stripe is a payment-processing service (http://stripe.com).

▪ Cortex by Orange Logic is a digital asset management system (http://orangelogic.com).

▪ IDAGIO is a streaming service for classical music (http://idagio.com).

▪ Vimeo OTT is a content monetization and digital streaming service (http://vimeo.com).

▪ DaVinci Resolve is a free post-production editing application.

▪ Sony Mirrorless Camera offers continuous live view, is perfect for shooting at tricky angles without needing to raise the camera to your eye, and it's great for shooting video. Many creatives choose to use their mirrorless as a video camera for this reason (http://electronics.sony.com).

- PTZ Camera (pan-tilt-zoom) cameras are built with mechanical parts that allow them to swivel left to right, tilt up and down, and zoom in and out of a scene (`http://ptzoptics.com`).

- DJI Spark Drone is a mini drone with intelligent flight control options, a mechanical gimbal, and a camera with incredible image quality (`http://dji.com`).

- Blackmagic Cameras are professional upgradeable cameras with multiple versions ranging from 4K to 4.6K, up to 60 fps at native resolution, and 12 to 15 stops of dynamic range, capable of both movie and broadcast recordings. In addition, the latest URSA Mini Pro supports 12K/8K/6K/4K formats in a single camera (`http://blackmagicdesign.com`).

- AJA Ki Pro GO Streaming Camera is a portable multi-channel H.264 recorder offering up to 4-channels of simultaneous HD and SD recording to off-the-shelf USB drives (`http://aja.com`).

- AJA Helo streaming camera is a compact, stand-alone unit with the ability to simultaneously stream your content to two destinations while recording (`http://aja.com`).

- vMix live video–editing software is a complete live video production and live streaming software solution. Create, mix, switch, record and live stream professional live productions on a Windows PC or Laptop (`http://vmix.com`).

Education, Mentorship, + New Work Development

- JotForm is a web-based form builder with over 150 integrations (`http://jotform.com`).

- Adobe Premiere Prois post-production editing software (`http://adobe.com`).

- Adobe Animate is a multimedia authoring and computer animation program (`http://adobe.com`).

Touring

- Lightwright is software that manages theatrical lighting data and paperwork (`http://lightwright.com`).

- Vectorworks is design software used by architects and stage designers (`http://vectorworks.net`).

- Microsoft Teams is a business collaboration application (`www` `.microsoft.com/en-us/microsoft-teams/` `group-chat-software?rtc=1`).

CHAPTER
7

The Arts Are for Everyone: Diversity + Accessibility

You've probably come across several acronyms for the topic this chapter focuses on—technologies being used for work in diversity and accessibility (D+A): DEI (diversity, equity, and inclusion), D&I (diversity and inclusion), and JEDI (justice, equity, diversity, and inclusion). Miami City Ballet Executive Director Juan José Escalante likes to adds the letter B (DIB—diversity, inclusion, and belonging), because "there has to be a sense of belonging, you know—that when you're here, you belong." And some have added the letter A make DEIA (diversity, equity, inclusion, and accessibility).

Technology can be a useful ally for creating a safe, equitable environment. This chapter covers many technologies for D+A, but what we really want to share is the way people are using it, because technologies are continually being updated or new ones created. We'll focus on specific D+A areas with technology solutions:

- Making venues, performances, and the artistic process more accessible for people with hearing and vision challenges

- Using podcasts and streaming as platforms to address D+A in the arts

- Tackling potential or perceived bias and making your organization more equitable, including HR and marketing pieces

"I've always seen my role as looking around and asking, 'Who's not here?,' and 'Why aren't they here?,' and 'How can we make it comfortable for them to be here and create an experience they want to come to?','" says Vanessa Braun, Manager of Employee Engagement and Director of Accessibility at Pittsburgh Cultural Trust. This is exactly the mindset needed to approach D+A work. We must move beyond potential bias about what patrons want or need by addressing our personal or institutional history of privilege to better meet their needs and truly represent our communities. That means talking with a diverse selection of people from your community to learn how best to improve communication and the experiences your organization offers. While it's true that ticket sales may increase when more people in your area feel welcomed, adjusting to include D+A isn't just about increasing attendance—it should be a part of every area of your organization. Technology can help.

"There's a business case for doing this work and there's an artistic case," according to Rocky Jones, Minnesota Opera's Equity, Diversity, and Inclusion Director:

> It's just going to make the product we create better, and that's going to put more butts in seats. So what I always say about it is that we're creating more joy for more people more of the time. Not to say that everything is perfect—it's lifelong work. And it's nonlinear. But we're a civic organization, and therefore, we have a responsibility to create a Minnesota Opera that reflects the entire community.

The organizations and technology included in this chapter are examples of success we felt would be useful and hopefully interesting to read about, but this is not an exhaustive list. Countless organizations and artists are finding new ways of integrating technology into their D+A work. For other examples, check out the websites of Goodman Theatre in Chicago (`www.goodmantheatre.org/about/accountability`) and Merrimack Repertory Theatre in Lowell, Massachusetts (`https://mrt.org/BlackLivesMatter`).

Whether you've already begun your journey with D+A or are just beginning the work, we've included a short list of additional resources at the end of the chapter for having internal discussions and for making a plan of action.

Hearing + Vision-Impaired Audiences

Several years ago, numerous companies were creating technology to be used for hearing- and vision-impaired patrons. However, many of them stopped production because the sales volume just wasn't there. Today, we can almost count on one hand the number of companies that focus on such products.

Smaller regional performing arts organizations must now rely on technology developed for huge clients such as sports arenas, touring music stars, or Broadway. That requires organizations to adapt the way they work with technology through workarounds that often require many more employee work hours—or lower performance expectations.

"Personal hearing devices are changing," notes Betty Siegel, Director of the Office of Accessibility and VSA at The John F. Kennedy Center in Washington, DC. "The three companies that are developing most of the assistive listening systems in the United States are now putting a lot of effort into Wi-Fi, and I think that's probably the system of the future."

But for Wi-Fi systems to work well, venues must offer strong public access. "We spent so much time telling people not to use their cell phones and limiting access to it in the building," Siegel adds, "and now we have to put in this whole infrastructure."

Deaf artist Monique Holt prefers open captioning apps such as Gala-Pro for shows with dialogue that moves quickly, such as *Hamilton* or *Abridged Shakespeare*. "If the Wi-Fi [in the theater] is good, then it's easy and enjoyable," she explains. "But if the Wi-Fi is bad, the captioning may stutter or shut down. Plus, it's a pain in the butt for patrons to have to hold their smartphones to watch the show and read subtitles."

GalaPro is a smartphone-enabled app for closed captions, audio description, and translations into other languages that's frequently used on Broadway and related national tours. The app offers other helpful capabilities, such as access to digital performance programs. Because those performances run for many months or even years, the initial work of setting up the timing and accuracy of the captioning for each show is easy to validate.

Asolo Repertory Theatre in Sarasota, Florida, started using GalaPro in 2019 to transcribe performances in Spanish or English. The app also dims the smartphone's screen to avoid disturbing surrounding patrons. The theater makes this service available after nine performances of a production, giving the technology time to be adjusted. This means that an employee spends nine performances plus the final rehearsals on stage before the show opens working with the text and timing before the service is offered to the public.

With a long run and a large budget or underwriting that will allow for the expense of having a designated employee for that time, the technology can be a great service for patrons. For organizations with shows that last only for a few weeks or less, an employee can live-push the text. This still requires the expense of a dedicated employee managing the technology at every performance.

Sometimes financial barriers or experience with technology prevent patrons from having devices with enough memory to download an app, so many venues offer devices already loaded with the required app to be used during performances. This approach also allows the venue to control certain aspects such as volume or screen brightness.

Technology can help elevate the magic of performances for the visually challenged. Miami City Ballet (MCB) offers a behind-the-scenes "Touch Tour" for prop-heavy productions such as *The Nutcracker* (see Figure 7.1). Before a scheduled performance, vision-impaired patrons are invited backstage for a tour, where they touch some of the props, costumes, and scenery as guides explain how those items further the storytelling. This gives a physical sense of part of the production's magic to those who have taken the tour. As they then sit with the rest of the audience for a performance, they wear audio description headsets through which descriptors explain basic plot points, the types of movement happening, and when those items they just interacted with are on stage.

MCB uses T-Coil (Telecoil) technology that transmits directly from their sound system, including the audio interpreter's microphone, to assisted listening devices provided to patrons upon request. That same technology can be used for hard-of-hearing patrons if they adjust their hearing aids to the T-Coil setting.

I get really excited about the curation of technology, because it requires human-centered design. I'm trying to move the needle beyond ADA [Americans with Disabilities Act] compliance so that we're creating spaces that are both brave and safe for people. That requires a deep investigation of the technology that's out there,

and listening to people who are living with a lack of sight or a lack of hearing.

Devon Ginn, Director of Inclusion & Community Partnerships
at Indiana Repertory Theatre (IRT)

Figure 7.1: Vision-impaired patrons experiencing a "Touch Tour" of props backstage at Miami City Ballet

Photo by Alexander Iziliaev

IRT uses T-Coil for hearing-impaired patrons and for audio description for the vision-impaired, but the organization is very open about the need to improve. Occasional patron complaints about using the system include issues like not being able to hear when a physical prop drops on stage. They can see the action, but it seems out of sync because they can't hear the prop hit the floor. There's also a slight time delay between the actual performance and the transmitted sound, which can give an echo-like quality. Ginn says, "When we recognize an issue, [we look at] what works and what doesn't work, trying to understand the technology fails. I know the folks I work with are hard at work making sure we address any issue as quickly as possible."

Another issue for patrons with disabilities or language barriers is knowing about the technology support offered if they don't already attend performances. While many organizations have detailed, robust pages on their websites about what they offer, patrons have to search that information out. This means that some sort of community engagement is needed to help inform targeted sectors. We don't have an easy answer, and we understand that staff and budgets are already stretched thin, but this is an important part of D+A to consider.

Programmable haptic suits from Music: Not Impossible (M:NI) allow people who are Deaf and hard of hearing to experience music in a new way. Their website describes the suits as a Vibrotextile™ wearable technology that translates sound onto the skin through vibration, providing a unique music experience. (`notimpossible.com/projects/music-not-impossible`).

"The concept of the Deaf holding balloons or [feeling music through] their feet in a concert to have a little bit of the musical emotion seemed preposterous," exclaimed M:NI's chief vibrational officer and co-founder Daniel Belquer. "I wanted to [create a way] for those people to come to a live concert and just get their minds blown with no learning curve."

The haptic suit he created consists of a vest with 20 actuators, or points of vibration, and one each on the wrist and ankle pieces (see Figure 7.2). "The vibration [function] is equal throughout the entire vest, wrist, and ankle pieces—the human body feels things differently in different parts of the body," explained Belquer. "And the 24 points are individually [programmable], so we can create all kinds of effects."

After several years of research and development, Belquer had heavy, handmade prototypes that were ready for testing at Lady Gaga concerts and the SXSW Music Festival in Austin, Texas. When the pandemic hit, he and his team of engineers continued making improvements. While there was increasing demand for the technology, it was inaccessible to most organizations due to expense and how complicated the suits were to program. So, Belquer changed the organization's business model in 2021 to become a full service rather than leasing the units and had lightweight suits manufactured while continuing to improve ways to program them to help cut down on time and costs.

In 2021, 2022, and 2023, Lincoln Center for the Performing Arts (LCPA) arranged for the haptic suits to be used during several of their outdoor events held at Damrosh Park and Josie Robertson Plaza in New York City.

"At Lincoln Center, we are always seeking new ways to make the arts accessible to the widest audience possible. Music: Not Impossible's work stood out as an innovative and unique way to create another entry point for guests to engage in live performance. Not only was it exciting for guests who were Deaf or hard of hearing – we even had our ASL interpreters use them – but also for guests with sensory processing disorders or who are non-disabled. It's truly an artistic experience through touch—a sense we don't often prioritize in the arts."

—*Miranda Hoffner, head of accessibility at Lincoln Center for the Performing Arts*

Figure 7.2: Haptic suits were provided at an outdoor silent disco at Lincoln Center's Josie Robertson Plaza for guests who are Deaf or hard of hearing to experience music in a new way. Different instruments are programmed to be mirrored through vibrations in 24 different areas, creating a fun, richer connection to the concert.

Photo credit: Lawrence Sumulong / © Lincoln Center for the Performing Arts. Photos of haptic vest, wrist and ankle components provided by Music: Not Impossible.

Belquer wanted to expand the use of the suits for indoor, more traditional types of music performances. "I respect the classical music world very much, so [adapting the suits for them] was a scary thing for me." Belquer and his team were invited to a closed rehearsal with the

Los Angeles Philharmonic Orchestra by their staff and higher management. "They told me if [the suits] make a beep, you guys are out because it's going to distract and the maestro is going to kill us," he said. "So they sat in the audience wearing the suits, and at the end they were crying. They said, this is amazing—it's going to change everything. So, I felt confident based on this new actual data."

This led to the suits being used for performances with the Mostly Mozart Festival Orchestra, Opera Philadelphia, and the New York City–based company Heidi Latsky Dance. There are many opportunities for these haptic suits to be used throughout the performing arts. "[Developing this technology] has been an interesting uphill experience," admitted Belquer. "But we have been receiving a lot of love from all fronts, and this is really rewarding—the part that motivates me personally and the team to move forward."

Meeting the Needs of Artists with Disabilities

Hiring diverse artists is part of making any performing arts organization a more truthful reflection of a community, including artists with disabilities. That allows for more opportunities for technology to create good working conditions in rehearsals and backstage.

Deaf artist Monique Holt works as an actress, director, lecturer, and Director of Artistic Sign Language (DASL), and has experienced numerous types of technology that have aided her work as a creative artist (see Figure 7.3).

"As an actor, I translate my own lines from the script into notated American Sign Language [ASL]," Holt explains. She uses Microsoft Word to create her own template; then her finished document is given to the DASL and stage manager, who add it to their script bible. "Plus, the understudy can learn their lines through [my document]," Holt adds.

Technology has helped the creative process for Holt in other ways as well. "The Artistic Director/Director asked me to play Aldonza/Dulcinea in Harlequin Productions' *Man of La Mancha* in Olympia, Washington, in 2019, but he didn't know ASL," Holt says. "The theater had no budget to hire an interpreter for rehearsal, so the director and I communicated through Cardzilla." She adds, "We got good reviews."

A downloadable app for Mac devices, Cardzilla allows deaf and hearing non-signers to communicate and was featured in the 2021 Apple film *CODA*. The app allows deaf people to key in messages, and it transcribes spoken word into text.

Figure 7.3: Deaf artist Monique Holt as Aldonza/Dulcinea in *Man of La Mancha* at Harlequin Productions

Photo by Seattle Actor Photos

Communication to deaf actors backstage during performances is also seeing advancement through technology. When Holt appeared as the Duchess of York in 2022's *Richard III* for the Public Theater's Free Shakespeare in the Park in New York City, they used a program called RadioWorld from Nemesis Research. Using Wi-Fi, the program converted the stage manager's announcements into text on a tablet installed in her dressing room.

When directing or working as the DASL for a theater production, Holt relies on Microsoft products Excel and PowerPoint to keep track of ASL animations for specific scenes and to share notes and concepts as she explains them to the cast or creative team. She sends the documents with *Google Docs*, *Sheets*, and *Slides*, which allows others to add comments and questions.

When asked what emerging technology or new ideas excite her, Holt remembers seeing a production at The Kennedy Center of *The Tempest* by the Montreal-based digital and multidisciplinary company 4D Art in 2007. "They used holograms for some characters—it was fantastic," she recalls. "What if we used holograms for ASL interpreters? That would be interesting." Holt is also helping develop Viscript, a deaf-friendly ASL-based video script template. And she's writing a *DASL Handbook* with a work scope breakdown.

Podcasts + Live Streaming

D+A should be woven into every area of your organization. Here are three examples that put that effort front and center in ways that expand your platform to raise awareness while promoting your organization.

The Score

Rocky Jones from Minnesota Opera produces *The Score*, a biweekly podcast about opera, classical music, and pop culture through the perspective of three black queer arts administrators (see Figure 7.4).

"We create a homey sort of vibe and just invite people into our tent, you know, whoever wants to come," Jones says. "So it's not necessarily that we just want to appeal to people of color—we want to appeal to opera nerds and to anybody who just wants to learn about our craft from a different perspective."

After Jones and Paige Reynolds helped create a new diversity charter for the Minnesota Opera that was approved in May 2020 (two weeks before George Floyd was murdered in Minneapolis), President and General Director Ryan Taylor asked what specific projects they would create. With fellow employee Lee Bynum, they came up with the concept for *The Score*. Jones explains:

> We decided to open [the podcast] up to talk to artists to get their experiences from all different marginalized communities, sharing the diverse community we have here in the Twin Cities with the whole world, because we have incredible artists who live here, and come through here, and work here. You know, it's also about keeping it real. No matter what we're talking about, including any horrible racist thing that's happened, we always end the show on a note of positivity and optimism. Because if we don't believe things can change, they're not going to change.

Figure 7.4: Hosts of *The Score*, Lee Bynum, Paige Reynolds, and Rocky Jones
Photo by Angela Divine Photography

As their podcast began finding its audience and people learned about the strong diversity, equity, and inclusion work at the company, big names in the opera world made themselves available to be interviewed. Jones says:

> You know, it's been an exciting ride. It's been great to have these fantastic guests come on. And sometimes we have people who are in the Minnesota Opera shows that are on stage, so it's also serving a marketing purpose. Every now and again, I've heard about people who have donated to the opera because they like what we're doing [with the podcast].

Minnesota Opera created a small recording studio for them, but due to COVID, the three creators began working from home and turned to Zoom, like many of us, to record their podcasts from separate locations. Bynum now lives in New York City and is the chief education officer at Lincoln Center for the Performing Arts, and Reynolds left the opera to create a company called The Freshwater Doula and remains an arts influencer in Minneapolis. The trio continues to record together, now bringing their expanded connections and experiences to the podcast:

The main thing we want to do is to demystify opera, to show that we're regular people, and to create a space of authentic belonging for everyone who comes in. Opera and classical music tell stories that resonate for all different sorts of communities.

—Rocky Jones, co-host of The Score

Content from their podcasts often appears in Minnesota Opera's monthly subscriber e-newsletters, and the company uses the podcasts during the hiring process. Job applicants are asked to listen to three episodes of *The Score* and then share what they learned and their personal perspectives. "I never thought about the podcast being used in that way," Jones says, "but that's pretty cool."

Jones uses Adobe Premiere Pro to edit the recorded segments and hosting platform Captivate.fm to distribute and promote *The Score*.

Live from Emmet's Place

Jazz pianist Emmet Cohen uses streamed weekly music sessions called *Live from Emmet's Place* and his subscriber newsletters as platforms for social justice. By including a wide diversity of musicians, he uplifts and represents the full jazz community. His newsletter often directly addresses injustice and discrimination, bringing attention to issues and continuing important conversations. "I try to use [*Live from Emmet's Place*] as an example of how humans can be at their best when working together. When our community is aligned, we're able to create something powerful for the greater good," Cohen says (see Figure 7.5).

For example, Cohen has used the weekly stream as fundraisers for efforts in New Orleans after Hurricane Ida in 2021 and for Ukraine at the beginning of the war in 2022, featuring an international roster of musicians. He's also done celebrations of Women's History Month and Gay Pride Month.

"I also feel like age [bias] isn't talked about a lot," Cohen says. "One of our main goals is to include the oldest generation of jazz musicians— the serious jazz masters." This has included singer Sheila Jordan at age 93 and saxophonist Houston Person at age 87. Cohen also features musicians in their early twenties who are just beginning their careers. "I want to show the breadth of age inclusivity," he says. "Age is something that can be overlooked, especially because society tends to reject older people. So that's really important to me."

Figure 7.5: Jazz pianist Emmet Cohen streams weekly live music sessions called *Live from Emmet's Place*

Photo by Gabriela Gabriella

During the first months of the pandemic in 2020, Cohen used Open Broadcaster Software (OBS) to stream sessions from his home in New York City's Harlem neighborhood. "It's free and constantly being updated—everyone was telling me I should try it because the quality is so much better than Facebook Live," Cohen says. OBS allows him to place the stream on Facebook and his YouTube channel. "I figured out that YouTube is actually much more powerful for streaming than Facebook for what we were doing," he says. "That's where there's real potential for growth and virality, and also for monetization." As the livestream developed, his team began using the Blackmagic Design ATEM Mini HDMI Live Stream Switcher, a compact broadcast switcher that allows them to go back and forth between multiple cameras from different angles so that the livestream isn't visually stagnant.

After nearly three years of writing weekly newsletters, Cohen occasionally uses OpenAI's Generative Pre-trained Transformer (GPT) to create a first draft when pressed for time. He'll plug in tour dates, subjects, and other information that need to be covered. GTP then references Cohen's past newsletters for the language and tone he typically uses and immediately creates something he can work with. "It spits out something that still needs to be edited," he admits, "but it's a tool that helps me with time management."

"I think AI will be an important tool in artists' lives in whatever capacity, and I'm not averse to any type of new technology," he adds.

Green Room Meditations

Indiana Repertory Theatre's (IRT) Devon Ginn (see Figure 7.6) produces a podcast called *Green Room Meditations*, with new episodes dropped on the third Friday of each month. The podcast is a space for theater makers and lovers to examine the industry through a lens of justice and defiant mindfulness. Guests include playwrights, actors, community leaders, such as playwrights Tamara Winfrey-Harris and Pearl Cleage. "I ask people on the podcast to show up for themselves and how theater can be one of many tools in the pursuit of justice and liberation," says Ginn.

Figure 7.6: Devon Ginn, host of Indiana Repertory Theatre's podcast, *Greenroom Meditations*
Photo by Cuong Tran for the Arts Council of Indianapolis

Ginn uses artificial intelligence (AI) through Descript to edit recorded interviews for his podcast, making the editing process seamless and smooth. "I found I have an affinity for using the word 'apparently,'" confesses Ginn. "The script will quickly find those and any use of 'um' or long pauses, which allows me to cut them out. Now that I have access to the script, I'll never be able to go back because editing and post would usually take several hours, whereas now it's under two."

He uses Libsyn to record and then to push podcasts out to apps and directories. Ginn says, "We're on Apple Podcasts, Amazon Music, Spotify, I Heart Radio—wherever people stream their podcasts and listen to music."

Human Resources + Marketing

There are numerous technologies available to help make sure your HR and marketing efforts truly reflect your organization and are as accessible as possible.

Bias in Written Materials

All of us have unconscious biases. Part of our personal and organizational journey with D+A is to recognize and confront them, but we may be unaware when those patterns creep into our work in HR or marketing.

AI technology can be used to help identify bias in written pieces—we've highlighted a few options. The Applied recruitment platform targets removing bias from the hiring process. Some of its strategies include removing job applicant information and randomizing the order in which recruiters see applicant answers. Applied also displays application question responses from all candidates rather than having recruiters review one full application at a time, to lower the chances that bias creeps in.

GapJumpers is a platform that allow organizations to hold anonymized job applications to help remove common biases such as those based on gender, race, and résumé history.

Developed as a free platform, Gender Decoder is a quick way to check whether your job ad has the type of subtle "gender-coding" that may discourage people from applying. Their website states that we all use language that is subtly gender-coded without realizing it. We have certain expectations about people and how they differ that may seep into the language we use. Their research has shown that masculine-coded language sometimes discourages women from applying for jobs.

It's worth noting that any technology may have some built-in biases because it was created by people, and the programs reference information from all over the Internet for your content, so the end result will still need to be carefully edited before being published.

Color Blindness

Color choice used in logos or graphics may not be distinguishable for people with color blindness. For example, if a logo or text is placed inside a color box and the two colors are seen as too similar to someone affected by color blindness, the visual statement you were trying to make will be lost. Here are three options that can help make sure images will be seen.

Colorblind Web Page Filter is a web-based tool that lets you copy a URL and view your original graphic and views of four common types of color blindness side by side. Color Oracle is an open source project that includes keyboard shortcuts, application agnosticism, and menu bar access. Stark is a Sketch plug-in that allows you to preview your graphic in eight different types of color blindness.

Diversity of People in Images

Pictures are worth a thousand words, right? For your marketing efforts, using photos of diverse people that accurately represent your community is important. No matter how eloquent the text you use may be, your photo or graphic image selection may negate your intentions. In researching websites for this book, it was a bit shocking to often find Black, Indigenous, People of Color (BIPOC) photos on D+A pages only; some prominent performing arts organizations across the United States were guilty of this. Make selecting photos and graphics that show diverse people consistent throughout all areas of your marketing.

Training

Whether you're using technology to make performances and venues more accessible or addressing bias and discrimination within your organization, training everyone is crucial. Not only does getting everyone on the same page clearly communicate your stance on issues, but it also allows others to be part of the discussions about opportunities for moving forward.

As we've repeated throughout this book, our industry is people-driven and technology can be an ally to help streamline and improve our work. As Betty Siegel from The Kennedy Center points out, "Technology is not replacing humans yet—not in the work we're doing. You know, one person who inadvertently and accidentally says just one wrong thing . . . that ruins the whole experience for [a patron]."

The same embarrassing example of why everyone needs to be trained (or at least knowledgeable) about D+A technology being used came up three times in interviews for this chapter. During a 2022 performance of *Hadestown* on Broadway, an actress saw an audience member holding up a device. Assuming they were illegally filming, the actress stopped the show to wrongfully chastise and embarrass the patron. If the cast and stage management had been aware that closed captioning was available on devices for the audience, the rain of bad press that followed that incident might have been avoided, not to mention the poor patron's bad experience. Of course, that means the ushers need to be trained to recognize the difference between patrons using captioning versus taking bootleg videos and photos—no easy task.

EXAMPLES OF WHO TO TRAIN

In this section, we've included many areas of organizations that should be trained about the D+I technologies you are using. As you think about your organization, there may be additional groups that should be included.

Ushers	At The Kennedy Center, according to Siegel, they use part-time paid ushers organized in tiers. "We identify specific ushers and train them intensively as Ambassadors—those who are just naturals with good customer service and seem to have the etiquette and socialization we need. Then we have a subgroup of that subgroup—the Liaisons. We train them on accessibility devices and related technology. How do you set up the audio description? How do you troubleshoot the receivers? How do you set up a captioned performance? How do you troubleshoot the captioning devices?"
Box Office/Ticket Scanners	Make sure all front-of-house staff know which devices are available for patrons, where to locate them in the lobby, and how to use them. Doing so will make the experience smoother and more pleasant for patrons. All staff should be able to help patrons if things have gotten hectic and no one else is available when the patron needs help.
Administrative Staff	For smaller organizations especially, repeat patrons and donors see the staff as all-knowing. All staff should at least be aware of each accessibility device available at performances, and some should know how to operate them. Sometimes, ushers or other front-of-house staff might not be available when a patron is having an issue. Resolving the problem as quickly and smoothly as possible is in everyone's best interest.

Continues

(continued)

EXAMPLES OF WHO TO TRAIN	
Board Members	Board members should be your biggest advocates and are often needed to obtain or approve funding for new technologies for your organization. They should have a complete understanding of all diversity + equity work happening at your organization, including improving the experience at your performances for patrons with disabilities. Plus, board members may bring additional ideas to the table.
Performers/ Musicians	Performing artists need to have a general understanding of the types of devices that may be in the audience, how they're being used, and why this technology is important. In addition to avoiding the previous example of the actress in *Hadestown*, those on stage need to understand what they may see in the audience to avoid being distracted. An accidental flash of a device illuminating a patron's face can easily pull a performer out of the moment if they aren't aware.
Stage Management/ Crew	These people run the show, which often includes a sort of crisis management or troubleshooting. Avoid miscommunication by giving the entire crew the same general understanding as you do the performers and musicians. That training might also alert them to any potential issues with the way the technology might affect the performance's sound or lighting.
Audiences	Times have changed, and patrons now need to understand what to expect from accessibility devices. While no one using a device wants to diminish anyone else's experience, awkward situations can be avoided. When we walk into theaters, we're already told by the people who scan tickets how long the performance will be, if there's an intermission, and if there are any sensory-related effects such as strobe lights. Why not include a quick mention that accessibility devices like headsets or apps on devices may be used by some patrons? Additional options include text/graphics in the performance program, signage in the lobby, and notes on event web pages and social media posts.

Systemic Racism

Indiana Repertory Theatre's Devon Ginn told us about *The Movement of 10,000 (MVMT10K)*, a useful piece of technology for anti-racism work. IRT has suggested use of the resource to their entire staff, and they follow up with all staff meetings for discussions.

MVMT10K is a digital platform created by the Indianapolis Foundation, a division of the Central Indiana Community Foundation (CICF). The goal is to inform, inspire, and ignite equitable change and justice with a goal of reaching at least 10,000 "movers" (users).

"Our main goal [with this app] is creating a space for people to build a community around anti-racism," says Kayla Knox, Opportunity, Equity, and Inclusion Officer at CICF, "and to create movement in the community based on that initial learning and the relationships that are built within the app—I think it's a good starting point for people to come together."

"We definitely don't consider ourselves experts, but as the content curator, I've studied race and racism through a master's degree from the University of Notre Dame, and have lived experience as a Black woman," continues Knox. "We've had several rounds of focus groups between internal staff members and external community stakeholders that have been very helpful in checking ourselves and making sure we're being representative of everybody."

Launched in October 2022, the app is a series of modules that feature articles and exercises about the history of racism in the United States, as well as actionable items that learners can take out into the community. In order to address financial equity with this training, use of the MVMT10K app is free and the vendor makes sure there are no paywalls for any resources they link to (see Figure 7.7).

The app was developed by Haystack with connections to their customer relationship management (CRM) system by Salesforce, CICF's partners in this project. "As the data systems person, I'm connecting the app to our database so we can send automated [email] messages based on engagement," explains Jena Brooks, CICF's data systems associate. "That's what is helping us not just have a static app, which is obviously an amazing piece of technology we're grateful to Haystack for, but we can also send 'Welcome to This Movement' or 'We haven't seen you in a while' messages to registered users." They also send an email when updated or new content has been added.

Knox and Brooks would like to have more accessibility features for people who are either visually impaired or learn differently and prefer listening; however, much of the content is from external third parties. "In the app, we'd like to host a recording of the content itself," explains Brooks. "We need the technology to catch up. And we would rather the recording be a human voice. I've used those kinds of assistive AI technologies in the past, and it sounds very much like a robot. It's a lot harder to connect with the material."

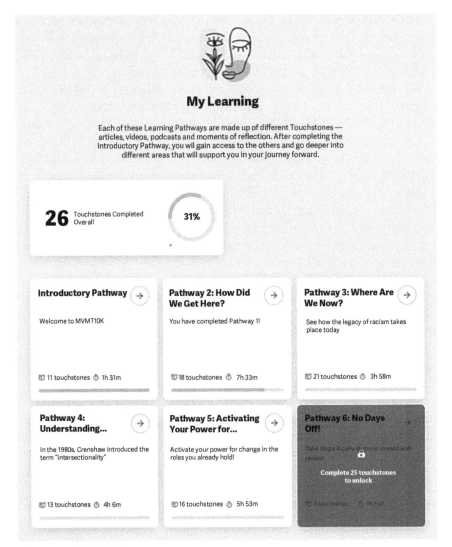

Figure 7.7: MVMT10K

Courtesy of MVMT10K

The user-friendly MVMT10K app guides people through six pathways and leads them through key learning points called "Touchstones" (articles, videos, podcasts and moments of reflection). In order to move forward to the next pathway, a certain number of Touchstones must be completed. Learn more at http://mvmt10k.org or at the Apple App Store.

Additional Resources

There are powerful online resources and books for D+A training available that can help your organization. Several people we spoke with have used these for staff training, and for resources to post on their websites to share the opportunity for learning with patrons and their larger communities.

TRAINING RESOURCES MENTIONED BY INTERVIEWEES

In this section, we'll discuss training resources that our interviews found helpful.

artEquity	▪ Launched in 2015 as a national initiative, *artEquity* provides tools, resources, and training at the intersection of art and activism. With over 5,000 individuals trained, and a growing alumni community, artEquity is building a broad base of individuals and organizations who are strategically poised to create and sustain a culture of equity, inclusion, and justice through arts and culture. Learn more at `http://artequity.org`.
Arts Connect International	▪ Founded in 2014, Arts Connect International is a Boston-based, globally reaching organization that seeks to build equity in and through the arts. Their website states, "There is a 'cultural equity gap' within the United States arts landscape, expressing an unequal representation of various identities in the arts, including, but not limited to race, disability, gender, sexual orientation, and socioeconomic status (class). This gap arises from systemic inequities in access to the arts as well as access to positions of power." Learn more about their resources and training at `http://artsconnectinternational.org`.
Leadership Exchange in Arts and Disability (LEAD®)	▪ As an integral part of The Kennedy Center's Access/VSA International Network, the *Leadership Exchange in Arts and Disability (LEAD)* program advances the full inclusion of people with disabilities in arts and culture. With a focus on expanding the breadth and scope of accessible programming, LEAD provides an opportunity for professionals in the field to develop best practices and resources; engage in conversations with colleagues and experts from around the world; and learn practical methods for designing inclusive arts experiences and environments. Learn more at `www.kennedy-center.org/education/networks-conferences-and-research/conferences-and-events/lead-conference`.
Books	▪ *Innovating for Diversity: Lessons from Top Companies Achieving Business Success through Inclusivity*, by Bertina Ceccarelli and Susanne Tedrick (Wiley Publishing, 2023).
	▪ *Impactful Inclusion Toolkit: 52 Activities to Help You Learn and Practice Inclusion Every Day in the Workplace*, by Yvette Steele (Wiley Publishing, 2023).

Summary

Audiences, artists, donors and staff expect performing arts organizations to include diversity + inclusivity work. There are numerous ways to use technology to incorporate this work into every corner of your organization. Try not to be overwhelmed by the big picture — begin with all-staff meetings with training opportunities. Your staff will help you see how D+I fits in every department.

Consider making D+I messaging part of how your organization communicates. This can include everything from making sure images show diverse people, to hiring diverse artists and staff, to making D+I part of the conversation in content you produce and push out.

Many organizations have included great resources and statements of intent about D+I on their websites. But people are watching for any organizations not following through on their statements or sliding back to non-inclusive patterns. Remember, this is on-going process.

Takeaways

- Doing diversity + accessibility work for your organization is a continual process. There is no easy fix, but D+A should become part of every area of your organization's approach to doing business.

- Technology is always changing. Before investing time or other resources in working in a specific program, research whether newer technology has been introduced or is in development that may better suit your needs.

- Be wise in selecting technology to incorporate in your organization's D+A work—there is no "one size fits all." Start by assessing what areas you wish to address and your budget; then contact similar organizations that are using technology for that purpose.

- Involving everyone in the entire organization in D+A technology training will help create a unified understanding of your objectives and individual responsibilities, as well as create an opportunity for valuable input on how your organization can move forward.

Technology Solutions

These are technology solutions mentioned throughout this chapter. Remember, this is not a comprehensive list of all the technologies available, but they might help to begin your research.

Meeting the Needs of Artists with Disabilities

- GalaPro is a smartphone-enabled app for closed captions, audio description, and translations into other languages that's frequently used on Broadway and related national tours. Other capabilities include access to digital performance programs (www.galapro.com).

- RadioWorld is a network-based messaging solution for backstage use (www.nemesis-research.com/radioworld).

Podcasts + Live Streaming

- Adoble Premiere Pro is a timeline-based and non-linear video editing software application (www.adobe.com/creativecloud).

- Captivate.fm allows uses to create and distribute unlimited podcasts, to get advanced analytics, to monetize, and promote (www.captivate.fm).

- Open Broadcaster Software (OBS) is a free and open-source, cross-platform screencasting and streaming app. It is available for Windows, macOS, Linux distributions, and BSD. The OBS Project raises funds on the platforms Open Collective and Patreon (https://obsproject.com).

- Blackmagic Design ATEM Mini HDMI Live Stream Switcher allows users to edit live events as it can record multiple video streams, including clean feeds of all inputs and programs (www.blackmagicdesign.com).

- OpenAI's Generative Pre-trained Transformer (GPT) is a language model relying on deep learning that can generate human-like texts based on a given text-based input. The transformer creates coherent paragraph-based information extracted from publicly available datasets.

- Descript is an AI tool used to write, record, transcribe, edit, collaborate, and share videos and podcasts. Editing video in Descript is as easy as using docs and slides (www.descript.com).

- Libsyn is a podcast hosting platform that offers distribution tools which include storage, bandwidth, RRS creation, and statistics tracking (https://libsyn.com).

Bias in Written Materials

- Applied targets removing bias from the hiring process. Some of its strategies include removing job applicant information and randomizing the order in which recruiters see applicant answers (`www.beapplied.com`).

- GapJumpers is a platform that will allow organizations to hold anonymized job applications to help remove common biases such as those based on gender, race and résumé history (`www.gapjumpers.me`).

- Gender Decoder is a free AI platform to check whether your job ad has the type of subtle gender-coding that may discourage people from applying (`http://gender-decoder.katmatfield.com`).

Color Blindness

- Colorblind Web Page Filter is a web-based tool where you can copy a URL and view your original graphic and views of four common types of color blindness side-by-side (`www.uxlift.org/tools/colorblind-web-page-filter`).

- Color Oracle is an open-source project for color blindness that includes keyboard shortcuts, application agnosticism, and menu bar access (`https://colororacle.org`).

- Stark is a Sketch plugin that allows you to preview your graphic in eight different types of colorblindness (`www.getstark.co`).

Interviewees

59 Productions is the Olivier and Tony Award–winning design studio and production company behind the video design of the Opening Ceremony of the London 2012 Olympic Games, globe-trotting smash hit *War Horse*, the design and creative direction of the record-breaking David Bowie exhibition, and the decor concept design for The Met Ball, hosted by Anna Wintour. Led by directors Leo Warner, Mark Grimmer, Lysander Ashton, Richard Slaney, Jenny Melville, and Anna Jameson, with the company's New York branch led by Ben Pearcy, 59 Productions are world-leading specialists in design for stage and live events, the go-to team for generating creative and technical ideas to realize ambitious artistic projects. For more information, visit http://59productions.co.uk.

Alliance Theatre is Atlanta's national theater, expanding hearts and minds onstage and off. Founded in 1968, Alliance Theatre is the leading producing theater in the Southeast and a recipient of the Regional Theatre Tony Award® in recognition of sustained excellence in programming, education, and community engagement. Known for its exemplary artistic standards and national role in creating significant theatrical works, Alliance has premiered more than 100 original productions. Alliance nurtures the careers of emerging writers through the Alliance/Kendeda National Graduate Playwriting Competition. Alliance is also deeply committed to Atlanta artists, showcasing the city's artistic community through the Reiser Atlanta Artists Lab, which provides developmental support and resources for locally sourced performance projects. For more information, visit `http://alliancetheatre.org`.

Alvin Ailey American Dance Theater has a mission through the Alvin Ailey Dance Foundation to further the pioneering vision of the choreographer, dancer, and cultural leader Alvin Ailey by building an extended cultural community that provides dance performances, training and education, and community programs for all people. This performing arts community plays a crucial social role, using the beauty and humanity of the African-American heritage and other cultures to unite people of all races, ages, and backgrounds. In the words of Mr. Ailey, "I am trying to show the world we are all human beings, that color is not important, that what is important is the quality of our work, of a culture in which the young are not afraid to take chances and can hold onto their values and self-esteem, especially in the arts and in dance. That's what it's all about to me." His words inform the organization's core values: Reaching Excellence – Innovation with Passion; Moved to Inspire – Inspired to Move; Build Community – Celebrate Diversity; and Progress with Purpose – Perform with Respect. For more information, visit `http://alvinailey.org`.

American Players Theatre (APT) is a professional theater located just outside Spring Green, Wisconsin. Situated on 110 acres of hilly woods and meadows, APT has two theaters: the newly renovated 1,075-seat outdoor amphitheater and the 201-seat indoor Touchstone Theatre. From June through November, APT produces nine plays in a rotating repertory. For more information, visit `http://americanplayers.org`.

Malia Argüello is the production manager at Indiana Repertory Theatre. A graduate of the Conservatory of Theatre Arts at Webster University, Argüello has worked in multiple fields from theater to ballet and symphony. With a background in stage management, her past companies include The Repertory Theatre of St. Louis, Wayside Theatre, BalletMet, A Noise Within, LA Dance Project, The Phoenix Symphony, Los Angeles Philharmonic, and Seattle Children's Theatre.

Aspen Music Festival and School (AMFS) was founded in 1949 in Aspen, Colorado. The organization is regarded as producing one of the top classical music festivals in the United States, noted both for its concert programming and its musical training of mostly young-adult music students. The typical eight-week summer season features more than 400 classical music events—including concerts by five orchestras, solo and chamber music performances, fully staged opera productions, master classes, lectures, and children's programming—and brings in 100,000 audience members. In the winter, the AMFS presents a small series of recitals and music education programs for local youth and families. For more information, visit http://aspenmusicfestival.com.

Attack Theatre was founded in 1994 in Pittsburgh, Pennsylvania, by Michele de la Reza and Peter Kope as a collaboration between two dancers and a city. They fuse modern dance, original live music, and interdisciplinary art forms to create engaging dance performances. "We create work at the intersection of art and community, resulting in productions that are personal, authentic, welcoming, and fearless." (Michele de la Reza and Peter Kope) For more information, visit http://attacktheatre.com.

Ballet RI (formerly Festival Ballet Providence), Rhode Island's premiere ballet company and New England's second-largest ballet company, delights audiences with a diverse repertoire of classical, neoclassical, and contemporary dance. Founded in 1978, the company enriches the lives of its audiences, inspiring the community by presenting world-class dance. The company performs in three venues in Providence throughout its September–May season, in addition to conducting year-round classes for aspiring dancers of all ages and in-school community engagement programs, striving to bring the transformative power of dance to the widest possible audience. For more information, visit http://balletri.org.

Daniel Belquer blends the world of music, composition, theater direction, invention, and technology into a unique oeuvre. Originally from Brazil, Belquer spent a fruitful period in Rio from 1998 to 2013, composing original scores for an impressive range of over 100 shows while pioneering his own productions that merged art with technology. In 2014, he expanded his horizons to the United States. His work has found expression in galleries across New York and Philadelphia, as well as in Prague, Czech Republic, and Berlin and Munich, Germany. His innovation and creativity have earned him recognition, resulting in notable awards like the Tribeca Film Festival Disruptive Innovation and the Everyday Genius from the Da Vinci Arts Alliance, along with acknowledgment from the Kimmel Center, among others. Since 2021, Belquer has been enriching the ExCITe Center at Drexel University, Philadelphia, as an artist in residence. In fall 2023, he became professor of Music Experience Haptic Design at Drexel University. For more information, visit `http://danielbelquer.com`.

Aubrey Bergauer has been hailed as "the Steve Jobs of classical music" (*Observer*) and "the Sheryl Sandberg of the symphony" (*LA Review of Books*). Bergauer is known for her results-driven, customer-centric, data-obsessed pursuit of changing the narrative for the performing arts. A "dynamic administrator" with an "unquenchable drive for canny innovation" (*San Francisco Chronicle*), she's held offstage roles managing millions in revenue at major institutions, including the Seattle Symphony, Seattle Opera, Bumbershoot Music & Arts Festival, and San Francisco Conservatory of Music. As chief executive of the California Symphony, Bergauer propelled the organization to double the size of its audience and nearly quadrupled the donor base. Bergauer helps organizations and individuals transform from scarcity to opportunity, make money, and grow the base of fans and supporters. Her ability to cast and communicate vision moves large teams forward and brings stakeholders together, earning "a reputation for coming up with great ideas and then realizing them" (*San Francisco Classical Voice*). With a track record for strategically increasing revenue and relevance, leveraging digital content and technology, and prioritizing diversity and inclusion on stage and off, Bergauer sees a better way forward for classical music and knows how to achieve it. For more information, visit `http://aubreybergauer.com`.

Black Ensemble Theater, founded in Chicago, Illinois, in 1976 by actress, producer, and playwright Jackie Taylor, has grown from a small community arts organization to be a vibrant internationally renowned arts institution. They are the only theater in the nation whose mission is to eradicate racism, utilizing theater and educational outreach programs to bring races together in a community that embraces similarities and fosters dialogue, understanding, and acceptance. For more information, visit `http://blackensembletheater.org`.

Boston Baroque was founded in 1973 by music director Martin Pearlman. North America's first permanent Baroque orchestra, the organization has garnered a global reputation for its lively, groundbreaking, emotionally charged performances and recordings that bring early music to life for modern audiences. Boston Baroque's orchestra is composed of some of the finest period instrumentalists performing today and is frequently joined by the ensemble's professional chorus and by a roster of soloists who grace the world's most renowned concert halls and stages. The ensemble performs Baroque and Classical music using period instruments and performance techniques that reflect the time in which the music was composed. Boston Baroque believes that Baroque and Classical music is music for all times. For more information, visit http://baroque.boston.

The Builders Association is a New York City–based, Obie Award–winning cross media performance company. They use the richness of new and old tools to extend the boundaries of theater, telling original stories that examine the impact of media on various cultures and communities. Founded in 1994 by Marianne Weems, The Builders' work is made by a core group of collaborators that includes Moe Angelos, Dan Dobson, James Gibbs, David Pence, Lawrence Shea, Austin Switser, and Jennifer Tipton, in addition to hundreds of collaborators across creative disciplines. For more information, visit http://thebuildersassociation.org.

Chun Wai Chan was born in Guangdong, China, and he trained at the Guangzhou Art School from 2004 to 2010. In 2010 he was a finalist at the Prix de Lausanne, which earned him a full scholarship to study with Houston Ballet's second company, Houston Ballet II. In 2012 Chan joined Houston Ballet as a member of the corps de ballet, and he was promoted to principal dancer at Houston Ballet in 2017. Chan joined New York City Ballet as a soloist in August 2021 and in May 2022 was promoted to principal dancer. For more information, visit http://chunwaichan.com.

The Cleveland Orchestra was founded in 1918 in Cleveland, Ohio. Over the ensuing decades, the ensemble quickly grew from a fine regional organization to being ranked among the top 10 orchestras in the world by numerous publications, including *BBC Music Magazine* and *The New York Times*. The orchestra performs a full season in Ohio, tours nationally and internationally, and has a residency in Miami, Florida, each year. For more information, visit http://clevelandorchestra.com.

Emmet Cohen, a multifaceted American jazz pianist and composer, is one of his generation's pivotal figures in music and the related arts. Leader of the Emmet Cohen Trio and creator of the Masters Legacy Series, he is an internationally acclaimed jazz artist, a dedicated educator, the winner of the 2019 American Pianists Awards, and a finalist in the 2011 Thelonious Monk International Piano Competition. Cohen headlines regularly at Jazz at Lincoln Center, the Village Vanguard, and Birdland, and he has appeared at the Newport, Monterey, and North Sea jazz festivals. His artistry has taken him to venues and festivals in over 30 countries. Cohen's entrepreneurial energies led to his developing "Live From Emmet's Place," a live-streamed "Harlem rent party" that unites a worldwide audience via tens of millions of Internet views. Cohen has released over 10 albums as leader and has performed or recorded with Ron Carter, Benny Golson, Jimmy Cobb, George Coleman, Jimmy Heath, Tootie Heath, Houston Person, Christian McBride, and Kurt Elling. For more information, visit http://emmetcohen.com.

Kathleen Breen Combes is originally from Rockville Centre, New York. Her early dance training was at the Fort Lauderdale Ballet Classique, the HARID Conservatory, and The Central Pennsylvania Youth Ballet before joining the Washington Ballet in 2000. Hailed by *The New York Times* as a "ballerina of colossal scale and boldness," she joined Boston Ballet in 2003, and was promoted to principal dancer in 2009, where she performed as one of the company's leading dancers until retiring from the stage in 2019. Alongside her performing career, she holds a Bachelor of Science degree and a Graduate Certificate in Nonprofit Management from Northeastern University. Breen Combes was appointed director of Ballet RI (previously Festival Ballet Providence) in January 2021.

Dallas Symphony Orchestra is the largest performing arts organization in the Southwest United States and committed to inspiring the broadest possible audience with distinctive classical programs, inventive pops concerts, and innovative multimedia presentations. Guided by internationally renowned music director Fabio Luisi, the Dallas Symphony Orchestra delivers uplifting, entertaining musical experiences and innovative, enriching educational opportunities—both within the inspiring Morton H. Meyerson Symphony Center and across the community. For more information, visit http://dallassymphony.org.

Michele de la Reza is co-founder and Artistic Executive Director of Attack Theatre. With **Peter Kope**, their work has been seen throughout the United States, Europe, and Asia, including the Avignon Festival, Indonesia Arts Festival, Monaco Danses Forum, Spoleto Festival USA, 7th Next Wave Dance Festival (Japan), and the Broadway production of "Squonk." They are sought-after collaborators and have worked with such organizations as the Pittsburgh Opera, Pittsburgh Symphony Orchestra, Carnegie Museum of Art, Quantum Theatre, and Andy Warhol Museum, among others. de la Reza was a founding company member of New York City–based Perks Dance Music Theatre and danced with Dance Alloy for eight years. She and Kope are recipients of Pennsylvania Council on the Arts fellowships, *Dance Magazine*'s "25 to Watch," the Hardie Educator of the Year award, and The Consortium of Public Education's "Champions of Learning" Award. With a core belief that movement is an essential part of living and learning, de la Reza brings dance and kinesthetic learning into classrooms and communities for learners of all ages.

Detroit Opera (formerly Michigan Opera Theatre), one of the nation's most vibrant nonprofit arts organizations, aspires to influence the future of opera and dance with a goal of invigorating audiences through new and reimagined productions relevant to current times. It is creating an ambitious standard for American opera and dance that emphasizes community, accessibility, artistic risk-taking, and collaboration. Founded in 1971 by the late Dr. David DiChiera, Detroit Opera is led by President and CEO Patty Isacson Sabee; Yuval Sharon, Gary L. Wasserman Artistic Director; Associate Artistic Director Christine Goerke; Music Director Roberto Kalb; Artistic Advisor for Dance Jon Teeuwissen; and Board Chairman Ethan Davidson. For more information, visit www.detroitopera.org.

Juan José Escalante is the executive director of Miami City Ballet and a board member of Dance NYC. With over 30 years of experience in arts management, he brings a wealth of knowledge and understanding. Previous positions have included executive director of The National Dance Institute, the José Limón Dance Foundation, and Orlando Ballet, director of finance and administration at El Museo del Barrio, and associate director of finance at New York City Ballet.

Erica Ezold joined People's Light in 2018 as director of finance, became director of finance and operations in 2020, and was promoted to managing director in 2023. She is passionate about producing and managing new theatrical work. Ezold grew up in the Philadelphia suburbs, moved to New York City for college, and spent the subsequent 15 years producing independently, working for large nonprofit institutions, and working in commercial theater management. Favorite productions from this time include *The Two Character Play* (Off-Broadway, 2013), *West Side Story* (Broadway, 2009), *August: Osage County* (Broadway, 2008), and *Spalding Gray: Stories Left to Tell* (Off-Broadway, 2007). Upon her return to the Philadelphia region in 2014, Erica served as general manager for Pig Iron Theatre Company, where she supported the company's innovative theater makers, as well as the next generation of devisers attending Pig Iron's master's program. Ezold holds a Bachelor of Fine Arts in Drama from New York University and a Master of Business Administration from Baruch College. She is on the adjunct faculty at University of the Arts teaching Theatre Management and is a member of the Forum of Executive Women in Philadelphia. She lives in Havertown with her husband Matt and two sons, Calvin and Wesley.

Jared Fine is the chief marketing officer at Jacob's Pillow. He previously served as director of marketing at New York's Public Theater, overseeing a large portion of the marketing staff and operations. Prior to joining the Public in 2015, Fine worked as creative director of marketing for the National Artists Management Company, which produces commercially on Broadway and around the world with productions including *Chicago The Musical*, and as the associate director of marketing and communications for the American Repertory Theater in Cambridge, Mass. He received his Bachelor of Fine Arts in Performing Arts from Hofstra University.

Larae J. Ferry has led the marketing, sales, and public relations strategies for both small and large performing arts organizations over the course of her 20 years as an arts administrator. This includes her time as the associate director of marketing at The Celebrity Series of Boston (Boston, Massachusetts) and as the vice president of sales and marketing at The Kimmel Center for the Performing Arts (Philadelphia, Pennsylvania). Ferry joined Alvin Ailey American Dance Theater (New York) in 2014 as the deputy director of marketing and transitioned to head of marketing in 2021. In her current role she is responsible for the marketing, ticketing and sales, digital strategy, design, content creation, and brand for the Alvin Ailey American Dance Theater, Ailey II, The Ailey School, and Ailey Arts-In-Education & Community programs. Ferry obtained her Master of Business Administration from Simmons College, and her Bachelor's in business administration from North Carolina Central University.

Dylan Giles, marketing director for Ballet RI, is passionate about the arts and their role in shaping our community. He earned a Bachelor of Science in Ballet Performance and a Journalism certificate from Indiana University before moving to Providence to join Ballet RI (then Festival Ballet Providence). He performed with the company for 10 years, while managing the company's marketing and communications, featuring successful campaigns for the new production of *The Nutcracker* as well as rolling out the company's rebranding to Ballet RI. An advocate for public transit and active mobility, Giles can usually be found on his bike headed to or from getting tacos.

Justin Gilmore has spent a decade working for a variety of nonprofit organizations, and he currently works for a major technology company as a pre-sales technical resource. Gilmore began his career working for advocacy and electoral organizations before graduating from the Masters of Arts Management program at Carnegie Mellon University. After graduation he led the Greater Pittsburgh Community Food Bank through multiple Salesforce implementations efforts focused on volunteers and programs. Gilmore is a board member of Brewhouse Arts, a nonprofit art center located in Pittsburgh's South Side.

Devon Ginn stewards the inclusion and community partnership initiatives at Indiana Repertory Theatre. Ginn also serves as a board member for BlackSpace Urbanist Collective and the Indiana Writers Center. This Indianapolis native was awarded fellowships with Americans for the Arts, the NEA/ Indiana Arts Commission, and the Indianapolis Arts Council. Ginn is a licensed 200-hour yoga and meditation teacher, a sound alchemist with Invoke Studio & Aura Self & Soul Care, and a published poet. As an artist, nonprofit administrator, and performance artist, his work examines the psychogeographies of the built environment through the lens of defiant joy and mindfulness.

Karen Graham is a speaker, trainer, writer, and consultant with expertise in technology leadership and innovation, nonprofit software, and digital strategy. Her consulting work includes strategic technology roadmaps, development of knowledge resources, and leadership coaching. Graham's past roles include executive director of the national nonprofit Idealware, as well as leadership roles in capacity building, arts, human service organizations, and a software startup. She holds a Master of Business Administration in Nonprofit Management from the University of St. Thomas. For more information, visit `http://karengrahamconsulting.com`.

Monique Holt is a deaf theater maker, director, actor, lecturer, assistant professor, and Director of Artistic Sign Language (DASL). She has worked with numerous prestigious organizations, including The Kennedy Center, New York Shakespeare Festival, Wooly Mammoth Theatre, Lincoln Center, Oregon Shakespeare Festival, and Arena Stage. Holt received her Bachelor of Fine Arts in Acting from New York University, and her Master of Fine Arts in Theater from Towson University. She is an assistant professor in the Theatre and Dance Program at Gallaudet University. Holt is a member of the Theatre Communications Group, the Registry of Interpreter for the Deaf (certified deaf interpreter), and the International Shakespeare Association (United Kingdom).

Indiana Repertory Theatre (IRT) is committed to building a vital, vibrant, and informed community through the transformational power of live theater. Founded in 1972, the IRT has grown into one of the leading regional theaters in the United States, as well as one of the top-flight cultural institutions in Indianapolis and Indiana. The IRT produces inclusive, top-quality, professional theater and thoughtful programming to engage, surprise, challenge, and entertain members of the whole community. For more information, visit `http://irtlive.com`.

The Indianapolis Foundation, founded in 1916, is a public charity and an affiliate of Central Indiana Community Foundation (CICF). As Indiana's oldest and largest community foundation, The Indianapolis Foundation aims to mobilize people, ideas, and investments to make this a community where all individuals have equitable opportunity to reach their full potential—no matter place, race, or identity. It awards nearly $7 million to support current and future community needs and is governed by a board of six publicly appointed directors. For more information, visit `http://cicf`

.org/about-cicf/funds-and-foundations/
the-indianapolis-foundation.

Jacob's Pillow is lauded worldwide as a "hub and mecca of dancing" (*Time Magazine*), "one of America's most precious cultural assets" (Mikhail Baryshnikov), and "the dance center of the nation" (*The New York Times*). "The Pillow" is a treasured 220-acre National Historic Landmark, a recipient of the prestigious National Medal of Arts, and home to America's longest-running international dance festival. The mission of The Pillow is to support dance creation, presentation, education, and preservation, and to engage and deepen public appreciation and support for dance. Each year thousands of people from across the United States and around the globe visit the Berkshires of Western Massachusetts to experience the Festival, with more than 50 dance companies and 500 free performances, talks, and events; train at The School at Jacob's Pillow, one of the most prestigious professional dance training centers in the country; explore the Pillow's rare and extensive dance archives; and take part in numerous community programs designed to educate and engage dance audiences of all ages. For more information, visit http://jacobspillow.org.

Rocky Jones is a writer, musician, and video artist, who has spent his life and career committed to the idea that art and artmaking can serve as catalysts for a more inclusive, equitable, and just world. A native of the Washington, DC, area, he is also an innovative marketing and communications professional with nearly 20 years of experience in industries as varied as retail, design, and nonprofit arts administration. Now based in St. Paul, Minnesota, Jones is currently the Director of Equity, Diversity, and Inclusion (EDI) at Minnesota Opera, as well as the chair of the company's EDI Council and the co-host/producer of MN Opera's bi-weekly podcast, *The Score*. In 2020, Jones was a primary author of MN Opera's landmark EDI Charter, a guiding set of principles that explicitly commits the company to bringing its work into alignment with antiracist and anti-oppressive values.

The Kennedy Center presents world-class art by the artists that define our culture today. In 1958, President Dwight D. Eisenhower signed bipartisan legislation creating a National Cultural Center in the nation's capital. In November 1962, President and Mrs. Kennedy launched a $30 million fundraising campaign for the Center's construction. Former President Eisenhower and his wife, Mamie, participated in the event, which demonstrated the bipartisan support for a world-class center for the performing arts in DC. In 1963, President Kennedy signed legislation to extend the fundraising deadline for the Center. Two months after President Kennedy's assassination, the nation's National Cultural Center was designated as a living memorial to President John F. Kennedy by an Act of Congress signed into law by President Lyndon B. Johnson on January 23, 1964. By this act, President Kennedy's devotion to the advancement of the performing arts in the United States was recognized. The Center's mission is established in its authorizing statute: present classical and contemporary music, opera, drama, dance, and other performing arts from the United States and other countries; promote and maintain the John F. Kennedy Center for the Performing Arts as the National Center for the Performing Arts; strive to ensure that the education and outreach programs and policies of the John F. Kennedy Center for the Performing Arts meet the highest level of excellence and reflect the cultural diversity of the United States; provide facilities for other civic activities at the John F. Kennedy Center for the Performing Arts; and provide within the John F. Kennedy Center for the Performing Arts a suitable memorial in honor of the late President. To fulfill the mission as the nation's cultural center, the Kennedy Center presents world-class art by the artists that define our culture today, delivers powerful arts education opportunities nationwide and embodies the ideals of President Kennedy in all the Center's activities provided throughout the living memorial. For more information, visit `http://kennedy-center.org`.

Kate Northfield Lanich is the vice president and general manager at Aspen Music Festival and School. In that capacity, she has transformed the operations of the company into a tech-forward enterprise. A lifelong musician and music manager, Lanich has worked in orchestras throughout her career. Prior to working at the Aspen Music Festival, she served as the orchestra personnel manager at the Juilliard School.

Czerton Lim teaches scenic design and other related topics as an associate professor for the Department of Theatre and Dance at FREDONIA. As a freelance set designer, his work has been seen regionally at Syracuse Stage; The Rev Theatre Company; Hangar Theatre Company; around the country at New York City, DC, Indiana, Michigan, Georgia, Virginia, and Washington, to name a few; and internationally as far as Melbourne, Australia, and Abu Dhabi in the United Arab Emirates. A proud member of USA Local

829, Lim is originally from the Philippines. For more information, visit `http://czlimdesign.com`.

Lincoln Center for the Performing Arts is an arts campus in New York City founded in 1956 that includes the Metropolitan Opera House, David Geffen Hall, the David H. Koch Theater, and the Lincoln Center Theater. Home to 11 resident arts organizations, including New York City Ballet, American Ballet Theatre, and the New York Philharmonic, Lincoln Center presents a tapestry of music, theater, dance, film, and opera. For more information, visit `http://lincolncenter.org`.

Tim Mangini, WGBH senior director of production technology, has been producing television and film projects large and small for over 40 years. Prior to heading up the WGBH Production Group, Mangini worked for 18 years directing the production and post-production of over 350 *FRONTLINE* documentaries. Before joining *FRONTLINE*, he worked domestically and internationally in the film, television, and multimedia industries as a director, producer, cinematographer, and editor. After beginning his career at Hanna-Barbera as a cartoon-character voice editor, Mangini worked for such clients as NASA, National Public Radio (NPR), Raytheon, and MCI. Later, he worked on an award-winning team as a motion picture sound editor and sound effects recordist. His list of film credits include *Pennies From Heaven*, *Under Fire*, *Poltergeist*, *48 Hours*, *Gremlins*, *Star Trek IV*, and the IMAX film *Behold Hawaii*.

Stephanie Martinez is an award-winning, Chicago-based choreographer. She has created over 70 ballets on companies and collegiate programs across the United States, including The Joffrey Ballet, Ballet Hispanico, Luna Negra Dance Theater, Charlotte Ballet, Sacramento Ballet, Bruce Wood Dance, Nashville Ballet, Tulsa Ballet, Kansas City Ballet, BalletX, and Milwaukee Ballet. In 2010, Martinez assisted Broadway legend Ann Reinking in setting the *Fosse Trilogy*, and in 2015 she was awarded The Joffrey Ballet's "Winning Works: Choreographers of Color" commission and the Chicago 3Arts Award in recognition for her work as a female artist of color. Most recently, Martinez choreographed *Carmen* at the Lyric Opera of Chicago and was dubbed "a chameleon" of choreography by *The Chicago Tribune*. Martinez is the founder and artistic director of PARA.MAR Dance Theatre. For more information, visit `http://stephaniemartinezchoreography.com`.

Chris McGinnis is the general manager of Second Stage Theater (2ST) on Broadway, where he recently managed the creative process for the Tony-nominated production of *Between Riverside and Crazy*. Prior to 2ST, he was the general manager at Bucks County Playhouse, which he joined in 2018, following a 10-year career in nonprofit management, directing, and producing in Philadelphia and New York City. He holds a Bachelor's in Theater from DeSales University and a Master's in Arts Management and Executive Leadership from Rider University. McGinnis has worked as an actor, director, and administrator with Walnut Street Theatre, Arden Theater Company, Act 5 Entertainment in San Francisco, the National Constitution Center (where he currently serves as a theater operations consultant), Media Theatre, and Pennsylvania Shakespeare Festival, among others.

Denise McGovern is the vice president of communications and media at the Dallas Symphony Orchestra (DSO). McGovern's role at the DSO encompasses public relations, broadcast media production, organizational relations, and archival planning. Since her arrival, the DSO has seen expansion of media coverage locally, nationally, and internationally, with pieces running in *The New York Times*, *Wall Street Journal*, *Washington Post*, and *Associated Press*. In 2020, McGovern led the establishment of a new broadcast studio in the Morton H. Meyerson Symphony Center. Since its launch, the broadcast team at the DSO has produced over 70 digital concert videos, nine nationally distributed television productions, and countless promotional pieces. Her leadership garnered the DSO its first Daytime Emmy nomination in 2022 for Outstanding Arts and Entertainment Program. McGovern is also in charge of expanding the historical documentation of the Dallas Symphony Orchestra, including the digitization of the performance catalog. McGovern has over 20 years of communications experience in classical music, culture, and the performing arts. Prior to her arrival at the DSO, she led the digital sales team at Universal Classics in New York, the U.S. home of Decca, Deutsche Grammophon, Decca Broadway, and ECM Records. She holds a Bachelor of Music in Flute Performance from Southern Methodist University and a Master of Music in Arts Administration from Indiana University.

Miami City Ballet was founded in 1958 in Miami, Florida, and has been described by *The New York Times* as "an exceptional troupe, by Balanchine standards, anywhere in the world." Miami City

Ballet is led by Artistic Director Lourdes Lopez and is considered a leader in the field, nurturing new choreographic voices, creating innovative collaborations, and opening new avenues of inclusivity within classical ballet. For more information, visit http:// miamicityballet.org.

Minnesota Opera was founded in 1963 with the commission of Minnesota composer Dominick Argento's *The Masque of Angels*, which sparked the creation of a small Twin Cities opera company spotlighting the rare and avant-garde. Over 55 years later, Minnesota Opera is a leading American company, admired as an innovative creator of compelling opera productions, programs, and new works. For more information, visit http://mnopera.org.

Jane Monheit is a jazz and adult contemporary vocalist with a deep passion for the Great American Songbook. With many highly acclaimed solo albums, countless awards and accolades, and over two decades of international touring experience, Monheit has not only been an extremely successful bandleader, but has had the privilege of making music with some of the greatest musicians, arrangers, and producers in jazz. Monheit has continued to tour the world nearly nonstop, including playing iconic venues such as Carnegie Hall and The Hollywood Bowl, and headlining at nearly every legendary jazz club on the planet, most notably New York City stalwarts such as the Village Vanguard and Birdland. In addition to touring, she writes English lyrics for Ivan Lins and uses the knowledge and experience she has gained both at Manhattan School of Music and on the legendary bandstands of the world to educate and uplift students worldwide. Monheit resides in Los Angeles with her husband of over 20 years, drummer Rick Montalbano, and their son. For more information, visit http://janemonheitonline.com.

Matt Morgan has 30 years of experience in technology, about half in web/digital and half in nuts-and-bolts information technology. His career includes leadership roles in several major cultural and educational institutions, such as the Brooklyn Museum, The Metropolitan Museum of Art, the New York Public Library, and the Curtis Institute of Music. At times since 2005, he has done strategic technology consulting work for over a dozen clients, including startup nonprofits and small businesses, and is now devoted exclusively to Concrete Computing. For more information, visit http:// concretecomputing.com.

Music Not Impossible is an immersive sensory experience inspired by the Deaf or Hard of Hearing (HOH) Community and goes beyond accessibility to radical inclusivity. It is the evolution of "The Art of Haptics" that uses the sense of touch to convey emotions and artistic expression. Music Not Impossible has also developed a complete platform for composing and sending vibrations wirelessly to the users' bodies with very low latency. For more information, visit http://notimpossible.com/music-not-impossible.

Nina Yoshida Nelsen, mezzo soprano, is an avid advocate for equity in the arts. She is perhaps most well known for her countless performances of Suzuki in *Madama Butterfly* with opera companies throughout North America and Europe. Also well known for her work in contemporary opera, Nelsen has sung in seven world premieres as well as their subsequent productions. Equally at home on the concert stage, she has performed in world-class halls, including Carnegie, Avery Fisher, and Royal Albert. Nelsen is the Artistic Advisor at Boston Lyric Opera and serves as president of the Asian Opera Alliance, an organization of which she is a co-founder. For more information, visit http://ninayoshidanelsen.com.

The New York Philharmonic is a symphony orchestra with its home at Lincoln Center for the Performing Arts in New York City. The organization has been at the forefront of every technological innovation, beginning with the first music recordings in 1917. Founded in 1842, they are the oldest major symphony orchestra in the United States and are consistently ranked as one of the top five orchestras in the world. For more information, visit http://nyphil.org.

Andrea Newby joined TheatreSquared in 2020 and became the director of marketing and communications in 2022. Since 2005, she has developed data-driven, patron-centric marketing, ticketing, and fundraising strategies to deepen the relationship between audience members and arts organizations—contributing to efforts that help to exceed overall revenue and retention goals, while increasing patron engagement and satisfaction. Newby holds a Master of Arts in Theatre from Louisiana Tech University and a Bachelor of Arts from Northeastern State University.

Julii Oh is an innovative senior marketing executive with a demonstrated track record of consistently delivering elevated and record-high results. She is an expert in brand strategy, integrated marketing, and sales strategy, with a keen eye for impactful implementation details. Oh offers a consultative focus in audience growth, revenue management, resource management, strategic marketing, brand strategy, and customer experience. She has years of experience with the New York Philharmonic and Miami City Ballet, and she is currently the principal strategist and chief marketing officer for San Francisco Ballet Company, The Cleveland Orchestra, and Detroit Symphony Orchestra. For more information, visit `http://linkedin.com/in/juliioh`.

Pacific Northwest Ballet, one of the largest and most highly regarded ballet companies in the United States, was founded in 1972. In July 2005, Peter Boal became artistic director, succeeding Kent Stowell and Francia Russell, artistic directors since 1977. The company of nearly 50 dancers presents more than 100 performances each year of full-length and mixed repertory ballets at Marion Oliver McCaw Hall in Seattle, Washington, and on tour. The company has toured in Europe, Australia, Taiwan, Hong Kong, Canada, and throughout the United States, with celebrated appearances at Jacob's Pillow and in New York City and Washington, DC. For more information, visit `http://pnb.org`.

Scott Penner is a Canadian-born set and costume designer based in Brooklyn, New York, and Hamilton, Ontario, Canada. Penner's approach to designing theater is passionate and fearless; his work explores how mass, shape, and form react and connect with the body in space. His work has been seen at the Prague Quadrennial, The Stratford Shakespeare Festival, Northlight Theatre, Shattered Globe Theatre, Aboutface Theatre (Chicago), The Grand Theatre (London), The Sudbury Theatre Centre, The Watermark Theatre (Prince Edward Island), The Globe Theatre (Regina), Buddies in Bad Times, Angelwalk Theatre (Toronto), and The Winnipeg Studio Theatre. His work includes design in classical theater, new and modern plays, musical theater, and dance. In television, Penner has served as an assistant costume designer for HBO Max's *Station Eleven* and Apple TV's *Five Days at Memorial*. He has a Master of Fine Arts from Northwestern University. For more information, visit `http://scottpennerdesign.ca`.

People's Light, a cultural and civic center with theater at its core, invites and creates opportunities for diverse communities to discover and celebrate our shared humanity. Founded in 1974, People's Light serves as one of Pennsylvania's largest professional nonprofit theaters, known for its resident company of artists, eclectic mix of productions, and innovative work with young people. In their 8–9-play season, they present stories drawn from ancient times through tomorrow that have direct relevance to its communities and their concerns. In support of this range, People's Light produces classics, contemporary plays, and commission and produces new work; of its 452 productions, over a third (171) have been world or regional premieres. For more information, visit `http://peopleslight.org`.

Sartje Pickett works as a freelance composer and sound designer in theaters across the United States, including Guthrie Theater, American Players Theatre, Yale Repertory Theatre, Oregon Shakespeare Festival, Folger Theatre, and Quantum Theatre. She also creates experimental sound design for installations, including with Bricolage Productions and Hypergraphica Productions. For more information, visit `http://sarahpickett.com`.

Pittsburgh Ballet Theatre (PBT) is one of the most exciting ballet companies in the United States and has built a legacy of excellence and innovation since 1969. The company's eclectic style and irrepressible energy have been shaped by a series of distinguished artistic directors over five decades. PBT has evolved into a critically acclaimed company with international reach. Today, the company ranks among the largest performing arts organizations in Pittsburgh and is home to 31 full-time dancers, who come from 12 states and six countries to live and perform in Pittsburgh. Sharing the same studio space, PBT School cultivates the next generation of professional dancers, who come from around the country—and the world—to train with PBT. Together with the celebrated PBT Orchestra under Maestro Charles Barker, PBT encompasses a rich family of dancers and musicians. Through more than 50 performances each year at home and on tour, PBT stays true to the vision of its founders—to be Pittsburgh's source and ambassador for extraordinary ballet experiences. For more information, visit `http://pbt.org`.

The Pittsburgh Cultural Trust, a nonprofit arts organization, has worked since 1984 to make the Steel City a place where the arts can flourish. Its efforts have focused on the cultural and economic development of the Cultural District, a 14-square-block area of downtown Pittsburgh. What was once a downtrodden red-light district now thrives as a vibrant center for culture, art, food, and community. Pittsburgh's Cultural District stands as a nationwide model for how the arts can play a pivotal role in urban revitalization.

Each year, millions of people visit the Cultural District to expand their horizons in its theaters, galleries, and public art environments. Patrons enjoy thousands of world-class performing arts events and visual arts exhibitions. Pittsburgh residents of all ages connect and learn with the Trust's comprehensive education and community engagement opportunities. Local arts organizations collaborate to build a stronger cultural community through the power of partnerships. The Cultural District acts as the anchor for all of that work. The Trust's superior venues and gallery spaces allow resident companies, community organizations, artists, and promoters to reach audiences large and small. In total, the Pittsburgh Cultural Trust manages more than one million square feet of real estate in the District. Step outside those buildings to find numerous public art installations that beautify Pittsburgh's largest arts neighborhood. Lauded as "the single greatest creative force in Pittsburgh because of its spirit of reinvention" by the *Pittsburgh Post Gazette*, the Trust strives every day to enrich the city of Pittsburgh's vibrancy, diversity, and prosperity. For more information, visit http://trustarts.org.

Matthew Principe is the director of live streams and artistic planning for Boston Baroque and, in partnership with WGBH Studios and IDAGIO, directs the live performance broadcasts of programs seen in six continents and over 60 countries. He also holds the position of director of innovation at Detroit Opera, where he works closely on digital media and innovative storytelling with artistic director Yuval Sharon. During the recent season, Principe oversaw the rebranding and naming of this institution from Michigan Opera Theatre, and the company experienced unprecedented new audience growth and highest attendance of opera and dance performances in 10 years. Prior, Principe was the line producer of the Metropolitan Opera's Grammy, Emmy, and Peabody Award–winning *Live in HD* series, which transmits live opera performances to movie theaters in 70 countries around the world, and associate producer of the Metropolitan Opera Radio Broadcasts on SIRIUS/XM Satellite Radio, broadcasting over 1,000 live broadcasts throughout North America as well as via the Met's website.

PXT Studio was started by Jason H. Thompson and Kaitlyn Pietras, husband and wife designers living in Los Angeles, California. They created PXT Studio out of a shared love for fusing art and technology and pushing the boundaries of what is possible in the world of storytelling. Together they share over 30 years of experience covering a wide variety of industries with their craft, including theater, opera, dance, museums, theme parks, corporate, and immersive environments. They have designed for major companies and theaters all over the world, including The Industry, Vienna State Opera, Oper Frankfurt, Walt Disney Creative Entertainment, Center Theatre Group, Lyric Opera of Chicago, LA Philharmonic, Oregon Shakespeare Festival, Carnegie Hall, The Cleveland Orchestra, San Francisco Symphony, New World Orchestra, The Public Theatre, Broadway, The Guthrie Theatre, Kansas City Rep, South Coast Rep, The Geffen Playhouse, Pasadena Playhouse, Artists Repertory Theatre, Rattlestick Playwrights Theatre, and Ars Nova. Collectively they have won two Los Angeles Ovation Awards and four Los Angeles Drama Critics Circle Awards, as well as having work showcased at the Prague Quadrennial in 2011, 2015, and 2019. For more information, visit `http://pxtstudio.com`.

Quantum Theatre is a kind of laboratory—an incubator for the amazing, christened in 1990, rededicated each year with the rites of spring to its mission to bring forth artists forging new theatrical ground. They are playwrights, directors, actors, influencers. They come from Pittsburgh, from around the country, and from around the world. Productions are staged environmentally in places that aren't theaters. Quantum's artists mine all kinds of nontraditional spaces for the sensory possibilities they offer when combined with creative design. They find it meaningful to place the audience and performers together, the moving parts inside the works. For more information, visit `http://quantumtheatre.com`.

Savannah Philharmonic is a community-focused arts organization that works to present exceptional concert programming and music education offerings of the highest caliber throughout Savannah, Georgia, and the southeast region. They remain dedicated to fostering community and inspiring a true appreciation of music through equitable access to performances and education programs—and ensuring there is "something for everyone" to enjoy. For more information, visit `http://savannahphilharmonic.org`.

Second Stage Theater was founded in 1979 in New York City to create and champion plays and musicals solely from living American writers. On its mainstage Broadway theater, the Hayes, and in its two Off-Broadway theaters over the past 45 years, Second Stage has developed and presented over 200 daring and provocative theatrical experiences by working with countless artists who have contributed their talents to its award-winning productions. As the only Broadway nonprofit company exclusively devoted to living American writers, Second Stage is dedicated to introducing the world to bold and diverse voices of American creativity. For more information, visit https://2st.com.

SFJAZZ is among the world's largest nonprofit jazz presenters. Located in San Francisco, California, the organization was founded in 1983 as a two-day festival. Today, SFJAZZ serves over a quarter of a million fans and students annually through year-round concerts, commissions, education programs, and now a digital platform called SFJAZZ at Home. For more information, visit https://sfjazz.org.

Lawrence Shea is an artist working with film, video, and interactive digital media. His work ranges from short experimental videos to video installation/interactive environments and recently, kinetic sculpture. He has exhibited his work at national and international venues, including The Mix Festival in New York; MIX Brazil; Outfest LA; The British Film Institute, London; and the Ars Electronica Festival, Lintz, Austria, as well as on cable and the Internet. Shea collaborates frequently with other artists on a range of projects, from theatrical visuals to museum exhibitions and large-scale public works of art. He created stage effects and environments for several of Mike Albo's monologue performances at PS 122 and HERE Arts Center, New York. Shea worked with artist Julia Scher for many years on her surveillance-art installations, including *Securityworld* (1996 at Galerie Hussenot, Paris); *Wonderland* (1998 Andrea Rosen Gallery, New York, and several European venues); and *Predictive Engineering 2* (1999 at San Francisco Museum of Modern Art). He was technical designer for Mary Ellen Strom and Ann Carlson's large-scale outdoor video projection and performance extravaganza *Geyserland*, taking place on an observation-car train trip from Bozeman to Livingston, Montana, in 2003 (www.1shea.org/geyserland.htm). Shea holds a Master of Fine Arts from The Massachusetts College of Art and a Bachelor of Arts from the University of Virginia, and has taught video production and installation art at The New School for Social Research, New York; The Pratt Institute, Brooklyn, New York; and Film Video Arts, New York. From 2000 to 2004 he was a full-time Visiting Artist at the School of the Museum of Fine Arts, Boston. From 2003 to 2005, he was executive director of the Internationally acclaimed MIX: The New York

Lesbian and Gay Experimental Film/Video Festival in New York. His work can be seen at www.lshea.org.

Gabryel Smith is director of archives and exhibitions for the New York Philharmonic. Since 2009 he has curated over 40 digital and physical exhibits for the Orchestra at David Geffen Hall, including touring exhibits to the Vienna Haus der Musik; the Austrian Cultural forums in New York and Washington, DC; and the New York Historical Society. Smith has lectured about the New York Philharmonic's history for audiences at Oxford, Princeton, Juilliard, New York University, and around Lincoln Center as well as at conferences such as the Society of American Archivists. He has written articles for Sony Masterworks; WQXR; *Playbill* magazine; and *The Swiss Journal of Musicology, Prelude, Fugue, & Riffs,* and he regularly contributes to the Philharmonic's weekly programs. In fall 2021 he joined the Juilliard Extension School faculty, teaching a course on Gustav Mahler's New York City.

Melissa Smith is the vice president of marketing at DipJar, where she is responsible for building the company's public outreach and brand relationships, including overseeing a growing social presence and sales partnership profile. She has worked extensively with local nonprofit businesses in the Pittsburgh area, including Humane Animal Rescue, where she led marketing programs to promote animal adoption. Through her work, Smith has gained extensive knowledge of the nonprofit sector, experience that enables her to understand DipJar customers and their needs. Smith is an avid animal lover with three cats of her own and a revolving door of fosters. Her passion for animals has driven her to spend her free time serving on the board for Biggies Bullies, a foster home–based dog rescue in Pittsburgh.

James Still is an American writer and playwright. Still grew up in a small town in Kansas and graduated from the University of Kansas. His plays have been developed at the New Harmony Project, the O'Neill Conference, Sundance, Seven Devils, the Colorado New Play Summit, Launch Pad, and many others, and have been produced throughout the United States, Canada, Europe, Japan, China, Australia, and South Africa. He is a four-time Pulitzer nominee for his work in the theater and a five-time nominee for his work in television. Still is the playwright in residence at Indiana Repertory Theatre, the artistic affiliate at American Blues in Chicago, and lives in Los Angeles, California. For more information, visit http://linkedin.com/in/james-still-7b636254.

Brandon Stirling Baker is an award-winning lighting designer, working internationally in the areas of dance, opera, and theater. His work can be seen on stages throughout the United States and abroad, including Lincoln Center, Kennedy Center, Hollywood Bowl, Walt Disney Concert Hall, New York City Ballet, San Francisco Ballet, Australian Ballet, Hong Kong Ballet, American Ballet Theater, Opera Philadelphia, Alvin Ailey American Dance Theater, Miami City Ballet, Boston Ballet, Joffrey Ballet, Houston Ballet, Pacific Northwest Ballet, Dutch National Ballet, Semperoper Dresden, Staatsballett Berlin, and many others. Since 2010, Baker has designed over 30 world premieres for choreographer Justin Peck. Additional collaborations include new works by Savion Glover, Sufjan Stevens, William Forsythe, Jamar Roberts, Lauren Lovette, Anthony Roth Costanzo, and many others. Baker was appointed lighting director of Boston Ballet in 2018 and is a recipient of the Knight of Illumination Award for his work in dance. For more information, visit http://stirlingbaker.com.

Nathan Stuber is a scenic designer and the properties director at American Players Theatre. His designs include *Born Yesterday, Endgame, The Two Gentlemen of Verona, Game of Love and Chance, Waiting for Godot, Crime and Punishment,* and *The Syringa Tree,* among others. Disclosing nontheatrical endeavors here would just confirm his deep-seated belief that he is a boring human. He wishes you could enjoy the idea of a nap that never comes as much as he does. "Thank you for supporting the arts and do yourself and everyone a favor by taking the long way back to your car if you have the time."

Price Suddarth is an award-winning American choreographer/dancer currently based out of Seattle, Washington. Suddarth received his early dance education first from the Central Indiana Dance Ensemble, followed by the School of American Ballet, and finally on a scholarship with the Pacific Northwest Ballet School where, upon graduation, he was offered a contract with Pacific Northwest Ballet. In 2018 Suddarth was promoted to the rank of soloist with the company. In 2011, he was nominated for a Princess Grace Award in dance, and in 2012, he was chosen as one of *Dance Magazine*'s Top 25 to watch. Since joining the company, Suddarth has originated leading roles in works by choreographers such as Marco Goecke,

Victor Quijada, and Twyla Tharp. Additionally, he has performed featured and leading roles in works by William Forsythe, Crystal Pite, Annabelle Lopez Ochoa, Alejandro Cerrudo, Justin Peck, Mark Morris, Jessica Lang, Christopher Wheeldon, Kent Stowell, Jerome Robbins, and George Balanchine. For more information, visit `http://pricesuddarth.com`.

Syracuse Stage is Central New York State's premier professional theater. Founded in 1974, they have produced a number of world, U.S., and East Coast premieres. Each season 70,000 patrons enjoy an adventurous mix of new plays and bold interpretations of classics and musicals featuring the finest theater artists. In addition, Syracuse Stage maintains a vital educational outreach program that annually serves over 30,000 students. For more information, visit `http://syracusestage.org`.

TheatreSquared offers bold new plays in an intimate setting, driving its growth to become Arkansas's largest theater, welcoming more than 80,000 community members to 350 performances and events each year. The company, located in Northwest Arkansas, offers a unique audience experience of immersive, professional productions in an intimate setting. Its pioneering work has been recognized with the 2022 Obie Award as well as critical acclaim from *The New York Times* ("Best Theater of 2020" list), *The New Yorker*, *The Wall Street Journal*, NPR's *All Things Considered*, and the American Theater Wing, founder of the Tony Awards. TheatreSquared's remarkable expansion—with a 20-fold increase in audience in just the past decade—parallels the emergence of its home region in the northwest corner of Arkansas as a booming population center and destination for American art. Since its founding in 2005, TheatreSquared's work has remained rooted in its founding vision, that "theater—done well and with passion—can transform lives and communities." For more information, visit `http://theatre2.org`.

Dane Toney holds a Bachelor of Fine Arts in Dance from Point Park University in Pittsburgh, Pennsylvania, and was a company dancer with Attack Theatre for 13 seasons before transitioning to their technology and creative productions manager. He trained intensively with Toneta Akers-Toler, founder and artistic director of the West Virginia Dance Company (WVDC), and has spent 18 seasons with Theatre West Virginia's Outdoor Drama Company. Toney has performed as a guest artist with the Liz Lerman Dance Exchange and Trillium Performing Arts Collective. Toney is a recipient of the

2017 BRAZZY Award, which recognizes two exceptional Pittsburgh dancers each year in honor of Leslie Anderson-Braswell. Toney moved back to West Virginia in 2021, where he raises goats and chickens on a farm. He is a choreographer and guest artist with WVDC, a freelance video editor, graphic designer, and a remote pilot.

Eve Trojanov is a versatile professional in the performing arts, with nearly a decade of dedicated service at People's Light. She has assumed various roles within the organization, spanning from dramaturgy, front of house, and box office to marketing. Notably, she briefly took on the role of interim events coordinator at The Farmhouse, a for-profit venture of People's Light. In her present capacity as the director of patron engagement, Trojanov oversees the box office, front of house, group sales, and telesales. One of her notable achievements is the establishment and expansion of an apprenticeship program, benefiting individuals throughout the organization. Prior to her tenure at People's Light, Trojanov honed her skills in advertising at Comcast. With dual bachelor's degrees in writing and photography, Trojanov brings a unique blend of creative and strategic skills to her role. She is deeply committed to fostering stronger bonds between People's Light and the broader community. Particularly, her focus is on reestablishing connections with subscribers, patrons, and volunteers post-pandemic and ensuring an inclusive, inviting environment for all audiences.

Michael Troutman is a father of three children, and he is currently marketing and communications director for People's Light as well as operations and communications manager for RadioPushers. He attained career mentorship, curriculum development, and nonprofit management experience, formerly working with Spectrum Health Services in Philadelphia and Junior Achievement NJ. Troutman concurrently worked as a broadcast producer and editor for Viacom subsidiaries Black Entertainment Television (BET) and MTV Networks. He obtained his Master of Business Administration from Keller School of Management through Devry University and is a graduate of Brown University with a double major, Bachelor of Arts in Economics and Bachelor of Arts in Visual Arts.

Stewart Urist currently serves as director of finance and administration at Pittsburgh Public Theater, where he oversees all aspects of the nearly $8 million–dollar company's budgeting, financial management, and accounting processes. Previously he served as executive director of Pittsburgh's site-specific Quantum Theater, which broke company records in earned and contributed revenue under his leadership. He has also worked at Ford's Theater Society in Washington, DC, and Broadway.com in New York. Urist is a strategically minded leader specializing in driving efficiency through savvy use of technological tools and creating efficient processes that can drive data-informed decision-making. He is a graduate of Kenyon College and Carnegie Mellon's Master of Arts Management program.

WGBH, branded on-air as GBH or GBH 2 since 2020, is the primary PBS member television station in Boston, Massachusetts. The organization is America's preeminent public broadcaster and the largest producer of PBS content for TV and the web, including *Masterpiece*, *Antiques Roadshow*, *NOVA*, *FRONTLINE*, and *This Old House*. By partnering with local and national organizations, WGBH provides audiences with direct access to the stories that enrich their world.

Katina P White is the Tessitura Support Administrator for the Pittsburgh Cultural Trust. She has a Bachelor of Arts in Theater from the University of Florida and a Master of Arts Management from Carnegie Mellon University. She has a passion for the performing arts and is obsessed with data. As a fan of well-told stories, in her spare time White enjoys many forms of media—from film to video games to podcasts—in her search for the next captivating tale. She calls Pittsburgh home with her husband, David, and her cat.

Amy Williams, DMA, is the executive director of the Savannah Philharmonic (SavPhil). Over the past three years, she has ambitiously and successfully built upon the Philharmonic's artistic excellence and significantly expanded its community impact, alongside Music and Artistic Director Keitaro Harada and the board of directors. Williams is a true bridge-builder in connecting an organization's internal community to that in which it lives, and has striven to be a leader in this capacity throughout her career. Prior to leading the SavPhil, Williams served as managing director at Camerata Pacifica, where she put in place the building blocks needed to create long-term sustainability. She also held the role of director of artistic administration and education at the Santa Barbara Symphony and began her arts administration path with the Los Angeles Chamber Orchestra. A classically trained bassoonist, Williams received her Bachelor of Music from Ithaca College; her Master of Music from University of Nevada, Las Vegas; and her Doctor of Musical Arts degree from Ohio State University.

She is a past board member of the Association of California Symphony Orchestras and has served on multiple committees over the years. Williams is both delighted and honored to be serving the Savannah community through her leadership of the Philharmonic and enjoys discovering all its vibrant region has to offer together with her husband, Paul.

Christine Wingenfeld began her journey into data analysis for the arts as an intern with Pittsburgh Ballet Theatre, where she then was hired as the External Affairs Analyst. She has a Master of Arts Management from Carnegie Mellon University and a Bachelor's degree in Business Administration from Duquesne University. Currently Wingenfeld is the partnership manager and data analyst for the Pittsburgh Cultural Trust, where she works to support the consortium of arts organizations.

Eric Winterling received his Master of Fine Arts in Fine Arts from Temple University and began his career as the resident costume designer for Houston Grand Opera (HGO). During his tenure with HGO, Winterling realized that his greatest interest was the keen and astute interpretation of design renderings. This discovery focused his career trajectory on costume construction. After moving to New York City, and following a couple of valuable stints in other shops, Winterling was able to realize his dream of opening his own studio. Eric Wintering, Inc. is one of New York City's premier custom costume studios. Working together with costume designers, the shop transforms their visions into one-of-a-kind costumes for stage and screen. For more information, visit `http://ericwinterlinginc.com`.

Acknowledgments

We are deeply grateful to all those who supported us throughout the process of researching and writing this book. You kept us moving forward with every encounter, as everyone shared our passion and enthusiasm for the work.

Thank you to those who shared their thoughts about our book focus and strategies as we began our research, including Tania Castroverde Moskalenko, Grant Palmer, Bradley Reynolds, Elizabeth Arnett, Michelle Paul, and Kevin O'Hora.

This book would not be possible without the generosity of the many interviewees who shared their time, wisdom, and experience. We were inspired by you throughout our journey, and we know our readers will be, too. We cannot thank you enough.

Our work was supported and improved by all those who provided feedback and support during the writing and editing process. A special thank you to Jessica Bowser Acrie, Dr. Dareen Basma, Dr. Anne Berkeley, Dr. Dan Green, Elizabeth Forrey, Maraika Lumbholdt, Lutie Rodriguez, Samantha Sonnet, Stewart Urist, and Christine Wingenfeld.

We could not have completed the book without the support of the Wiley Publishing team. Thank you to Dabian Witherspoon, Moses Ashirvad, Saravanan Dakshinamurthy, and the editorial, production, marketing, and sales teams. And special thanks to Wiley Senior Editor Kenyon Brown. Without his guidance and vision, this book would never have happened.

We are grateful to our family and friends who supported and stayed with us throughout the process. And to Brenda Johnston, who introduced us. A monumental thank-you to Sandy Murphy for her patience, love, and support while writing this book.

In gratitude, we know it takes a village to transform our worlds. We are genuinely in awe and humbled by the opportunity to work with and learn from all those acknowledged.

About the Authors

One of the best parts of writing this book for us was getting to know each other. Our paths did not cross naturally, and we owe a trove of gratitude to Brenda Johnston, who introduced us once she heard about Paul's idea. In addition to having a shared passion for the performing arts and careers engaging with management and production technologies, we quickly discovered we had a lot of other things in common. For one, we both have dogs. But more importantly, we work well together. An additional bonus was that while our experience with technology in the workplace was similar enough, we had expertise in very different areas that allowed us to offer significant breadth in the book. Brett had implemented new technology systems, from CRMs to moving an organization to the cloud and structuring new knowledge and communication systems. Paul's expertise in marketing offered expertise in branding, and his experience in touring expanded that area even further. Hence, we wrote the book together but often took the lead where our expertise allowed.

Brett Ashley Crawford, PhD teaches arts and entertainment management at Carnegie Mellon University in Pittsburgh, Pennsylvania, and leads a research center, the Arts Management and Technology Laboratory. She started the platform because of a need for more materials available to the performing arts industry. She learned about success stories and compiled data and resources about exciting emerging technology through her research. Before her time at CMU, she was a tech-forward manager.

As a box office manager in the 1990s, she helped move organizations from spreadsheets to databases. As a graduate student, she earned extra money coding HTML for small organizations as they mastered the Internet. As a managing director, she transitioned her theaters to robust technology systems. The power of technology and data to improve the reach and impact of performing arts organizations was undeniable.

Paul Hansen lives in Indianapolis, Indiana, and was working in arts administration for a dance company, performing as an actor, and teaching at Butler University. As marketing director for Dance Kaleidoscope for nearly 12 years and as a department of one, to quote Blanche Dubois from *A Streetcar Named Desire*, Paul relied on the kindness of strangers to help guide him with numerous tactical uses of technology. With limited resources and reacting to ever-changing algorithms and best practices, Paul reached out to form a cohort of other arts leaders for brainstorming (and shared moral support). Before that, Paul's decades of work as a professional actor/dancer based in New York City taught him much about using technology to further the business of being a performing artist.

Index

3D printing, Raise3D Professional
Desktop 3D printer, 97–99
59 Productions, 203

A
Adobe Animate, 176
Adobe Creative Cloud, 126, 144
Adobe Premiere Pro, 176, 201
AI (artificial intelligence)
branding and, 126–127
ChatGPT, 82, 90
CRMs and, 46–48
Descript, 201
LLMs (large language models), 81–82
video design, 106–108
AIDA (Awareness, Interest, Desire, and
Action), 62
Airtable, 14, 15–17, 24, 57, 65
AJA Helo, 176
AJA Ki Pro GO Streaming Camera, 176
Alliance Theatre, 203–204
Alvin Ailey American Dance Theater
(AAADT), 204
touring and, 171–174
Amazon Web Services (AWS), 112
American Players Theatre (APT), 204
Anatomy of Work study (Asana), 13–14
Archtics, 34–35, 57
Argüello, Malia, 204
ArtsVision, 17–20, 24
Asana, 15, 24

ASIMUT, 57
Aspen Music Festival and School (AMFS),
17–20, 205
Attack Theatre, 6–7, 205
Airtable, 14
LGL (Little Green Light), 31
Slack, 10–11
Audience View, 145
augmented reality (AR), 112
authentication, two-factor, 45
automation, 47–48
communication, 60–62
Google Analytics, 67–68
marketing, 60–62
Prospect2, 67–68
TheatreSquared, 67–68

B
B2B (business-to-business),
communications, 8
Baker, Brandon Stirling, 225
Ballet RI, 205
Belquer, Daniel, 205–206
Bergauer, Aubrey, 206
Black Ensemble Theater, 206
email, 74
video, 71
Blackbaud, 56–57
Blackmagic Camera, 176
Blackmagic Design ATEM Mini HDMI
Live Stream Switcher, 201

Boston Baroque, 206–207
branding
  Adobe Creative Cloud, 126
  AI and, 126–127
  brand protection, 126–127
  Canva, 126
  Gravit Designer, 126
  Sketch, 126
  social media and, 128–134
  style guide, 127
  technologies, 125–126
Brightcove, 175

C

Canva, 126, 144
Captivate.fm, 201
casting, 123
  Google Jamboard, 119
  Still, James, 118–119
CCPA (California Consumer Privacy Act), 44
CDP (customer data profile), 28
  CRM design, 48–49
Chan, Chun Wai, 131–132, 207
change management, 3
ChatGPT, 82, 90
Cinema 4D, 108–109
CMS (customer relationship management
    system), 27, 91
codification strategies, 4–7
Cohen, Emmet, 72, 75, 208
collaborative work
  email and, 9
  Slack, 9–12
Color Oracle, 202
Colorblind Web Page Filter, 202
Combes, Kathleen Breen, 208
communication, 60–62
  email, 74–75
    as disruption, 9
  internal, 8–13
  social media, 71–74
  video, 70–71
  websites, 69–70
Cortex, 175
costume design
  Penner, Scott, 101–102
  Winterling, Eric, 99–101
COVID-19 pandemic, 3
CPRA (California Privacy Rights Act), 44
CRM (customer relationship
    management), 27
  AI (artificial intelligence) and, 46–48
  Attack Theatre, 31

data cleaning, 34
  designing, 48–49
  inputs, 33
  installation preparations, 55–56
  integrating systems and, 33–34
  LDL (Little Green Light), 31
  Melissa and, 35
  needs assessment, 50–51
  onboarding, 40–43
  outputs, 33
  price considerations, 53–54
  security, 53
  Survey of Ticketing Software, 50
  system structure, 30–31
  training, 40–43
  vendors, 51–53
customer journey, 62–68
customer tracking, 27–29. *See also* CDP
    (customer data profile); CMS
    (customer relationship management
    system); CRM (customer relationship
    management)

D

D+A (diversity and accessibility),
    179–181
  artists with disabilities, 186–188
  hearing impaired audiences,
    181–186
  human resources and, 193–194
  marketing and, 193–194
  podcasts
    Green Room Meditations, 192–193
    The Score, 188–190
  streaming, *Live from Emmet's Place,*
    190–192
  training and, 194–199
  vision impaired audiences, 181–186
Dallas Symphony Orchestra, 208
Dance Studio Manager, 145
dashboard analysis, 37–39
data analytics
  dashboard analysis and, 37–39
  for marketing, 90
  planning and, 36–39
  projections, 39–40
  strategy and, 36–39
data collection
  CDP, 28
  CMS, 27
  CRMs, 27, 33–36
DaVinci Resolve, 175
DAW (digital audio workstation), 116

de la Reza, Michele, 31–32, 209
Descript, 201
Detroit Opera, 209
digital content, 147
  Boston Baroque, 154–156
  Dallas Symphony Orchestra (DSO),
    160–162
  Jacobs Pillow, 148–150
  NY Phil (New York Philharmonic),
    150–152
  Second Stage Theater, 153–154
  SFJAZZ, 156–160
directing, 123
  Still, James, 118–119
Disguise Media Server, 110
DJI Spark Drone, 176
documentation, Guru, 41
donations, 83
  DipJar, 84–86
  NFTs (non-fungible tokens), 87–88
  QR codes, 86–87
Drive, 24

E
education, 162–171
Egnyte, 6–7, 23
email
  as disruption, 9
  marketing and communication,
    74–75
  solutions, 90
Eos (Electronic Theatre Control), 104
Escalante, Juan José, 209
Ezold, Erica, 210
  data for projection, 39–40

F
Ferry, Larae J., 210–211
Fine, Jared, 210
FreeSpeak network, 116–117

G
GalaPro, 201
GapJumpers, 202
GDPR (General Data Protection
  Regulation), 43–44
Gender Decoder, 202
Giles, Dylan, 211
Gilmore, Justin, 30, 211
Ginn, Devon, 211
Google Alerts, 144
Google Analytics, 67–68

Google Jamboard, 119
GPT (Generative Pre-trained
  Transformer), 201
Graham, Karen, 212
Gravit Designer, 126, 144
Guru, 41, 57

H
Helix network, 116–117
Holt, Monique, 212
hybrid work, 3

I
iCal, ArtsVision and, 19
IDAGIO, 175
Indiana Repertory Theatre (IRT), 212
  lighting design, 104–105
  set design, 94–96
  sound design, 114–115
internal communications, 8–13
  Matter Most, 24
  Slack, 24
  Yammer, 24

J
Jacob's Pillow, 213
Jones, Rocky, 213
JotForm, 176

K
KnowBe4, 45, 57
knowledge management, 4
  codification, 5
  Drive, 24
  Egnyte, 23

L
ladder of engagement, 27, 28
Lanich, Kate, Northfield, 214
laser cutting, costume design,
  101–102
LastPass, 45
LED light, video design, 103–105, 107
legal compliance
  CCPA (California Consumer Privacy
    Act), 44
  CPRA (California Privacy Rights
    Act), 44
  GDPR (General Data Protection
    Regulation), 43–44
  PCI (payment card industry), 43
Libsyn, 201

lighting design, 120–121
  Baker, Brandon Stirling, 102–104
  Boston Ballet, 102–104
  Electronic Theatre Control Eos, 104
  Indiana Repertory Theatre (IR),
    104–105
  LED light, 103–105, 107
  OLED (organic light-emitting diode), 111
  Peck, Justin, 102–104
Lightwright, 176
Lim, Czerton, 215
Lincoln Center for the Performing Arts, 214
Little Green Light, 57
Long Haul Audience Development Model,
  63

M
Mangini, Tim, 215
marketing, 60–62
  AIDA (Awareness, Interest, Desire,
    and Action), 62
  D+A and, 193–194
  data analytics, 90
  email, 74–75
  social media, 71–74
  teams, 68–75
  video, 70–71
  websites, 69–70
Martinez, Stephanie, 133–134, 215
Matter Most, 24
McGinnis, Chris, 216
McGovern, Denise, 216
Melissa, CRMs and, 35
mentorship, 162–171
Miami City Ballet, 216–217
Microsoft Teams, 176
Minnesota Opera, 217
Monheit, Jane, 128–130, 217
Morgan, Matt, 30, 217
music composition. See sound design
Music Not Impossible, 218

N
NCOA (national change of address), 34
Nelsen, Nina Yoshida, 132–133, 218
Newby, Andrea, 34–35, 218
North Carolina Symphony, 34

O
Oh, Julii, 140–142, 218–219
onboarding, CRMs, 40–43
Open Broadcaster Software
  (OBS), 201

P
Pacific Northwest Ballet (PNB), 164–168,
  219
PARA.MAR Dance, social media, 74
passwords, LastPass, 45
Patreon, 81
PCI (payment card industry)
  compliance, 43
Penner, Scott, 219
People's Light Theatre, 35–36, 39, 219–220
  email, 74–75
  social media, 72–73
  website, 69–70
personalization strategy, 4
Pickett, Sartje, 220
Pittsburgh Ballet Theatre (PBT), 220
Pittsburgh Cultural Trust, Tessitura, 32
playwriting, 123
  Still, James, 118–119
Principle, Matthew, 221
privacy
  CCPA (California Consumer Privacy
    Act), 44
  CPRA (California Privacy Rights Act), 44
  GDPR (General Data Protection
    Regulation), 43–44
  PCI (payment card industry), 43
project management
  Airtable, 24
  ArtsVision, 24
  Asana, 24
  solutions, 89–90
Prospect2, 67–68
PTZ camera, 176
PXT Studio, 221–222

Q
QLab, 116
Quantum Theatre, 222
  Slack, 10–11

R
RadioWorld, 201
Raise3D Professional Desktop 3D
  printer, 97–99
rebranding
  Ballet RI, 135–138
  Detroit Opera, 138–140
RegFox, 31, 57
Reiser Atlanta Artists Lab, 168–171
residencies, The Cleveland Orchestra
  (TCO) and, 140–142
RFP (request for proposal), 49

S

Savannah Philharmonic, 222
Second Stage Theater, 222–223
security
  digital literacy and, 45
  passwords, 45
  two-factor authentication, 45
set design, 120
  Adobe Creative Cloud, 96
  American Players Theatre (APT),
      97–99
  AutoCAD, 96
  Indiana Repertory Theatre (IRT),
      94–96
  laser cutting machines, 96
  Raise3D Professional Desktop 3D
      printer, 97–99
  Vectorworks, 96
SFJAZZ, 223
Shea, Lawrence, 223
ShowClix, 57
Sibelius, 115
simulcasts, 147–162
Sisense, 37
Sketch, 126, 144
Slack, 10–11, 24
  communication and, 9–12
  project management and, 10
  Quantum Theatre, 10–11
Slate, 18
Smith, Gabryel, 224
Smith, Melissa, 224
social media
  branding and, 128–134
  CapCut China, 144
  marketing and communication,
      71–74
Sony Mirrorless Camera, 175
sound design, 122
  Benedum Center for the Performing Arts,
      116–117
  DAW (digital audio workstation), 116
  FreeSpeak network, 116–117
  Helix network, 116–117
  Indiana Repertory Theatre (IRT),
      114–115
  Pickett, Sartje, 115–116
  QLab, 116
  scalable sound systems, 117–118
  Sennheiser Mobile-Connect, 117
  Sibelius, 115
special events, solutions, 90
Stark, 202

statistical modeling, 48
Still, James, 224–225
strategy, data analytics and,
    36–39
streaming, 147–162
Stripe, 31, 57, 175
Stuber, Nathan, 225
subscriptions, 91
  Patreon, 81, 91
  Savannah Philharmonic, 75–81
Suddarth, Price, 225–226
SurveyMonkey, 144
Syracuse Stage, 226
systemic racism, 196–198

T

teams, marketing and, 68–75
technology
  hybrid work, 3
  selecting, 21–22
  theater management, 2–3
  user adoption and, 40–41
The Builders Association, 207
The Cleveland Orchestra (TCO),
    140–142, 207
The Indianapolis Foundation, 212
The Kennedy Center, 213–214
The New York Philharmonic, 218
The Pittsburgh Cultural Trust,
    220–221
The Tessitura Network, 32–33,
    35–36, 57
  automation and, 67–68
  dashboards, 37–38
  Pittsburgh Cultural Trust, 32
  White, Katina, 29
theater, management, technology
    and, 2–3
TheatreSquared, 35, 67–68, 226
Ticketmaster, Archtics, 34–35
TicketSpice, 31, 57
Toney, Dane, 226–227
tools, selecting, 21–22
touring, 171–174
training, 20–21
  CRMs, 40–43
  D+A and, 194–199
  process recommendations,
      41–42
  Slack, 12
Trojanov, Eve, 36, 227
Troutman, Michael, 227
two-factor authentication, 45

U

Urist, Stewart, 227–228
user adoption, success and, 40–41
UX (user experience) design, 62

V

Vectorworks, 176
video
  marketing and communication, 70–71
  solutions, 89
video design, 105–106, 121–122
  509 Productions, 106–108
  AI in, 106–108
  Cinema 4D, 108–109
  Disguise Media Server, 110
  green screen, 110
  LED screens, 107, 110–111
  OLED (organic light-emitting
      diode), 111
  Pearcy, Benjamin, 106–108
  Pietras, Kaitlyn, 108–112
  PXT Studio, 108–112
  Shea, Lawrence, 112–114

Thompson, Jason, H., 108–112
WATCHOUT media server, 108
Vimeo OTT, 175
vMix, 176

W

WATCHOUT media server, 108
Wealth Engine, 48
websites, marketing and communication,
    69–70
WGBH, 228
White, Katina, 29
Williams, Amy, 228–229
Wingenfeld, Christine, 32–33, 229
Winterling, Eric, 229
WordPress, 145
workflow
  Airtable, 15–17
  Asana, 14–15
  three W's, 13

X–Y–Z

Yammer, 24